THE MACMILLAN SPECTRUM

INVESTOR'S CHOICE GUIDE TO

▼

Building and Managing an Investment Portfolio

THE MACMILLAN SPECTRUM
INVESTOR'S CHOICE GUIDE TO
▼

Building and Managing an Investment Portfolio

GORDON K. WILLIAMSON

Macmillan/Spectrum
New York

Macmillan/Spectrum A Simon and Schuster Macmillan Company 1633 Broadway New York, NY 10019

Library of Congress Cataloging-in-Publication Data: 97-071160

ISBN: 0-02-861440-2

Manufactured in the United States of America

99 98 97   9 8 7 6 5 4 3 2 1

Cover Design: Kevin Haneck
Book Design: A&D Howell Design

CONTENTS

▼

ABOUT THE AUTHOR

▼

Gordon K. Williamson, JD, MBA, MSFS, CFP, CLU, ChFC, RP is one of the best trained and experienced financial advisors in the country. Dr. Williamson has written over 20 books, including the most popular book ever written about mutual funds, *The 100 Best Funds You Can Buy* (which is updated annually). Gordon authored the first two books ever written about annuities: *All About Annuities* and *The 101 Best Annuities You Can Buy*. Besides writing books, he has also been the financial editor of a number of newspapers and magazines.

Mr. Williamson has also worked as a teacher. He taught investment classes for ten years at the University of California and was the chairman of the Business and Finance Department for continuing education. Currently, Gordon is the Executive Director of the Institute of Certified Fund Specialists, an educational program that leads to the designation CFS. The CFS program has been in existence for over six years and is not only the first mutual fund designation, it is also the only independent fund designation. For information about this 60-hour program or to find a CFS in your area, phone (800) 848-2029.

Gordon spends most of his time counseling clients and conducting investment research studies. Even though he lives in La Jolla, California, Dr. Williamson's clients are located throughout the country and around the world. If you would like more information about his brokerage and advisory services (minimum account size of $100,000), telephone (800) 748-5552 or fax (619) 454-4660.

▼

CHAPTER 1

DESCRIBING ASSET ALLOCATION

WHAT WE ARE GOING TO TALK ABOUT IN THIS CHAPTER:

- ► Nine General Approaches to Structuring a Portfolio

- ► Understanding Different Types of Return

- ► Defining the Three Different Types of Asset Allocation

Asset allocation is the process of determining how to divide your money among different investment categories. In its simplest form, asset allocation helps you figure out what percentage of your portfolio should be in stocks, bonds, real estate, and money market instruments. Each of these four broad categories has different risk and return characteristics. Understanding these characteristics is just one part of the asset allocation decision.

An Introduction to the Financial Planning Process

Money market accounts have little risk but provide little in the way of returns, particularly once the effects of income taxes and inflation are factored in. Nevertheless, if your objective is to eliminate any chance of a short- or long-term loss and you are willing to give up the potential for a high return, a money market fund is an appropriate choice.

At the other end of the spectrum is common stocks. Stocks are an investment that, depending upon the type of stock, can be high in risk and high in return potential. Thus, if your objective is to end up with what might turn out to be a huge gain and you are also willing to sustain low, moderate or large losses, common stocks are an appropriate selection.

Example 1.1—The Five Best and Five Worst Years for Stocks and Bonds

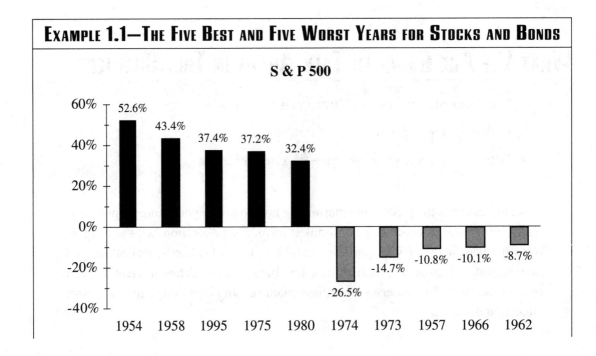

S & P 500

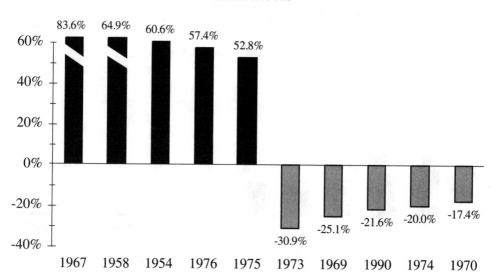

Small Stocks

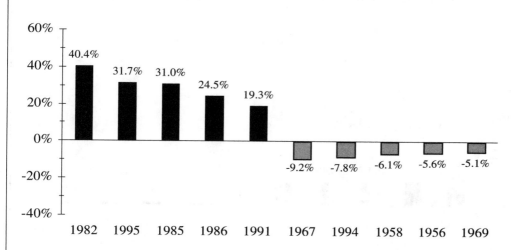

Long-Term Government Bonds

continues

Example 1.1—The Five Best and Five Worst Years for Stocks and Bonds [continued]

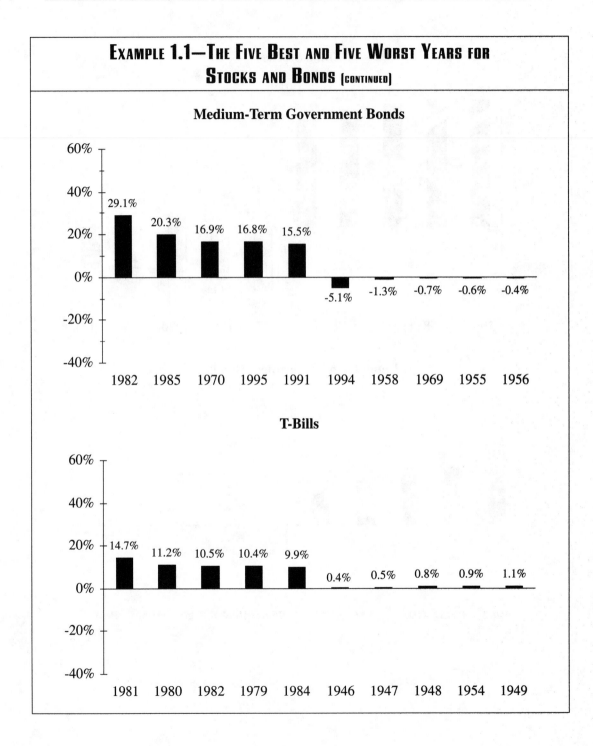

Medium-Term Government Bonds

Year	Return
1982	29.1%
1985	20.3%
1970	16.9%
1995	16.8%
1991	15.5%
1994	-5.1%
1958	-1.3%
1969	-0.7%
1955	-0.6%
1956	-0.4%

T-Bills

Year	Return
1981	14.7%
1980	11.2%
1982	10.5%
1979	10.4%
1984	9.9%
1946	0.4%
1947	0.5%
1948	0.8%
1954	0.9%
1949	1.1%

Bonds, particularly long-term, high-quality corporate or U.S. government issues, have risk-reward characteristics that are somewhere in between those of money market accounts and common stocks. Long-term (defined as securities with a remaining maturity of more than ten years) bonds have experienced periods of very positive returns (e.g., 1995 and from 1981 to 1988) and they have also gone through periods of loss (e.g., 1994 and from 1976 to 1981). However, most of the time, long-term bonds exhibit modest to moderate gains accompanied by modest volatility. So, if common stocks appear to be too risky and money market instruments are not exciting enough, bonds may be a good fit for your portfolio.

Real estate comes in many forms (e.g., your personal residence, raw land, income-producing property, a real estate investment trust or a small part of several different types of properties). The risk-reward characteristics depend upon the type of real estate and the extent of any leverage (mortgage or trust deed). The return potential and risk level of real estate can be quite small (e.g., you own a building that you have leased out to AT&T for ten years with an inflation adjustment), or quite large (e.g., you own some raw land for which you put 30% down and financed the remaining 70%, hoping that a developer will pay you top dollar for the property).

So far we have touched on the major investment categories (cash, stocks, bonds and real estate), describing, in general terms, their respective risk-reward characteristics. Asset allocation looks at these different characteristics and helps guide you in deciding what percentage, if any, these categories should represent as part of a complete portfolio. The following sections detail what your decision-making process is based upon.

EXAMPLE 1.2—THE DECISION-MAKING PROCESS

1. **Time Horizon:** e.g., seven years until child goes to college and twenty years until retirement

2. **Risk Level:** e.g., moderate risk with 70% of portfolio and fairly aggressive with balance

3. **Financial Goals:** e.g., $125,000 for college fund and $700,000 at retirement

4. **Current Holdings:** e.g., $50,000 in bank CDs, $30,000 in government bond fund

5. **Extraordinary Events:** e.g., will inherit about $50,000 within five years

6. **Preferences or Biases:** e.g., never sell GM (cost basis is too low)

7. **Tax Bracket:** e.g., 45% state and federal combined (consider using tax-free bonds)

Time Horizon

Time horizon refers to how long money can be invested before it is mostly or fully withdrawn. Your time horizon is usually based upon your financial goal(s). For example, if you plan on retiring in eight years, your time horizon is at least eight years (presumably much longer since it is extremely doubtful that an entire retirement account will be fully spent after even several years of retirement). Investors often have multiple time horizons. As an example, a couple may need college money for the kids in five years and again in 12 years (for the second child) in addition to having a strong desire to pay off the remaining mortgage at the end of 15 years.

Time horizon is a very important consideration when selecting investments. For most investors, the shorter the period of time, the more conservative the portfolio should be; a time horizon of only a couple of years means that less volatile investments should be included in the portfolio. Volatility is obviously a two-way street, but few investors want to take the risk that the stock, bond or real estate market might be depressed just at the time that money is needed.

The greater one's time horizon, the more aggressive the portfolio can be. A moderate or fairly risky portfolio will go up and down more dramatically than a conservative portfolio, but its overall average annual return will most likely be much higher than a stable portfolio, given a time horizon of at least five years.

In general, if your time horizon is five years or more, most of the portfolio should be in equities such as stocks and perhaps some real estate. If the period of investment is closer to five years or more, nearly 100% of the assets should be in equities. Similarly, if your time horizon is only a couple of years, most, if not all, of the holdings should be in debt instruments such as money market accounts, short-term bonds, intermediate-term bonds, plus some hybrids such as convertibles and high-yield bonds. Despite these generalities, your risk level is a critical ingredient in determining how the portfolio should be structured.

Risk Level

Risk level refers to how much downward fluctuation you can stomach. Historical charts and graphs showing great returns are of little consolation if you are unable to sleep at night because you are worried about the market. Quite simply, if you cannot handle the ups and downs of the stock market, or perhaps the volatility of long-term bonds, then a more conservative portfolio with at least fairly predictable returns is warranted. An advisor or the financial media should not make you something that you are not, regardless of whether they are trying to get you out of equities or into them.

There are several ways to determine risk level. Some of these methods are described in later chapters. Some people become overly concerned if even a part of their portfolio drops in value; for these investors, asset allocation will provide only moderate comfort. For most people, the overall return of the entire portfolio is all that really matters. This is a more sound approach to investing since we cannot assume that all of our investments are increasing in value all of the time unless our holdings are limited to money market accounts, bank CDs, T-bills and fixed-rate annuities.

One of the tricky things about risk is that there is often a big difference between the conceptual and the real world. Thus, you may look at a historical chart that shows that investment X was down 25% in one quarter but then went on to post a 5% gain for the entire year, followed by a 20% return for the following year, and you may feel comfortable owning investment X. This feeling may be in stark contrast to the feelings that might result after you own X and it then drops by 15 to 20%. Being an armchair quarterback is much safer than actually being on the gridiron.

Financial Goals

Financial goals, the third part of the investment decision-making process, refers to what you are trying to do with your savings and investments. The most common financial goals are: (1) saving for a home; (2) a college fund for the children; and (3) a comfortable retirement. One's financial goals should also include any liquidity needs. If an unexpected expense arises, what source(s) can be tapped for quick cash and what is the "cost" of such liquidation?

Liquidity needs may be greatly diminished if the investor is adequately insured. Proper coverage means reviewing auto, home, life, and medical insurance policies. Opting for a larger deductible and higher coverage is usually a smarter course of action than paying for a smaller deductible. It is not the $500 or $2,500 deductible that will alter your long-term financial goals—it is the fluke $50,000 operation you or a family member needs that is somehow not covered by your current policy.

Example 1.3—Liquid Investments (or Emergency Funds)

► money market fund (taxable or government-backed)

► short-term bond funds (with an average maturity of less than two years)

► bank CDs that mature in less than two years

► fixed-rate annuities (depending upon any withdrawal penalty)

► cash value of a life insurance policy

Once you have determined your liquidity (or emergency) needs, short- and long-term goals can be established. Successfully reaching those financial goals will be dependent upon your portfolio averaging a certain rate of return. Obviously, the higher the rate of return needed, the more aggressive the portfolio and the less likely that things will work out exactly as planned.

Money Talks:

The words "liquidity" and "marketability" are often considered to be synonymous, but there is a big difference. An investment or asset is considered to be liquid if the investor can sell it for the same price he paid for it (or a price very close to the original purchase price). An investment is considered to be marketable if it can be easily bought and sold, regardless of price. Most common stocks you are familiar with are quite marketable—they can easily be sold by a brokerage firm on a major stock exchange. However, the price you receive for your shares of IBM or GM may be much less (or more) than what you paid for the shares last month or a decade ago. Money market funds are extremely liquid because their price per share remains at a constant one dollar. Money market funds have little marketability because the only one that will buy back your shares (plus the additional shares that represent interest) is the entity that issued the shares to begin with.

The riskier the portfolio, the greater the volatility of returns and, therefore, the less predictable the returns. Fortunately, a large part of risk is eliminated with time and by selecting investment categories that have generally performed well over time. Long-term winners include: long-term bonds, high-yield bonds, foreign securities, real estate, and, of course, common stocks. Long-term losers include: "cash equivalents" such as U.S. T-bills, bank CDs, and money market accounts; most forms of option and commodity trading; penny stocks; and almost all limited partnerships.

CURRENT HOLDINGS

Current holdings, another step in the asset allocation process, are important for two reasons. First, it gives us some insight into what the investor is comfortable with; it may also help us in determining one's level of investment knowledge or sophistication. Second, part or most of the current holdings may coincide with what the actual asset allocation should be. This means reduced transaction costs, triggering fewer taxable events (which can happen whenever a non-sheltered investment is sold) and increasing the comfort level of the investor (since change often translates into uncertainty).

EXTRAORDINARY EVENTS

Extraordinary financial events are those situations wherein a moderate or large amount of money comes into your hands (e.g., an inheritance, gift, sale, or bonus) or leaves your hands (e.g., buying a boat or a new car, lending money to the kids, paying for an operation). If it is expected that a large expense is going to be incurred during the next few years, provisions must be made for such a possibility. This means a more conservative posture for part of the portfolio. On the other hand, a windfall of several or tens of thousands of dollars means that at least part of the portfolio can be more aggressively invested than originally thought.

PREFERENCES (OR BIASES)

Preferences are an important part of everyday life and play a major role when it comes to investing. An investor's preferences or biases may be grounded on sound financial advice or may be ill-founded (e.g., you just read a doomsday book that stresses the importance of owning gold bullion or your favorite financial guru just came out with a position paper on oil wells). Any such biases or preferences need to be brought out and openly discussed. These investment preferences need to be scrutinized the same way that you should approach any investment. This means that there are no "free passes" for any investment. Each investment must be viewed in light of your time horizon, risk level, financial goals and tax bracket.

TAX BRACKET

The investor's tax bracket is the final step of the asset allocation process. Every investment has tax ramifications either now or in the future. Retirement accounts are tax sheltered vehicles but eventually become taxable as monies are withdrawn. Municipal bonds may provide tax-free interest payments, but there may be a capital gain or loss when the bonds are sold, redeemed, or exchanged. Some stocks pay much higher dividends than others. This does not mean that a stock that does pay a dividend is better or worse than one that does not, but it does mean that we need to be conscious of any such dividends and at least consider placing such stocks inside a qualified retirement plan.

When it comes to the asset allocation process, the tax ramifications of an investment or even an entire portfolio are usually much less important than one's time horizon, risk level, or financial goals. Often times, people are "blinded" by the tax ramifications of a particular investment—meaning that they focus too much on tax minimization instead of looking at the major attributes of an investment such as its safety, marketability and actual performance track record. This is one of the main reasons that investors have lost tens of billions of dollars in limited partnerships over the years.

EXAMPLE 1.4—FEDERAL TAX BRACKETS

Taxable Income

Single	*Joint Return*	*Tax Rate*	*6% Tax-Free = The Same As*
$22,751–55,100	$38,001–91,850	28%	8.33% taxable
$55,101–115,000	$91,851–140,000	31%	8.70% taxable
$115,001–250,000	$140,001–250,000	36%	9.38% taxable
10% federal surtax over $250,000	—	39.6%	9.93% taxable

Nevertheless, it would be wise for the investor to look at his tax return to see how much he is paying in interest income and capital gains. By making such a review, he may discover that investments such as bank CDs, taxable money market accounts, and government securities could be repositioned into tax-advantaged investments that are similar in safety and maturity but have higher after-tax returns (e.g., municipal notes and bonds, fixed-rate annuities and tax-free money market funds).

NINE GENERAL APPROACHES TO STRUCTURING A PORTFOLIO

There are several approaches investors can take to managing their own money or that of their clients. The more popular methods of money management include:

1. Investing only in those assets that have a known rate of return, those that are considered "risk-free," or are guaranteed (i.e., bank CDs, fixed-rate annuities, money market accounts, Series EE Bonds and U.S. T-bills).

2. Investments that have traditionally been considered safe but offer yields more attractive than those found with "risk-free" investments, meaning securities with longer maturities (i.e., U.S. Treasury bonds, high-quality corporate and municipal bonds).

3. Investments that seek the highest possible current yields (i.e., high-yield corporate bonds, high-yield municipal bonds, and certain preferred stocks and convertible securities).

4. Investments that include a "balance" between stocks, bonds, and what are referred to as "cash equivalents" (i.e., money market accounts, bank CDs and U.S. T-bills).

5. A globally balanced portfolio that would include U.S. as well as foreign stocks and bonds.

6. A pure U.S. blue chip stock portfolio that would be comprised of stocks from very large domestic corporations plus perhaps some utility stocks.

7. A domestic stock portfolio that might encompass the entire range of U.S. stocks: small, medium and large cap stocks (meaning stocks of corporations whose market capitalization, or "cap" is less than $1 billion in the case of small cap, between $2 and $10 billion in the case of medium cap, and over $10 billion in the case of large cap) as well as stocks that are further characterized as being either "value" (the price of the stock is depressed but is expected to recover) or "growth" (the company has done well in recent quarters or years and is expected to continue doing as well).

8. A globally balanced stock portfolio comprised mostly of large company domestic and foreign stocks with perhaps a modest weighting in what are referred to as "emerging markets" (i.e., Latin America, China, Vietnam and former Eastern Bloc nations).

9. A pure foreign stock portfolio comprised of small, medium, and large cap stocks from established and mature economies (i.e., Japan, the U.K., Germany, France, Canada and Italy—what is referred to as the "Group of 7" or "G-7 Nations" if you were to include the U.S.) as well as high growth regions (i.e., Thailand, South Korea, Taiwan and Indonesia) and emerging markets.

As exciting or secure as some of these approaches sound, each has its advantages and disadvantages. As you read through this book, you will see why there are good and bad aspects to any form of money management—including asset allocation.

Asset allocation, in its most general terms, can be defined simply as trying to get someone the best risk-adjusted returns possible over a particular period of time, given a known level of risk. There is no such thing as the "best" investment or portfolio since different investors have different risk profiles. Instead, asset allocation is a series of trade-offs. Examples of some of these trade-offs include: (1) if you are seeking a certain rate of return, then a certain level of risk must be assumed; (2) if you want X to represent a portion of your portfolio plus you are only willing to accept Y amount of risk, then other investment categories must be included, assuming you are looking for Z amount of return; and (3) you are willing to continue to maintain your current risk level, but if you want a higher rate of return, then some or most of your existing holdings need to be repositioned.

Asset allocation is best utilized once an investment strategy has been developed. Your investment strategy is highly personal, covering such things as: your risk level, your time horizon, your investment biases, the value of your current holdings, how much (if any) can be saved and invested each year, and your tax bracket. Investment strategy is detailed in a later chapter.

UNDERSTANDING DIFFERENT TYPES OF RETURNS

A commonly used phrase throughout this book is "risk-adjusted" returns. It is important to understand what both "risk-adjusted" and "returns" mean. An investment's return (which is really an abbreviation for "total return") is the sum of its current yield or interest (in the case of bonds) plus any appreciation (an increase in the price per share or unit) or minus any depreciation (a decrease in the price per share or unit). It is important to understand that an investment may have what is considered to be a high yield (such as lower-rated bonds, preferred stocks, convertible securities, or second trust deeds) but a negative return. In such a case, this would mean that the loss of principal (e.g., a 10% bond that drops in value 12%) exceeds any current income.

EXAMPLE 1.5—UNDERSTANDING TOTAL RETURN

Suppose you own a very small apartment building that has no mortgage. You paid $100,000 for the building and after all expenses (i.e., property taxes, management company, upkeep, advertising, etc.), you net $10,000 a year from the building. At this point, your total return is 10% ($10,000/$100,000). After owning the building for 10 years (and netting $10,000 each year), you sell the building and net $150,000 after all selling expenses. Your total return for this investment is the amount of income you received each year ($10,000 × 10 = $100,000) plus the net profits from the sale ($150,000−$100,000 = $50,000). Total return in this example is $150,000.

Let us change the facts somewhat. Suppose that instead of an apartment building, you used the $100,000 and bought 30-year U.S. government bonds that had a yield of 7% ($7,000) a year. After ten years you sell the bonds (which still have a remaining maturity of 20 years) and net $99,000. Your total return for this investment would be $70,000 (the $7,000 you received in interest payments for ten years) minus $1,000 (you are getting back $1,000 less than what you paid for the bonds). Total return for this second example is $69,000.

All too often, investors rationalize losses by thinking that when something falls in value, it is "only on paper" or it is a "paper loss" since the asset has not actually been sold. True, this kind of loss we are talking about has not been what the IRS refers to as "realized"; it is still a loss. Your net worth is based on what your investments are presently worth—not what they were worth when the markets were peaking or at some other point you now fondly remember.

A risk-adjusted return looks at how much risk was taken, or is expected to be taken, to get an expected or actual total return (yield or interest plus appreciation or minus a loss in value). One of the easiest ways to understand what "risk-adjusted" means is to draw two sets of stairs next to each other; one set represents risk and the other set represents return (total). If, for every step of return added a step were also taken for risk, this would be considered a fair trade-off. The S & P 500 or a government bond would be examples of a fair trade-off. Whether or not it would be appropriate would depend upon one's risk level.

If, for every step of return added, something more than a step of risk was also taken, this would represent an inadequate or poor risk-adjusted return (meaning too much risk was being accepted for an incremental addition in return). Futures contracts, penny stocks, and most limited partnerships would be examples of investments that usually have poor risk-adjusted returns.

Finally, if for every step of return added, something less than a step of additional risk was taken, this would represent a good or excellent risk-adjusted return (or trade-off). Global stocks funds, utility stocks, and high-yield bonds are examples of investments that have very good risk-adjusted returns more often than not.

EXAMPLE 1.6—PUTTING "RISK-ADJUSTED" RETURNS IN PERSPECTIVE

I have two investment choices for you, B and C. Over the past three years, investment B, which is a mutual fund that invests in conservative stocks and bonds, has had some ups and downs but has managed to turn in a cumulative return of 30% (roughly 10% compounded per year), despite the fact that during one of the three years it was down as much as 8% in a single quarter. Over the past three years, investment C has not had any down years or quarters. In fact, over the past three years, investment C has had a cumulative return of 100%.

Before writing out a check to investment C, you might like to know that "investment C" represents a trip to Las Vegas that I make once a year. During that trip, I make a single bet of 33.3% of your money. Whether I win or lose, I only make one bet and then get back on the plane and come home. Over the past three years, I have won three out of three bets.

Given such an extreme example, it is very doubtful that you would now want to go into investment C. Why? Because I have explained what the investment is; most people know that the odds in Las Vegas are against you, no matter what game you play. You are probably not attracted to this kind of "investment" once you realize that your loss potential is 33% a year.

Investment C becomes attractive once more if we alter the facts of this example and include the following: "If I ever make a losing bet, I will personally reimburse you for 90% of the loss." With such a reimbursement program, your loss potential each year drops from 33% to only 10% of 33% (or 3.3%). If your loss potential per year is 3.3% but your return potential is 33% (remember only one bet is made each year), risk-adjusted returns become extremely attractive. In fact, using two sets of stairs as a visual analogy, for every ten steps of return you take, you are only taking one step of risk.

So far we have discussed the nine most common ways investors structure their portfolios, a broad definition of asset allocation, why paper losses are still losses, what total return is (abbreviated throughout the rest of the book as simply return), and the meaning of risk-adjusted returns. Let us now talk about time.

The Proper Holding Period

Investments are normally described in terms of historical returns and levels of risk. What is not commonly talked about is their holding period. Some investments have expected or guaranteed returns that are narrow enough that their holding period can be relatively short without causing the investor much, if any, chance of loss. Conceptually, such investments, such as cash equivalents (e.g., bank CDs, money market accounts and T-bills), should not be owned for more than one or two years. This is because cash equivalents have a poor long-term performance record once you factor in the effects of income taxes and inflation; more often than not, real returns (meaning adjusted for inflation and income taxes) on these investments have actually been negative. Other investments, such as long-term quality bonds, high-yield bonds, utility stocks, REITs (real estate investment trusts) and large company stocks should be owned for about five years or longer. A few investment categories, such as balanced mutual funds and variable annuity subaccounts, convertible securities, and global bond funds fall somewhere in between and should generally be owned for at least three or four years. Some investments, such as limited partnerships, are structured such that they perform best if held for over ten years.

The reason that knowing your expected holding is so important, and time-saving when structuring a total portfolio, is that you do not want to own investments that extend beyond this time. You also want to limit those investments whose recommended holding period is too short—such investments should only be added as a means of reducing the portfolio's overall volatility. Structuring a portfolio is easier when certain investment categories can be eliminated in a wholesale fashion.

EXAMPLE 1.7—ELIMINATING INVESTMENTS BASED ON YOUR TIME HORIZON

Imagine that you have come to me for investment advice and have given me the following limited background information: (1) your only goal is to buy a home and the $10,000 you have to invest is, and will be, the only money or asset available for a down payment; (2) you want the money invested for just three years; (3) in a couple of years you can afford a mortgage payment of up to several thousand dollars a month; (4) the house you buy will depend upon how much your $10,000 grows to in three years; and (5) your risk level is somewhere between conservative and moderate.

Based on these facts alone, some of the investments that can immediately be eliminated from consideration are:

Investment Category	Reason for Elimination
Limited Partnerships	Holding period is typically 10 to 15 years.
Rare Coins or Stamps	Mark-ups (fees) can't be recovered in three years.
Real Estate	Amortizing buying and selling costs over just three years will eat into most or all of any profit.
Long-term Zero Coupon Bonds	Volatility could be too high over three years.
Most Common Stocks	Volatility (risk level) could be too high.

THREE TYPES OF ASSET ALLOCATION

Asset allocation involves all of these ideas: existing holdings (such as one of the nine portfolios described at the beginning of the chapter), total return, risk-adjusted returns, and time. Financial planning or investment counseling deals with things such as whether or not a paper loss should be realized and in what calendar year, as well as the tax consequences of an investment or course of action, life, health and disability insurance, as well as retirement and estate planning. Some of these topics will be covered in this book, but only those areas of financial planning that relate directly to asset allocation or increasing your after-tax return will be included.

There are three forms or types of asset allocation: (1) strategic, (2) tactical, and (3) dynamic.

STRATEGIC ASSET ALLOCATION

Strategic asset allocation is a passive approach that focuses on long-range policy decisions to determine the appropriate mix. It is a passive strategy in that it does not attempt to predict or time the market. The portfolio is fully invested at all times. Risk is reduced by using several different investment categories. This form of asset allocation becomes semi-active whenever the portfolio is rebalanced back to its initial or revised asset weightings. The focus of this book will be on strategic asset allocation but, when appropriate, attention will be given to the other two schools of thought.

EXAMPLE 1.8—STRATEGIC ASSET ALLOCATION

Based on your investment strategy and risk level, it has been determined that your portfolio should be divided as follows: 20% small company growth stocks, 20% large company growth stocks, 30% foreign stocks, 10% emerging markets stocks and 20% in high-yield corporate bonds.

A few months after you have implemented the asset allocation described above, there is a severe downturn in the stock market and parts of your portfolio are now in negative territory, showing losses as great as -9%. What should you do? Nothing. As a follower of strategic asset allocation, no changes should be made based on the ups and downs of the stock market or bond market. Instead, changes should be considered at the end of six months or a year, based on the original weightings for each category. Thus, if small company stocks no longer represent 20% of your total portfolio but instead represent 17% (due to a drop in the stock market), then another part of your portfolio that is now overweighted needs to be partially sold off (e.g., high-yield bonds may now represent 23% of the whole pie either due to superior performance or because the category did not drop nearly as much as some other parts) and used to "bring up" the small stock portion so it once again represents 20%—no matter how you feel about stocks at the time.

TACTICAL ASSET ALLOCATION

Tactical asset allocation is an active approach that generally uses market predictions to change the asset mix in order to exploit superior predictive ability through such techniques as sector rotation or market timing. This strategy believes that market inefficiencies can constantly be found and that short-term trading can take advantage of such inefficiencies.

EXAMPLE 1.9—TACTICAL ASSET ALLOCATION

Based on your investment strategy and risk level, it has been determined that your portfolio should be divided as follows: 20% small company growth stocks, 20% large company growth stocks, 30% foreign stocks, 10% emerging markets stocks and 20% in high-yield corporate bonds.

A few months after you have implemented the asset allocation described above, there is a severe downturn in the stock market. What should you do? As a believer in tactical asset allocation, stocks should now be more heavily weighted than originally planned. Right after a downturn, these stocks are on sale and such "sale prices" should be taken advantage of. Furthermore, if there is a specific area of the stock market that now looks particularly bad but is fundamentally good (e.g., technology stocks), then such a sector should represent much more of the whole pie than it normally would. Both of these quick moves may only last several months or a year or two before another "buying opportunity" arises elsewhere.

DYNAMIC ASSET ALLOCATION

Dynamic asset allocation is an active technique that reacts to changing market conditions by making relatively frequent changes in the asset mix with the goal of providing downside protection in addition to upside participation. Managers that use this approach actively alter clients' portfolios but do so by being reactive (after the fact) instead of proactive (forecasting).

EXAMPLE 1.10—DYNAMIC ASSET ALLOCATION

Suppose your portfolio started with 70% in bank CDs earning 5%, with the remaining 30% of your portfolio in common stocks. You may decide that if the stock portion of your portfolio drops by, say 4%, one half of the stock portion will be sold, and the proceeds are to be added to the CDs. If your remaining stocks drop another, say 2%, you might then sell off the balance of the stocks and have 100% in CDs.

The "trigger" points that help you decide when to move parts of your stock holdings to cash may be more sensitive (for conservative investors) or less sensitive (for moderate or aggressive investors), depending upon your risk level. Similarly, how much you start off with in stocks will also be dependent upon how much risk you can live with.

SUMMARY

Before getting into the specifics of asset allocation, it is important that you first have a strong grounding in determining your financial objectives, a historical perspective about the risk and return of different investment categories, the different forms of risk and how they are measured, as well as how investments interact with each other. The early chapters of this book cover the use of financial tables, which can be found in the appendix. If you already know how to use financial tables, skip this first part of the book. If you do not feel comfortable with financial tables, do not feel intimidated. Learning how to use these tables is quite simple and can be quite rewarding.

 Dollars & Sense:
One of the quickest ways to explain asset allocation to my new clients is to tell them that their portfolio is like a garden, filled with different kinds of vegetables and fruits. My job is to make sure part of their garden is always in bloom. No investment should be expected to be in bloom the entire year. Asset allocation greatly increases the likelihood that parts of the portfolio will be in bloom throughout the year.

LET'S REMEMBER THIS:

▶ The advantages of asset allocation.

▶ Understanding different types of return.

▶ The three different types of asset allocation.

▼

SHORT-TERM VS. LONG-TERM PERFORMANCE

WHAT WE ARE GOING TO TALK ABOUT IN THIS CHAPTER:

- ▶ Stock Ownership Translates into Business Ownership

- ▶ Keeping an Eye on Bond Maturity

- ▶ The Wisdom of Brokers

Whenever there is a stock market crash, correction, or even a series of single-day losses, I receive somewhere between zero and two phone calls from all of my clients combined. My clients are just like everyone else; they have the same hopes, fears and concerns. The one thing that makes them different from other investors is that I have made sure they are educated about the ups and downs of the market. My clients do not panic or become nervous because they understand and have come to expect downturns.

There are a number of things that you can do to be prepared for bad financial news; things that will ensure that you stay the course. To better cope with losses, keep in mind the following:

- ▶ What stock ownership represents

- ▶ The maturity date of your bonds

> ► There is a difference between expected and guaranteed rates of return

> ► Every investment has an expected range of returns

> ► The long-term historical record of your investments

What Stock Ownership Represents

When the stock market has just experienced a particularly bad day, week, month, quarter or even year, it is easy to lose sight of what owning a stock means. Owning a stock means that you own a very small part of a corporation—an entity whose employees want to be successful. Companies are in business to make money. These businesses are made up of people just like you and me. It is human nature to want to succeed. Whether a corporation has just reported record profits or losses, one thing is certain: They want to do better the next quarter or year, and no matter how successful they might be next year or next quarter, they will want to make even more money the following period.

Dollars & Sense: There has been an upward bias in the stock market for well over 100 years. If George Washington had $1 and invested that $1 in U.S. stocks at the beginning of his presidency, that $1 today would be worth over $15.4 billion, assuming stocks averaged the same 12% rate of return they have for the past half-century. If he had averaged 16.5%, which is what small company stocks have averaged over the past 50 years, his original $1 would have been worth $53 trillion by the end of 1996. A $53 trillion portfolio would pay off the national debt several times over.

As a shareholder, you should never lose sight of this human equation. The company(s) you "own" is interested in its future just as much, if not more, than you are. The people that work at these corporations have rent or mortgages to pay, mouths to feed, things they want to buy, and concerns about their retirement. Let us look at Ford Motor Company as an example.

Suppose you own shares of Ford and are thinking about buying even more shares of the company. Initially you are reluctant to invest more money because you have just learned that Ford stock has just plummeted. Instead of selling for $50 a share, it is now selling for $30 a share. Let us further suppose that when Ford stock was selling for $50 a share, that meant that it was selling for 20 times earnings (also known as a p/e, or price/earnings, ratio of 20).

If a company is selling for "20 times earnings" this means that if one had enough money to buy 100% of that company for cash (eliminating any outstanding debt including the company's bonds and notes), they would recoup all of their investment in 20 years—assuming only current earnings in future years. The reality is that most major corporations have increasing earnings almost every year. So someone paying 20 times earnings may end up having to wait only 10 to 15 years before recovering 100% of the purchase price.

Waiting 10 to 20 years to be made whole again may seem like a long time, but look at this ficticious purchase in its proper context: (1) during the "recovery" period, profits are being earned so the new owner is getting a return on his investment; (2) ownership of a large corporation means that you have the flexibility to try to expand market share or even to go into new, perhaps unrelated, products—a new invention or product line could mean a windfall profit; (3) owning a company such as Ford means that you have instant worldwide recognition and that sales will at least be decent, even if you sometimes produce a mediocre or noncompetitive automobile; (4) any type of new competition is either nonexistent or limited at best since start-up costs would run into the billions; and (5) the chances that you could duplicate the success of Ford, IBM, General Electric (or whatever company you admire) if you were to start a similar business are remote at best.

Keeping the aforementioned points in mind, buying Ford at 20 times earnings suddenly seems like a great deal. If Ford stock drops by 40%, from $50 to $30 a share, so does its p/e ratio. If a price/earnings ratio of 20 was a great deal, a p/e of 20 is a steal! A similar argument could be made for any other well-established corporation, whether it is in manufacturing, retail, service, or public utility.

When Ford has a bad quarter, year, or even a couple of bad years in a row, you do not hear the executive officers say, "Gee, maybe we ought to sell the company and go into something else." As ridiculous as this sounds, it is exactly what investors do when they bail out. They equate success with short-term performance. If you do not have patience, then you should probably never own stocks. People that need guarantees, assurances or who simply lack patience can find solace in investments such as money market accounts, bank CDs and short-term bonds.

The point of all of this is that you should not lose sight of what you are buying when you buy shares of a stock or a mutual fund, variable annuity, or variable life insurance policy that invests in stocks. You are buying a stake in a business—presumably a successful business that wants to be even more successful in the future. But, like any other business or profession, there are going to be down times. You cannot expect anyone or any business to turn in record profits every year.

MATURITY DATE OF YOUR BONDS

I am not a strong advocate of bond ownership for most people. More precisely, I believe that owning debt instruments, which includes bonds, CDs and money market accounts, is a bad long-term investment. This does not mean that I do not recommend debt instruments as part of a portfolio in order to reduce overall risk or as a comparatively safe haven when stocks, real estate, and other investments look uncertain or are going through some kind of correction.

Tens of millions of people own bonds, either directly or indirectly (a mutual fund, variable annuity, or variable life insurance). Long-term bonds (those with remaining maturities of more than ten years) have the greatest return potential but also the greatest loss potential. Losses suffered in the bond market are usually not nearly as great as those suffered in the stock market, but many people have lost money in debt instruments. What makes bond losses so frustrating is that they tend to last longer than those in stocks. Interest rate increases (or the belief that there will be increases) tend to last longer than investors expect, whereas a loss in a stock tends to be quicker and more unexpected.

Several studies show that the total return from a bond is basically its current yield. This means that any appreciation (caused by falling interest rates) tends to cancel out any depreciation (caused by rising interest rates) and vice versa. Thus, if you have bonds that have been taking a beating in the market, be patient. Interest rates always change, sometimes for the better and sometimes for the worse.

The three charts below (Example 2.1) show the income (interest payments), total return (interest payments plus bond appreciation or depreciation), and volatility or risk (as measured by standard deviation) of long-term U.S. government bonds.

The first chart covers a 50-year period of time (1946 to 1995) and shows the consistency of bond income and the wild swings in total return that were due to interest rate changes.

The second chart shows the amount of risk taken over the past 50 years by long-term bond investors. Notice that on a risk-adjusted return basis, the income from a bond is much more appealing than the volatility associated with total return—most of which comes from bond appreciation or depreciation due to interest rate changes. In fact, the relationship between income return and risk is over two to one (6.0% vs. 2.94%); the relationship between total return and risk is a disappointing one to two (5.4% vs. 10.43%).

The third chart again covers the same half-century period of time (1946 to 1995) and shows that despite one's holding period, interest payments (shown as "Income Return") represent a very high percentage of the total return.

When viewed as a set, these three charts show that the added volatility or risk associated with a long-term bond is not worth the additional return.

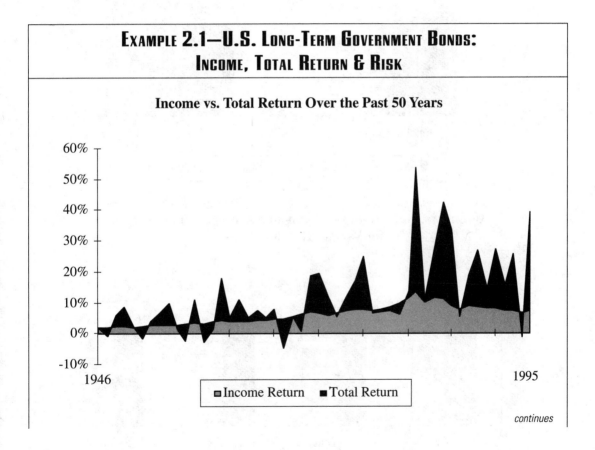

EXAMPLE 2.1—U.S. LONG-TERM GOVERNMENT BONDS: INCOME, TOTAL RETURN & RISK

Income vs. Total Return Over the Past 50 Years

continues

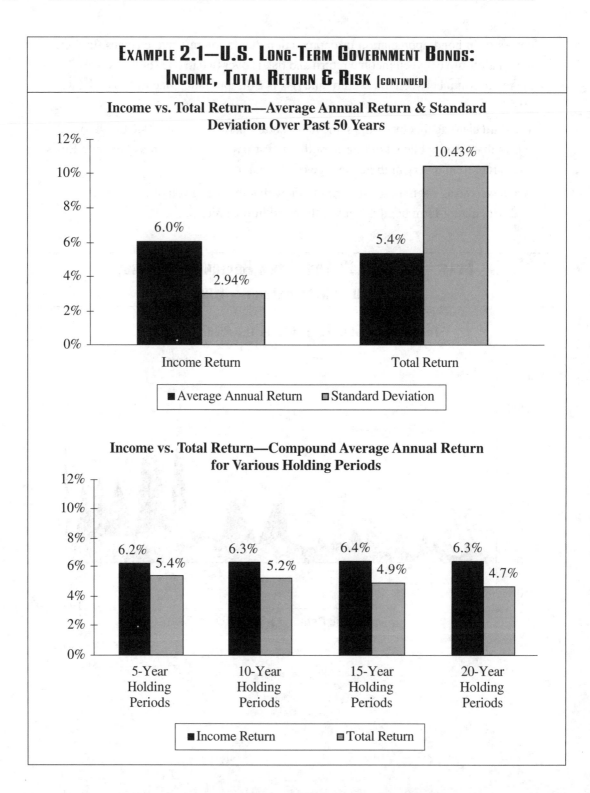

Example 2.1—U.S. Long-Term Government Bonds: Income, Total Return & Risk [continued]

Income vs. Total Return—Average Annual Return & Standard Deviation Over Past 50 Years

- Income Return: Average Annual Return 6.0%, Standard Deviation 2.94%
- Total Return: Average Annual Return 5.4%, Standard Deviation 10.43%

Legend: ■ Average Annual Return □ Standard Deviation

Income vs. Total Return—Compound Average Annual Return for Various Holding Periods

- 5-Year Holding Periods: Income Return 6.2%, Total Return 5.4%
- 10-Year Holding Periods: Income Return 6.3%, Total Return 5.2%
- 15-Year Holding Periods: Income Return 6.4%, Total Return 4.9%
- 20-Year Holding Periods: Income Return 6.3%, Total Return 4.7%

Legend: ■ Income Return □ Total Return

If the bond market moves against you, try to remember why you bought the bond(s) in the first place. You bought bonds either for current income, safety, or both. The fact that interest rates have increased (or are expected to) does not make the bond any less safe or have any affect on current income. A change of interest rates does mean that the bond's current value has changed and that possibly a loss will be suffered if the bond were sold at that time. Until the bond is sold, the loss is only a paper loss, just like a stock that drops in value but is still held.

PREDICTING INTEREST RATES

Trying to predict interest rate movements is as difficult as trying to guess what the stock market will do next. Looking at interest rate or stock market charts, certain patterns appear obvious, and this is where a false sense of predictability comes into play. You and I could look at charts of the Dow Jones Industrial Average or the benchmark 30-year U.S. Treasury bond over the past year (or several years) and point to what now looks like obvious turning points. When investors do this, comments such as, "Oh yeah, I would have gotten out here and gotten back in over here" abound. Yet, when the movements are actually taking place, such "trends" do not appear to be so obvious. More than one well-respected brokerage firm has gone broke trying to predict interest rate changes (e.g., E. F. Hutton).

Since no one is particularly good at predicting interest rates, the question then becomes what should an investor do when interest rates start to rise and bond prices begin to fall? Well, just like stocks, you have to review why bonds were bought in the first place. If those reasons remain intact, the bonds should be held. If circumstances have changed (e.g., the investor wants to be more conservative or more aggressive), then a sale may be warranted. If, for example, the bonds were originally purchased for preservation of capital, then any long-term bonds should be sold and replaced with short- or intermediate-term securities. This would mean that buying long-term bonds was a mistake from the beginning due to their volatility.

On the other hand, unlike stocks, bonds do have a maturity date and patience does have its rewards. The longer you own a bond, the less time you have to wait until the bond matures and full face-value is realized. The bond is also making semi-annual interest payments along the way. Such payments can greatly help to minimize or reduce any paper losses caused by rising interest rates. Most importantly, the bond market could unexpectedly change directions, and any losses in value could be recovered in less than a year.

The Truth About Computerized Trading

Most rational people know that no one knows what the stock market will do tomorrow, much less next week, month, or year. The belief that someone or some computer program knows what the market will do even ten minutes from now is ridiculous. Think about program trading for a moment. When a "program" gets a "sell" signal and proceeds to sell baskets full of stocks, options, or futures contracts, who is the computer selling to?

The fact is that there is a pretty good chance that another computer program is generating a "buy" signal at the same time. When the stock market drops, say 100 points, a brokerage firm's computer program says, "More often than not, when the market drops 100 points, chances are that the losses are just beginning." At that same moment, another trading company's computer program might be saying, "When the market drops 100 points, our research shows that 70% of the time there is a quick recovery . . . hurry up and buy stocks or call options."

The general public has the illusion that brokerage firms have some kind of special knowledge when it comes to the stock and bond markets. There is this further impression that computer programs run in some kind of synch; that is, when one gets a "buy" or "sell" signal, they all do. Well, the truth is that all of these programs are based on certain assumptions and historical data. One company's research might show that over the past ten years, when the market starts to fall so many points disaster is soon to follow. Another company may use the same data but over the previous 15, instead of 10, years. Over a 15-year period, it may be shown that when stocks (or bonds) start to fall in value, there is going to be a rally.

If someone or some company had the formula or program for successfully determining when to get in and out of the market, they would not need you or me as customers. In fact, they would not need any offices or 99% of their staff. Net worth would increase several fold each year. Why hassle with employees or customers who are generating you $100 or $1,000 in commissions when you can trade in your own account and make millions in the first year and billions in later years.

Even though most people instinctively know that no one can predict the future of the market, market timers, newsletters, and financial "gurus" continue to flourish. And when the market starts to look dark and the smell of blood is in the air, their numbers seem to multiply, similar to some kind of vampire fest. When it comes to predicting the direction of interest rates, and therefore bond prices, there is a belief that such predictions are easier to make and more accurate than stock market forecasts. However, this thinking is wrong.

Dollars & Sense:

To show you the absurdity of claiming to be able to time the market, let us go back 50 years to the beginning of 1946. Assume that 50 years ago, you were able to correctly predict what the best performing asset category was going to be for every single month (12 months × 50 = 600 possible market moves). Finally, assume that your choices for investment were: small stocks, the S & P 500, long-term corporate bonds, long-term U.S. government bonds, intermediate-term government bonds and U.S. Treasury bills that had a remaining maturity of just one month.

Starting with $1 (and never adding to this $1), by successfully switching into what would be that month's best peforming asset category (using one of the six categories described in the paragraph above), your $1 would have been worth $4,034 trillion or $4 quadrillion (70.05% annualized).

EXPECTED AND GUARANTEED RATES OF RETURN

Before going into any investment, it is important to understand the difference between "expected" and "guaranteed." When you hear or read that the expected return is going to be X, pick up a dictionary and look up the word "expected." Notice that the definition does not mention any form of guarantee. In fact, there are only a few investments that can legally use the word guarantee. Guaranteed rates of return can only be found with bank CDs insured by the FDIC, fixed-rate annuities, certain types of whole life insurance policies, and securities issued by the U.S. government if they are held to maturity.

EXAMPLE 2.2—INVESTMENTS THAT HAVE EXPECTED AND GUARANTEED RETURNS

Investment	*Status*
T-Bills, T-Notes, & T-Bonds	Only current yield is guaranteed; face value is guaranteed if the security is held to maturity.

continues

Example 2.2—Investments That Have Expected and Guaranteed Returns (continued)

Savings Bonds	Quoted interest rate is guaranteed only if these bonds are held for at least several years.
Fixed-Rate Annuities	Rate is guaranteed for one quarter up to ten years; withdrawals during any penalty period could lower the effective yield.
Money Market Funds	No guarantees; rate can change slightly each day.
Bank CDs	Rate is guaranteed if FDIC insured; early withdrawal penalty could eat into part or all of any interest earned—principal could also be hurt.

An expected return should be based on an investment's long-term track record. A track record that should encompass positive as well as negative periods of time. Long-term figures are fairly predictive and accurate, but the problem is that most people do not stick with an investment for the long haul. Short-term performance can be very misleading. Short-term movements in the market can, and will, deviate greatly from the norm. Moreover, the more aggressive the portfolio, the more likely it will not have an "average" quarter or year.

If you need short-term guarantees, stay away from stocks or mutual funds that invest in stocks. You should also stay away from intermediate- and long-term bonds. The more you need short-term assurances, the more you should be in short-term debt instruments such as money market instruments and bond maturities of a couple of years or less.

Range of Returns

Before going into any investment that is not guaranteed, find out what its range of returns has been. Standard deviation measures an investment's range of returns over the past 36 months. An investment's standard deviation is calculated by first determining its average annual rate of return over the past 36 months, drawing a single line to represent this return and then plotting the monthly returns (which have now been annualized to be consistent with the annualized return line) on the same graph. The result, a scatter graph, shows the ups and downs (the plotted points) of an investment against its "norm" (the straight line).

Standard deviation is often used in the financial press as a measurement of risk. This is a fairly accurate measurement of risk, but it does have its shortfalls. First, standard deviation, by its own definition, includes the words "expected returns," and we now know that "expected" is not the same as "guaranteed." Second, standard deviation measures both downward (points on the graph below the average line) as well as upward (points above the line) volatility. This means that a mutual fund, stock, bond, real estate or gold bullion can be punished for higher than normal returns to the same degree it is punished for negative returns. I say "punished" because few investors or advisors like investments with large standard deviations. Finally, standard deviation shows what you can expect every two out of three years. Even if you could substitute the word "guaranteed" for "expected," this would still only cover 66 to 67% of the time. What happens the other third of the time will most likely be outside of the range of returns.

All of this discussion about standard deviation does not mean that it is not a valuable tool. Since there is no precise way to gauge how a nonguaranteed investment will perform, standard deviation remains one of the better measurements. One of its real values is that standard deviation points out that there is a positive and often negative range of returns for most investments. This is something that should be kept in mind the next time one of your investments starts to head south.

LONG-TERM PERFORMANCE

The misleading part about using long-term figures as a gauge of what the investor can expect in the future is that these figures do not include any footnotes or references as to the kinds of ups and downs that were experienced along the way. Virtually every great mutual fund, individual stock, variable annuity subaccount, or piece of real estate has gone through some pretty awful periods of performance over the past decade.

In order to gain a better perspective of what can happen, pick a handful of your favorite mutual funds (or use a publication's top five or top ten list). Next, get a printout showing the performance figures of those funds for every month (or quarter) for the past decade. You can get these printouts from a brokerage or financial planning firm; they may also be obtained from mutual fund tracking services such as CDA/ Weisenberger, Lipper Analytical Services, Morningstar, or Value Line. Finally, look for those periods such as 1987 and 1990 (and 1996 for the more aggressive mutual funds) when there were several negative figures during the year. Ask yourself if you could hold tough if similar periods were to happen in the future. Although "past results are no guarantee of future returns," the past can give you a good idea as to what you can expect as far as bad results are concerned.

REVIEW

When part or all of your investment portfolio begins to drop in value, it may be a good idea to review what you are trying to do with your money. Look at long-term annualized return figures, the investments' standard deviation, plus a number of the negative periods that the investments in question have been through. Such a review may be just what is needed to rekindle your faith in the marketplace. Remember what it means to own shares of a company. Keep in mind that the stock market has had an upward bias for more than 100 years. No matter when you, your children, your friends' children, or your grandchildren were born, stocks are higher now than they were on any of their birthdates.

Money Talks:

The word "guarantee" is one that is used commonly. When it comes to investing, the word is often misused. There are only a handful of investments that the word "guarantee" can be used with: government securities (interest payments are guaranteed but principal is only guaranteed if the security is held until its maturity date), fixed-rate annuities (principal is guaranteed at all times and so is the locked-in rate of return), bank CD interest rates (principal is not guaranteed because the potential penalty can eat into principal), and certain forms of life insurance (the death benefit and/or the growth rate of any cash value). The word "guarantee" cannot be used with municipal bonds, corporate bonds, common stocks, mutual funds, mortgages, real estate or collectibles.

SUMMARY

This chapter covers a number of elements you will come across in greater detail in future chapters. The main emphasis of this chapter is to show how patience pays off and to give you a better appreciation of what stock ownership represents.

The following chapter deals with the media. Over the past few years, the media's impact on investment decisions has become enormous, as the amount of financial news coverage has increased by several fold. This increased exposure is good, but as you will learn, a heavy price is paid for such up-to-the-minute information.

LET'S REMEMBER THIS:

► How bond maturities affect value.

► The limitations of broker advice.

► The difficulty of making predictions.

CHAPTER 3

▼

WHY THE MEDIA CAN BE YOUR WORST ENEMY

WHAT WE ARE GOING TO TALK ABOUT IN THIS CHAPTER:

- ▶ By Being a Media Contrarian You Can Prosper

- ▶ Financial Magazine Ratings

- ▶ Examples of Confusing Media Information

By its very definition, the "news" is events that are out of the ordinary. Newspapers, television and radio news shows, and magazines are not in the business of reporting. They are in the business of market share. Every one of these sources wants a bigger listening, reading, or viewing audience. Market share is how advertising and subscription rates are determined. Without subscribers and advertisers, none of these publications would exist.

Few things sell as well as fear and greed. Let me rephrase that. Nothing sells better than fear, greed and sex. The press thrives on disaster, both human and financial. When was the last time you saw a headline that read "2,500 Planes Landed Safely Today" or "12,000 Publicly Traded Corporations Reported Profits Last Year"? Out of fairness to the media, such events are not reported because they do not really fall within the definition of news; they are ordinary events.

Since the stock market goes up more often than not, it is not considered news when stock prices go up. As a side note, over the past 65 years, there have been more days when stocks have gone down than up. The percentages change once you start looking at weekly, monthly, quarterly, or annual figures. Nevertheless, when stocks have a few bad days or weeks in a row, the bear market soothsayers start coming out of the woodwork. These "experts" are interviewed and we are supposed to believe that they must have predictive powers—otherwise, why would they be in the national news?

The Financial Periodicals

One of the investor's worst enemies can be the monthly financial magazine. As an example, after the 1987 stock market crash, the next 15 cover stories for one such publication were about safe places to invest your money (i.e., places other than directly into the stock market). It does not take a genius to look back at the last half-century and see that when stocks drop by 20% or more, a great buying oppor-tunity exists. We like to buy things when they are on sale. We might even buy more things if the discounted price is great enough. If stocks are a good deal when they are down 5 to 10%, they become a screaming buy when they fall 20 to 50%.

Dollars & Sense: To get a better, hands-on feeling of why news stories and articles can sometimes be misleading as well as confusing, you only need to look at *The Wall Street Journal* or *Investor's Daily* for a week, any week. On a given day you will find one or more positive articles or paragraphs and one or more negative viewpoints about the same company or stock about the direction of the stock market.

Financial periodicals would be much more responsible, but perhaps sell fewer copies, if they were to give investors a historical perspective about the markets after there has been a particularly good runup or downturn in prices. When you think about it, it is not in a periodical's best interest to fully inform you. If readers knew the whole pic-ture, there would be no need to ever buy or subscribe to a financial magazine whose chief appeal is giving readers "insight" into what they should be doing next with their portfolios. After all, if the solution were, which it most often would be, simply "hold tight," there would be no mystery and no need to find out what the financial gurus were dishing out next month.

Obviously, many of these periodicals provide a wide range of information and do not deal solely with the "flavor of the month" (i.e., where to invest your money now).

However, that impulse to buy a magazine greatly diminishes when the cover story is "Ten Places to Retire" instead of "Ten Safe Places to Invest Your Money Now" (now that the stock market has crashed).

THE MAGAZINE RATINGS GAME

Each month, financial magazines have to come up with a catchy cover title and story to attract newsstand readers (the impulse buyers). They must also find a way to make their many subscribers anxious to see what's inside that month's issue. Since mutual funds are perhaps the most popular investment vehicle (and since most of the magazine's advertisers are no-load mutual fund companies), it is natural that the magazine would tend to come up with snappy feature stories about funds.

For example, listed below are six feature *Money Magazine* article titles from February 1992 through February 1996. What is amazing about this roster is that there is only one fund repeated from issue to issue. Are we supposed to assume that a mutual fund that is "great" in 1992 is no longer worthy in 1993, 1994, 1995, or 1996? And are we further supposed to conclude that no fund is "best" or "great" for more than one year, no matter what year we look at?

Money Magazine: **Mutual Fund Repeats**		
Date	*Title*	*Number Of Repeats From Any Previous Issue*
Feb. 1992	"Great Mutual Funds to Buy Now"	—
Feb. 1993	"Funds to Buy Now"	1/20
Feb. 1994	"The 9 Best Funds to Own Now"	0/32
Aug. 1994	"The 10 Best Funds Today"	0/41
Feb. 1995	"The 8 Most Dependable Mutual Funds"	0/51
Feb. 1996	"Undiscovered Stars"	0/60

With recommendations like these, is it any wonder that investors in mutual funds have dramatically different results from the mutual funds themselves? A study conducted by a mutual fund company covering the past five years shows that the average stock (equity) fund had an average annual return of 12%. The study tracked a few hundred people that were actually in these funds. At the end of five years, the investors in these funds had an average annual return of -2%. This means that instead of having $100,000 that grew to $176,234 (12% compounded for 5 years), the $100,000 shrunk to roughly $90,392 (-2% compounded for five years).

If these investors were "actually in these funds," how come they lost close to $10,000 instead of making, on average, over $76,000? Well, the answer is that these investors kept switching their money from one fund to another. When a fund they owned did not perform as expected over some short period of time, it was swapped for one that had just done well or was touted as being the next "best" or "great" fund.

Are the financial magazines the only ones to blame for these kind of results or investor knee-jerk reactions? No. There are also commission-driven (or simply impatient or ignorant) brokers and financial planners who should rightfully share in the blame. Think of the tens or hundreds of billions of dollars that are lost every year by mutual fund investors alone who do not stay the course and are often influenced by the ill-advised brokers and financial magazines of the world. What a waste.

Full Disclosure

It should be quickly pointed out (before any scathing reviews about me or my books appear) that each year I write a book titled *The 100 Best Mutual Funds You Can Buy*. The book is now in its seventh edition and is a best-selling book on mutual funds. I am proud of the book on several counts: (1) I was the first book author to include money market funds; (2) I was the first to show the tax efficiency of the mutual funds included in the book; (3) I was the first to point out the difference between "volatility" (standard deviation) and "risk"; and (4) I was the first to point out that there is no relationship between a fund's turnover rate and its tax ramifications (something most of the financial press has still not figured out even though I first started writing about this topic several years ago). Despite all of this self-praise, one could argue that I am being hypocritical (based on the title of the book).

Yet, there is a big difference. I have lots of repeats from year to year. And, unlike many of the financial magazines, I do not favor one type of fund (no-load) over another (load, also known as those that charge a commission). This is easy for me to do since I do not rely on advertisers. Part of the reason I write the book each year is that with approximately 8,000 funds, the task of selecting a mutual fund can be difficult at best.

A number of funds tell you that they are number one, and while this may be true during select periods of time, the real quantifier should be whether or not a particular fund coincides with what you are trying to do with your money based upon your risk level, time horizon, biases, existing holdings, and tax bracket. These are all key points covered in the book each year. However, most importantly, I point out that just because a fund does not make my top 100 list or does not reappear in some subsequent edition does not mean that it is still not an excellent fund. To say that there are only 100 great funds is ridiculous.

One last self-grandising point I would like to make before moving on. I recommend funds in every major category, even those categories that have not performed well over the past couple of years. Unlike other writers, I do this because it should be obvious to any student of financial history that a poor performing category has a very good chance of being the next great performing category. Not only has this repeatedly been true throughout the history of the mutual fund industry, it also coincides with the required mutual fund disclaimer (that must appear in any mutual fund advertisement that refers to performance figures) that "past results are no guarantee of future returns."

MORE CONFUSION

To be fair to the financial magazines, let me quickly uncover some other confusing sources of information:

- ▶ If you have ever watched *Wall Street Week* on PBS, you know about the "Elves" index—a panel of 10 stock market "experts." What may surprise you is how wrong this blue ribbon panel has been. Since the introduction of this 10-member panel on October 3, 1989, the panel has been the most positive on January 3, 1992 (six bullish, four neutral, zero negative). Yet, during the following three months, results were negative: January 1992 (-1.9%), February 1992 (+1.2%), and March 1992 (-1.9%). The panel was the most negative on October 12, 1990 (because the market's low point for the year was one day earlier, October 11, 1990 when the Dow bottomed at 2365.10). During the next three months, the market did surprisingly well: October 1990 (-0.4%), November 1990 (+6.4%), and December 1990 (+2.7%).

- ▶ Oftentimes, the experts are simply wrong. Consider the following quotations: (1) "The summer rally could be the last rally in this bull market. If Bush is going to lose, it is the last rally." (Robert Farrell, chief market analyst, Merrill Lynch in *Barron's* 6/29/92); (2) "This is the early stage of a bear market . . . something truly serious is going on." (Justin Mamis of The Technical Analyst in the *New York Times* 7/8/92); (3) "Earnings expectations are just too high. I think the bull market ended in February for most stocks."

(Michael Metz, Oppenheimer & Co. in *Business Week* 8/3/92); (4) All future rallies will fail . . . It'll be steady agony in 1993." (Stan Weinstein, from *The Professional Tape Reader,* in *USA Today* 9/92); (5) "We've got maybe 4 to 6 weeks of the bull market left. Then run for the hills." (Ralph Acampora, Prudential Securities, in *Publication* 4/2/93); (6) "Stocks and bonds are in for a bloodbath. The financial pain will be awesome." (Charles Minter, Comstock Partners, in *USA Today* 5/21/93).

▶ A 1994 column in *The Wall Street Journal* contained the following statement: " . . . market statistics show that anyone who bought stocks at the top of the market in 1973, instead of investing in Treasury bills, would have had to wait until the mid-80s at best to break even." Does this mean an investment in stocks in 1973 was a money-loser for 12 long years? No, and perhaps it is worthwhile to clarify exactly what did happen.

The Dow Jones Industrial Average peaked at 1051.70 on January 11, 1973 and then began a long slide, bottoming at 577.60 on December 6, 1974. One dollar invested in S & P 500 stocks (with dividends reinvested) on January 1, 1973 was worth $0.63 by year-end 1974, but recovered to $1.01 by June 1976. In a "horse race" between S & P 500 stocks and one-month Treasury bills, the stock portfolio does not pull ahead of the T-bill fund until May 1985, when it reached $2.88 (vs. $2.78 for T-bills).

▶ Few issues of *Barron's* are awaited as eagerly as those issues that highlight the magazine's Roundtable interviews with Wall Street superstars such as Mario Gabelli, John Neff, and Peter Lynch who reveal their favorite stocks. According to a study conducted by the Tulane University Business School, a reader who bought each stock one trading day after publication, and held for a year, would have earned a mere 21/100 of a percentage point more than a sample control group. The study looked at all 1,599 stock picks made in the 24-year period between 1968 and 1991. Over two years, and also over three years, the Roundtable picks did slightly worse than the norm.

▶ Most prominent among the mutual fund information providers are Morningstar, Inc. in Chicago and Lipper Analytical Services, Inc. in Summit, N.J. In the summer of 1994, Lipper produced the results of a study that showed that Morningstar five-star stock funds underperformed the market in the ensuing 12-month period. The analysis included funds rated in 1990, 1991, 1992, and 1993.

▶ A mutual fund that finished at the pinnacle of the investment rankings in any one year is a matter of chance and gives you no indication of how the fund will perform the following year. The funds that ranked one, two, three, and four on the basis of investment return for 1989 finished with rankings of 389, 1701, 1707, and 1689 respectively for 1990.

▶ It is disturbing that so many investors are using ratings to pick mutual funds because about 90% of the returns from a particular mutual fund are due to that fund's asset allocation or investment style. Many services do not consider the individual investment style of a fund when they assign its ratings. Rather, the performance of a particular asset class can be overemphasized. The table below shows how the Morningstar ratings can be influenced by asset class performance. DFA Japanese Small Company is an index fund—shouldn't it therefore have the same rating all of the time? Is it only a coincidence that the fund actually did better when it had one star than when it had five stars? Do you want your rating system to work like that?

DFA Japanese Small Co. Star Ratings at Beginning of Year vs. U.S. Stock Returns

Year	Stars	DFA Japan Fund	S & P 500
1990	5	-33.4%	-3.1%
1991	5	17.1%	30.5%
1992	3	-26.1%	7.6%
1993	1	14.2%	10.0%
1994 1st quarter	1	28.4%	-3.8%

▶ According to a 1994 study by Morningstar, there were close to 220 growth funds that had track records of at least five years; the average return for this group was 12.5% per year. Surprisingly, the average annual return for actual investors in growth funds for this same five-year period was -2.2% per year. Obviously, investors in stock funds are not being patient enough. The average redemption rate in mutual funds is a little over 18% per year.

▶ FundMinder reviewed the performance of 200 no-load growth mutual funds from 1989 to 1994 and compared these gains with the gains of actual investors who bought and sold these funds, during the same time. Average annual returns for no-load growth funds were 12% vs. only 2% for investors who were in and out of these funds during the same period. Thus, the return that the typical investor actually realizes has more to do with his or her behavior (i.e., not being patient) than a fund's investment results.

▶ "We do not have, never have had, and never will have an opinion about where the stock market, interest rates, or business activity will be a year from now."(Warren Buffett, considered one of the very best investors in history.)

▶ On August 13, 1979, *Business Week* declared on its cover, "The Death of Equities." At the time, the Dow Jones Industrial Average was 875. In 1899, Charles H. Duell, director of the U.S. Patent Office, stated, "Everything that can be invented has already been invented."

▶ In February, 1989, *Business Week* published its list of mutual funds, boasting that these "fund picks have really paid off" and ranking funds solely according to their risk-adjusted returns for the previous five years (1984–88). *Business Week*'s top-rated funds for those five years had a collective annualized rate of return of 19.3%. Their lowest-rated funds had a puny 1.1% per year return as a group. Yet, if an investor had rented a time machine and gone back seven weeks to December 29, 1988 to buy all of the top-rated funds, he would have received 9.5% per year for the next three years. However, had he bought *Business Week*'s lowest-rated funds instead, his return would have been 20.6% per year!

▶ *Business Week*'s top-rated funds as published in their February 1992 issue gained 21% per year as a group from 1987 through 1991. For the next two years they returned 6.3% per year. In comparison, their lowest-rated funds, which had gained 69% per year (1987 to 1991), advanced by 15.4% per year during 1992 to 1993. All of this goes to show that the past is truly not a good indicator of future results.

Instant Karma

One of the things financial advisors like me dread is the clients who come in for a quarterly or annual review with their own list of winners. These people have good intentions, but even if the intentions were somehow not so noble, who can complain—after all, it is their money we're talking about. They have done some reading and are at least somewhat convinced that I (or whomever their advisor or broker might be) have made at least some mistakes. In short, they want to know why none of the funds that they are in (and were recommended by the advisor) are included in the list they have recently cut out of a newspaper, newsletter, or magazine. Moreover, some of these same investors are a little miffed (to put it nicely) that the funds selected by the advisor have underperformed some, most, or all of those on "the list."

The conversation might go something like this: "John (the advisor), I know we agreed that this was going to be a long-term commitment, but after being with you a year, I (the client) have some concerns. I have clipped out this article from my local paper (or whatever source) and I see a number of funds that have gone up more than mine. In fact, I have come to learn that most (or all) of the funds you have for me have not even done as well as the S & P 500 over the past year. What's the deal?" (A variation of this discussion is, "I could have done better investing in bank CDs . . . and they're a no brainer and much safer.")

Before even looking at the list, certain questions need to be addressed:

▶ Are investment recommendations going to be based on an article?

▶ If outside sources are to be used, what will happen when they (or a similar source) come out with a new list?

▶ Since these lists do not deal with risk, is the issue of risk no longer being considered?

▶ Does it no longer matter how the different parts of the portfolio are correlated?

▶ Is it now okay to load up heavily on one investment category (most lists are highly concentrated in one category such as "growth" or "emerging markets")?

▶ Are short-term records now more important than long-term performance figures?

▶ What do you hope to accomplish by following this new list?

▶ Which funds are to be chosen if there are two or more lists from different publications?

> ► If publication X picks a certain fund but publication Y pans it, what do we do?

> ► Are weekly publications a better source than monthly, quarterly, or annual periodicals?

> ► Are book lists better or worse than one from a periodical?

> ► What kind of background does the financial writer have?

This last point is something no one ever discusses. The person writing the article probably has little, if any, real world experience. They may have been with the magazine for a number of years, but how many of those years have they covered mutual funds? Do you ever wonder why few, if any, of these writers have any kind of financial credentials? Why do investors seek out designated advisors but will blindly follow a writer that has no degrees or credentials that are relevant to what is being written about?

There is an old saying: "Those who can't, teach." The vast majority of people who edit and write these articles could not make it in the real world. The pay they receive is a fraction of what a decent advisor makes. And, although I do not believe that intelligence has much to do with one's annual income, you have to wonder if these people are so accurate, why aren't they making much more money trading in their own accounts or working in the financial services industry?

What You Should Do

There is a world of difference between the media's criteria for selecting a mutual fund (or other kind of investment vehicle) and what your agenda should be:

Media's Criteria for Investment Selection	What Your Investment Criteria Should Be
short-term performance	risk level
inadequate concern for risk level	time horizon
amount in any one category is not importantlong-term track record	the "fit" with the rest of of your holdings loss potential bad periods
	tax consequences
	management tenure

Legg Mason, a well-known money management firm did a study to review the effectiveness of magazine rankings of mutual funds. The study took a random sample of 25 recommended growth and income funds from *Business Week, Forbes, Kiplinger,* and *Money Magazine* in 1992. Each of these 25 funds' 1992 ratings were compared to how well the fund performed in 1993 plus its three-year record, ending in 1994. The study found no correlation between these fund ratings and their future performance.

There are additional issues that are rarely mentioned by these publications when they present their new list of recommendations. First, when you make a change, a tax event is triggered. Even if you make an exchange within the same fund family, a sale and purchase tax are placed and the IRS is notified (via a 1099) of such change(s). Second, there may be some transaction costs (a commission or fee) if a change is made. Third, the publication may be biased—only no-load funds are being recommended because the publication caters to do-it-yourselfers or because most of the advertisers are no-load mutual fund companies.

Future Lists

The number of lists is only going to increase in the future. Magazines have found that these kinds of articles help increase periodical sales. Plus the number of financial publications is only growing. It is very easy to write about what has performed well, just like there is little risk in being an armchair quarterback. With close to 8,000 different mutual funds (and the list keeps growing), there will always be a number of funds that outperform yours over any given day, week, month, quarter, or even year.

Despite what I have just described, most people will continue to make their own investment decisions based on an ad or rating service. These people will fail to make the connection that this form of investment selection is not much different than looking at the racing forms and attempting to pick today's winning horses based solely on how they placed the last race.

We Are All in the Dark, to One Degree or Another

The truth is, none of us knows what the top 10 or best 100 investments are or will be. Despite this reality, an investment plan or strategy can still be of tremendous help. As an investor, a known strategy will save you quite a bit of time—steering you away from investments that are either too conservative or too risky. The amount of time you have to invest is also another filter that should be used to sort through. Before closing on this topic of the media, let me give you one last example:

At the beginning of 1995, a mutual fund magazine surveyed a couple of hundred equity fund managers (presumably these people polled are biased in favor of stocks since these are the kinds of securities they deal in). The consensus of these stock fund managers was that stocks would have a total return of somewhere between 0 and 5% for the 1995 calendar year. A January 1995 front-page article in *The Wall Street Journal* referenced a poll taken by pension fund managers across the country. The 100 to 200 managers surveyed felt that 1995 would be a flat year for stocks. Finally, I went to a two-day seminar put on by one of the largest mutual fund companies in the country (they also have one of the best track records). This fund company has a couple of dozen funds, domestic and international. The majority of their offerings are stock funds but they also have some bond funds. It was their belief that 1995 would be a flat to slightly positive year for stocks. As you may recall, 1995 turned out to be one of the best years ever for common stocks. The stock market was up about 37%.

Money Talks:

When someone mentions "the stock market" to you, there is a strong likelihood that they are referring to the Dow Jones Industrial Average (also known as "the Dow"). The Dow is comprised of just 30 stocks; companies are not frequently added or taken off of this list. Most stock market performance charts use figures from the Standard & Poor's 500 (also known as the S & P 500). As you might suspect, this index is much more representative of all U.S. stocks since it is comprised of 500 different issues and the list is revised on a more frequent basis. Most equity money managers are measured by their bosses against the S & P 500 and not the Dow.

Summary

The media's job is to report the news, things that are out of the ordinary. Unfortunately for investors, stock market crashes and downturns are out of the ordinary. I say "unfortunately" because such stories cause investor panic and confusion. If you can learn to focus on your objectives and not be overly influenced by short-term market activity, you will not only get better results, your life will be calmer.

The next chapter starts to lay the groundwork necessary for you to construct your own portfolio and make your own future projections. Chapter 4 is used in conjunction with the appendix.

Dollars & Sense: Years ago, I used to have a computer screen on my desk that was connected to a service that gave me stock quotes and market activity by the second. My performance and the performance of my clients suffered during this period because I made the critical mistake of being caught up in the moment. What I sometimes thought were positive or negative "trends" often turned out to be the exact opposite an hour or day later.

Let's Remember This:

- ▶ Why you should be leary about the media's role in reporting.

- ▶ Why a contrarian view is often best.

- ▶ Examples of what happens when the financial press starts making recommendations and "top 10" lists.

USING FINANCIAL TABLES

WHAT WE ARE GOING TO TALK ABOUT IN THIS CHAPTER:

▶ Getting Friendly with Financial Tables

▶ Determining What Annual Contributions Will Grow To

▶ Reaching a Specific Dollar Goal

Financial tables are the core of any financial software. These tables enable the program to compute the projected growth of one dollar in so many years, the projected growth of five dollars invested each year, the effects of inflation, and what happens to principal when a certain percentage is taken out each year. The only thing you or I have to do is to plug in a couple of numbers.

The financial tables in the appendix work exactly the same way. But, instead of using a computer, you simply look up a number (often referred to as a "factor") in one of the tables and multiply that factor by another number, either a lump-sum figure or a series of equal investments or withdrawals. The multiplication can either be done by hand or with a very basic hand-held calculator.

The purpose of this chapter is to familiarize you with just four financial tables. These financial tables can answer just about any question you have about money, interest, inflation, and withdrawals. The reason you will want to know how these tables work is that the tables are an integral part of any financial plan and, therefore, the asset allocation decision.

Money Talks: The term "financial tables" can refer to any set of numbers or figures. The four financial tables used in this book show you how to make some important but simple multiplication or division calculations. Your bookstore or local library should carry a number of books devoted solely to financial tables; a number of these books are designed to be used by people in specific areas (e.g., insurance, financial planning, banking, real estate, etc.).

Deciding whether or not you should have 30% of your portfolio in medium-term government bonds or high-yield bonds cannot be made until it is first determined what you are trying to do with your money—how much growth or income is necessary and over what period of time. In turn, the "how much growth" and the "period of time" are based on the lump-sum you are trying to obtain (the use of Table 1 or Table 2, as you will see below). The other two tables are used when the situation becomes more complex—while trying to obtain a goal of X dollars, a withdrawal is made and needs to be replaced in even installments (Table 3) or all at once, but some time in the future (Table 4). The final table (Table 4 again) will also show you the cumulative effects of inflation, either on a dollar or an entire investment portfolio.

You can also have some fun or play some games with these tables by answering the questions such as: (1) how much would $1 have grown had President George Washington been able to invest it in the stock market; (2) the difference between compound interest and simple interest on a $5 deposit in a hypothetical bank that Columbus walked into when he first landed on North America; (3) how long it would take to end up with $1,000,000; (4) deciding whether to take $1,000 today or take $1 the first day, $2 the second day, $4 the third day and so on, for 20 days; or (5) what would happen if inflation averaged 15% a year.

Dollars & $ense: I use these financial tables in my investment advisory practice on an almost daily basis. These tables are much easier, and often quicker, then relying on a software program. The beauty of these tables is that they never go out of date—interest rates and returns will change over time, but not these tables. The tables, shown in detail in the appendix, normally cost about $15 if you buy a complete bookfull. The tables provided in the appendix, although only 20 pages in length, should satisfy 99% of all investors and financial planners.

Most of this chapter is a series of examples, divided into four parts or tables: Table 1, "When A Single Sum Grows For One Or More Years"; Table 2, "When a Series of Equal Deposits Grows For One or More Years"; Table 3, "How Much Is Needed to be

Invested Each Year to End Up With a Certain Amount"; and Table 4, "How Much a Lump-Sum in the Future is Worth Today." As you will see, these tables will also show you the effects of a single or multiple withdrawal as well as the effects of inflation.

Table 1: When a Single Sum Grows For One or More Years

Table 1 and Table 2 are the most frequently used tables when it comes to financial planning and asset allocation. Table 1 is popular because it is used whenever someone is looking at their current situation and wants to calculate what his portfolio will be worth in the future. The future could be next year or several decades from now.

Table 1 is often used in conjunction with Table 2 because Table 1 can only "look ahead" with current assets; it cannot be used for any additional investments that might be made in the future (e.g., monthly, quarterly, or annual retirement plan contributions). There are only three things you need to know in order to use Table 1: (1) the amount of time the money can be left alone to grow; (2) the lump-sum figure; and (3) the actual or assumed rate of growth for that lump-sum figure. Listed below are some examples as to when you would use Table 1.

Example #1

John and Mary have $20,000 in bank CDs. They want to know what their $20,000 will be worth in 17 years when John retires. The couple plans on keeping all of the money in CDs and they assume that their CDs will continue to yield 6% per year.

	Rate 6%			
Year	Table 1 Compounding Factor for 1[1]	Table 2 Compounding Factor for 1 Per Annum[2]	Table 3 Sinking Fund Factor[3]	Table 4 Discount Factor[4]
1	1.06	1.00	1.00	.943
etc.	—	—	—	—
17	2.69	28.21	.036	.371

[1] What an initial amount becomes when growing at compound interest.

[2] Growth of equal year-end deposits all growing at compound interest.

[3] Level deposit required each year to reach 1 by a given year.

[4] How much 1 at a future date is worth today.

Answer: (a) Go to the appendix and find the page titled "Rate 6%"; (b) go down the first column until you get to "Year 17"; (c) go to the right, under the first column (since we are dealing with a single, lump-sum figure) and find the factor "2.69"; (d) multiply that factor by $20,000; (e) the resulting figure $53,800 (2.69 × $20,000) is the answer.

Example #2

Ben has $7,000 in a mutual fund and has just received $5,000 as a gift from his parents. Ben is curious and would like to know what his assets ($12,000 total) will be worth in 5, 10, and 15 years. He is assuming that his mutual fund will continue to grow at 8% per year.

	Rate 8%			
Year	Table 1 Compounding Factor for 1[1]	Table 2 Compounding Factor for 1 Per Annum[2]	Table 3 Sinking Fund Factor[3]	Table 4 Discount Factor[4]
1	1.08	1.00	1.00	.926
etc.	—	—	—	—
5	1.47	5.87	.171	.681
etc.	—	—	—	—
10	2.16	14.49	.069	.463
etc.	—	—	—	—
15	3.17	27.15	.037	.315

[1] What an initial amount becomes when growing at compound interest.

[2] Growth of equal year-end deposits all growing at compound interest.

[3] Level deposit required each year to reach 1 by a given year.

[4] How much 1 at a future date is worth today.

Answer: (a) Go to the appendix and find the page titled "Rate 8%"; (b) go down the first column until you get to "Year 5"; (c) go to the right, under the first column (since we are dealing with a single, lump-sum figure) and find the factor "1.47"; (d) multiply that factor by $12,000; (e) the resulting figure $17,640 (1.47 × $12,000) is the answer. To find the value in 10 and 15 years, repeat the same steps but use different factors—2.16 for 10 years and 3.17 for 15 years.

Example #3

Susan has been offered an early-retirement package from her employer. Besides providing her with some medical and life insurance benefits for a number of years, they are also offering her $150,000. If she accepts the offer, Susan will go to work for a friend and will be able to live off the lower salary. Susan is 57 years old and wants to know the projected growth of $150,000 in eight years when she is eligible for full Social Security benefits. She has been reading about investments and feels comfortable in a balanced portfolio that historically has grown at 10% annually.

		Rate 10%		
Year	*Table 1 Compounding Factor for 1[1]*	*Table 2 Compounding Factor for 1 Per Annum[2]*	*Table 3 Sinking Fund Factor[3]*	*Table 4 Discount Factor[4]*
1	1.10	1.00	1.00	.909
etc.	—	—	—	—
8	2.14	11.44	.087	.467

[1] What an initial amount becomes when growing at compound interest.

[2] Growth of equal year-end deposits all growing at compound interest.

[3] Level deposit required each year to reach 1 by a given year.

[4] How much 1 at a future date is worth today.

Answer: (a) Go to the appendix and find the page titled "Rate 10%"; (b) go down the first column until you get to "Year 8"; (c) go to the right, under the first column (since we are dealing with a single, lump-sum figure) and find the factor "2.14"; (d) multiply that factor by $150,000; (e) the resulting figure $321,000 (2.14 × $150,000) is the answer.

Example #4

Dan has just become a grandfather. He is interested in contributing $5,000 to his granddaughter's college fund and wants to know what the $5,000 will grow to in 18 years. Dan has been told that U.S. stocks have averaged 12% per year over the past half-century.

		Rate 12%		
Year	Table 1 Compounding Factor for 1[1]	Table 2 Compounding Factor for 1 Per Annum[2]	Table 3 Sinking Fund Factor[3]	Table 4 Discount Factor[4]
1	1.12	1.00	1.00	.893
etc.	—	—	—	—
18	7.69	55.75	.018	.130

[1] What an initial amount becomes when growing at compound interest.

[2] Growth of equal year-end deposits all growing at compound interest.

[3] Level deposit required each year to reach 1 by a given year.

[4] How much 1 at a future date is worth today.

Answer: (a) Go to the appendix and find the page titled "Rate 12%"; (b) go down the first column until you get to "Year 18"; (c) go to the right, under the first column (since we are dealing with a single, lump-sum figure) and find the factor "7.69"; (d) multiply that factor by $5,000; (e) the resulting figure $38,450 (7.69 × $5,000) is the answer.

Example #5

Judi, age 40, has the following portfolio (with the assumed future rates of growth shown in parentheses): (a) $12,000 in CDs (5%); (b) $17,000 in the XYZ growth fund (13%); (c) $26,000 in the ABC tax-free bond fund (6%); and (d) $71,000 in the LMN fixed-rate annuity (7%). Judi is interested in knowing what her portfolio will be worth when she is 60 and 65. If the projected figure is high enough, she may retire at age 60.

		Rate 5%		
Year	Table 1 Compounding Factor for 1[1]	Table 2 Compounding Factor for 1 Per Annum[2]	Table 3 Sinking Fund Factor[3]	Table 4 Discount Factor[4]
1	1.05	1.00	1.00	.952
etc.	—	—	—	—
20	2.65	33.07	.030	.377
etc.	—	—	—	—
25	3.39	47.73	.021	.295

[1] What an initial amount becomes when growing at compound interest.

[2] Growth of equal year-end deposits all growing at compound interest.

[3] Level deposit required each year to reach 1 by a given year.

[4] How much 1 at a future date is worth today.

Answer: (a) Go to the appendix and find the page titled "Rate 5%"; (b) go down the first column until you get to "Year 20"; (c) go to the right, under the first column (since we are dealing with a single, lump-sum figure) and find the factor "2.65"; (d) multiply that factor by $12,000; (e) the resulting figure $31,800 (2.65 × $12,000) is what the CD money will be worth when Judi turns 60. Use similar steps to find out what the rest of her portfolio will be worth when she turns 60; make sure you use different "rate" tables since she has various investments growing at different expected rates of return. To find out what Judi's portfolio will be worth in 25 years, when she turns 65, use the same tables but use the factors listed next to "Year 25".

As you can see from all five of these examples, a lump-sum figure is involved. In one case, two figures are added together to get a single sum. In the final example, four different computations are involved because four different sums and four different rates of return are assumed, projected, or guaranteed.

TABLE 2: WHEN A SERIES OF EQUAL DEPOSITS GROWS FOR ONE OR MORE YEARS

Table 2 is more popular with younger people because it is based on the assumption that a certain amount of money is being saved or invested each year. It is used whenever you hear someone say something like, "I'm investing $2,000 each year into my IRA" or "My boss contributes $5,500 every year into my retirement account."

Table 2, like Table 1, "looks" to the future and will show you what you will end up with at the end of one year or in dozens of years. Table 2 is often used in conjunction with Table 1 because many people have a portfolio (a lump-sum figure that would use Table 1) and they can add money to their portfolio every year (a series of equal deposits that would require the use of Table 2).

An important point to keep in mind about Table 2: it is simpler to use than most people would suspect. As an example, if you can save $100 a month, simply assume that $1,200 can be invested each year. Similarly, if you think you can save between $3,000 and $4,000 each year, use $3,500 per year.

Like Table 1, there are only a few things you need to know before using Table 2 to make your own projections: (1) how much can be invested each year; (2) how many years can you continue to make similar investments; and (3) the rate of return you want to assume the invested dollars are growing. Listed below are some examples as to when you would use Table 2.

Example #1

John and Mary can save $3,000 a year. John and Mary are both 35 years old and want to know what the $3,000 in annual savings will grow to when they retire at age 60. The couple loves the ABC Aggressive Growth Fund and plans to invest the $3,000 each year into this fund which has averaged 15% annually over the past 15 years.

		Rate 15%		
Year	Table 1 Compounding Factor for 1[1]	Table 2 Compounding Factor for 1 Per Annum[2]	Table 3 Sinking Fund Factor[3]	Table 4 Discount Factor[4]
1	1.15	1.00	1.00	.870
etc.	—	—	—	—
25	32.92	212.79	.0047	.030

[1] What an initial amount becomes when growing at compound interest.

[2] Growth of equal year-end deposits all growing at compound interest.

[3] Level deposit required each year to reach 1 by a given year.

[4] How much 1 at a future date is worth today.

Answer: (a) Go to the appendix and find the page titled "Rate 15%"; (b) go down the first column until you get to "Year 25"; (c) go to the right, under the second column (since we are dealing with a series of deposits) and find the factor "212.79"; (d) multiply that factor by $3,000; (e) the resulting figure $638,370 (212.79 × $3,000) is the answer. The factor, 212.79, is so high because it takes into account annual investments over 25 years.

Example #2

Ben has just found out that he is getting a $150 a month raise. He has decided to invest all of this money each month into an IRA account. Ben's banker tells him that the money can conservatively be invested at 6% per year. Ben's stockbroker says that he should be able to average 11% in a fairly conservative mutual fund. Before deciding what to do, Ben wants to know what each investment will be worth in 20 years.

		Rate 6%		
Year	Table 1 Compounding Factor for 1[1]	Table 2 Compounding Factor for 1 Per Annum[2]	Table 3 Sinking Fund Factor[3]	Table 4 Discount Factor[4]
1	1.06	1.00	1.00	.943
etc.	—	—	—	—
20	3.21	36.79	.027	.312

[1] What an initial amount becomes when growing at compound interest.

[2] Growth of equal year-end deposits all growing at compound interest.

[3] Level deposit required each year to reach 1 by a given year.

[4] How much 1 at a future date is worth today.

Answer: (a) Go to the appendix and find the page titled "Rate 6%"; (b) go down the first column until you get to "Year 20"; (c) go to the right, under the second column and find the factor "36.79"; (d) multiply that factor by $1,800 (the $150 a month that can be saved each month equals $1,800 per year); (e) the resulting figure $66,222 (36.79 × $1,800) is the answer.

		Rate 11%		
Year	Table 1 Compounding Factor for 1[1]	Table 2 Compounding Factor for 1 Per Annum[2]	Table 3 Sinking Fund Factor[3]	Table 4 Discount Factor[4]
1	1.11	1.00	1.00	.901
etc.	—	—	—	—
20	8.06	64.20	.016	.124

[1] What an initial amount becomes when growing at compound interest.

[2] Growth of equal year-end deposits all growing at compound interest.

[3] Level deposit required each year to reach 1 by a given year.

[4] How much 1 at a future date is worth today.

Answer: (a) Go to the appendix and find the page titled "Rate 11%"; (b) go down the first column until you get to "Year 20"; (c) go to the right, under the second column and find the factor "64.20"; (d) multiply that factor by $1,800; (e) the resulting figure $115,560 (64.20 × $1,800) is the answer.

Example #3

Susan has been offered an early-retirement package from her employer. Besides providing her with some medical and life insurance benefits for a number of years, they are also offering her $2,000 a month; the money will be paid out for as many years as she worked for the company (14 years). Using other savings, Susan can invest $1,500 of the $2,000 for the entire 14 years. If she accepts the offer, Susan wants to know what she can expect to have when the early-retirement package runs out. She feels comfortable with a 9% assumed rate of growth.

	Rate 9%			
Year	Table 1 Compounding Factor for 1[1]	Table 2 Compounding Factor for 1 Per Annum[2]	Table 3 Sinking Fund Factor[3]	Table 4 Discount Factor[4]
1	1.09	1.00	1.00	.917
etc.	—	—	—	—
14	3.34	26.02	.038	.299

[1] What an initial amount becomes when growing at compound interest.

[2] Growth of equal year-end deposits all growing at compound interest.

[3] Level deposit required each year to reach 1 by a given year.

[4] How much 1 at a future date is worth today.

Answer: (a) Go to the appendix and find the page titled "Rate 9%"; (b) go down the first column until you get to "Year 14"; (c) go to the right, under the second column and find the factor "26.02"; (d) multiply that factor by $18,000 ($1,500 a month times 12 months); (e) the resulting figure $468,360 (26.02 × $18,000) is the answer.

Example #4

Dan has just become a grandfather. He is interested in contributing $1,000 a year toward his granddaughter's college fund and wants to know the growth of his annual contribution after 17 years. Dan has been told that foreign stocks have averaged 14% per year over the past 15 years.

		Rate 14%		
Year	Table 1 Compounding Factor for 1[1]	Table 2 Compounding Factor for 1 Per Annum[2]	Table 3 Sinking Fund Factor[3]	Table 4 Discount Factor[4]
1	1.14	1.00	1.00	.877
etc.	—	—	—	—
17	9.28	59.12	.017	.108

[1] What an initial amount becomes when growing at compound interest.

[2] Growth of equal year-end deposits all growing at compound interest.

[3] Level deposit required each year to reach 1 by a given year.

[4] How much 1 at a future date is worth today.

Answer: (a) Go to the appendix and find the page titled "Rate 14%"; (b) go down the first column until you get to "Year 17"; (c) go to the right, under the second column and find the factor "59.12"; (d) multiply that factor by $1,000 (he will make only one deposit a year); (e) the resulting figure $59,120 (59.12 × $1,000) is the answer.

Example #5

Judi, age 40, has been reading a lot about retirement planning but has only recently taken the matter seriously. She is now committed to invest $700 from each paycheck toward her retirement. Judi gets paid twice a month and can continuously lend family members money and charge them 10% per annum. She plans on lending money to family members until she reaches her hoped-for retirement age of 62.

		Rate 10%		
Year	Table 1 Compounding Factor for 1[1]	Table 2 Compounding Factor for 1 Per Annum[2]	Table 3 Sinking Fund Factor[3]	Table 4 Discount Factor[4]
1	1.10	1.00	1.00	.909
etc.	—	—	—	—
22	8.14	71.40	.014	.123

[1] What an initial amount becomes when growing at compound interest.

[2] Growth of equal year-end deposits all growing at compound interest.

[3] Level deposit required each year to reach 1 by a given year.

[4] How much 1 at a future date is worth today.

Answer: (a) Go to the appendix and find the page titled "Rate 10%"; (b) go down the first column until you get to "Year 22"; (c) go to the right, under the second column and find the factor "71.40"; (d) multiply that factor by $16,800 ($700 times 2 pay periods per month times 12 months); (e) the resulting figure $1,199,520 (71.40 × $16,800) is the answer.

As you can see from all five of these examples, a series of payments or savings is involved. In several of the examples, money is being set aside on a more frequent basis than annually. However, it is still a good idea to add up what these contributions total each year and then use Table 2. Like the examples for Table 1, the time period and assumed rate of growth (or yield) is known, assumed, or projected.

TABLE 3: How Much Is Needed to be Invested Each Year to End Up With a Certain Amount

Table 3 is used for those of us who like to dream. People who want to know how long it will take to become a millionaire or pay off a home mortgage faster than normal. By seeing "the light at the end of the tunnel," Table 3 provides some encouragement and discipline. The saver knows that if things go as planned, there is a pot of gold at the end of the rainbow.

Table 3, like Table 2, assumes that you can save a certain amount each year. Table 3 shows that you will end up with "1" at the end of X number of years, assuming a certain amount is invested each year. The "1" you will end up with could be $100, $1 million or some odd number such as $123,500.

Like Table 1, there are only a few things you need to know before using Table 3 to make your own projections: (1) how much you want to end up with; (2) how many years you can invest; and (3) the rate of return you want to assume the invested dollars are growing. Listed below are some examples as to when you would use Table 3.

Example #1

John and Mary have just started earning some money and would like to buy a house in the future. They can handle the monthly mortgage payments but need $30,000 for the downpayment. Assuming a growth rate of 10%, they want to know how much they will need to save each year to end up with $30,000 within five years.

		Rate 10%		
Year	Table 1 Compounding Factor for 1[1]	Table 2 Compounding Factor for 1 Per Annum[2]	Table 3 Sinking Fund Factor[3]	Table 4 Discount Factor[4]
1	1.10	1.00	1.00	.909
etc.	—	—	—	—
5	1.61	6.11	.164	.621

[1] What an initial amount becomes when growing at compound interest.

[2] Growth of equal year-end deposits all growing at compound interest.

[3] Level deposit required each year to reach 1 by a given year.

[4] How much 1 at a future date is worth today.

Answer: (a) Go to the appendix and find the page titled "Rate 10%"; (b) go down the first column until you get to "Year 5"; (c) go to the right, under the third column and find the factor ".164"; (d) multiply that factor by $30,000; (e) the resulting figure $4,920 (.164 × $30,000) is the answer—how much needs to be saved each year.

Example #2

Ben has just found out that he won the lottery and will be receiving monthly install-ments of $10,000 over the next 10 years. Ben would like to know how much of the $10,000 he receives monthly needs to be invested so that he ends up with $1,000,000 in nine years. Ben's accountant tells him that Ben should be able to get about an 11% return on an investment portfolio that includes utility stocks, high-yield bonds, and blue chip stocks.

		Rate 11%		
Year	Table 1 Compounding Factor for 1[1]	Table 2 Compounding Factor for 1 Per Annum[2]	Table 3 Sinking Fund Factor[3]	Table 4 Discount Factor[4]
1	1.11	1.00	1.00	.901
etc.	—	—	—	—
9	2.56	14.16	.071	.391

[1] What an initial amount becomes when growing at compound interest.

[2] Growth of equal year-end deposits all growing at compound interest.

[3] Level deposit required each year to reach 1 by a given year.

[4] How much 1 at a future date is worth today.

Answer: (a) Go to the appendix and find the page titled "Rate 11%"; (b) go down the first column until you get to "Year 5"; (c) go to the right, under the third column and find the factor ".071"; (d) multiply that factor by $1,000,000; (e) the resulting figure $71,000 (.071 × $1,000,000) is the answer.

Example #3

Susan has been offered an early-retirement package from her employer. Besides providing her with some benefits for a number of years, they are also offering her $3,000 a month for the next seven years. Susan wants to know if she invests $1,800 of the $3,000 each month ($21,600 a year) whether or not it is even possible to have that money grow to $250,000 at the end of those seven years. She knows nothing about investments but is willing to consider investing aggressively if that is what is needed to end up with a quarter of a million dollars.

	Rate 16%			
Year	Table 1 Compounding Factor for 1[1]	Table 2 Compounding Factor for 1 Per Annum[2]	Table 3 Sinking Fund Factor[3]	Table 4 Discount Factor[4]
1	1.16	1.00	1.00	.862
etc.	—	—	—	—
7	2.83	11.41	.088	.354

[1] What an initial amount becomes when growing at compound interest.

[2] Growth of equal year-end deposits all growing at compound interest.

[3] Level deposit required each year to reach 1 by a given year.

[4] How much 1 at a future date is worth today.

Answer: This one is a little tricky. By trying different rates of return you can see what is too high (e.g., 17%) and what is too low (16%). As you will see, even at 16%, Susan is going to fall short. (a) Go to the appendix and find the page titled "Rate 16%"; (b) go down the first column until you get to "Year 7"; (c) go to the right, under the third column and find the factor ".088"; (d) multiply that factor by $250,000; (e) the resulting figure $22,000 (.088 × $250,000) is what Susan needs to save each year to end up with $250,000. If she were to somehow average 17% a year, $21,600 would definitely be enough.

Example #4

Dan has just become a grandfather. He has been reading some articles about the high cost of college. Dan figures that his granddaughter will need $160,000 by the time she enters college in 19 years. Since "time is on her side," Dan wants to invest the money aggressively and believes that despite the ups and downs of the stock market, the invested money will grow at an average annual rate of 15%. Dan wants to know how much he will have to invest each year so that his granddaughter will end up with $160,000.

	Rate 15%			
Year	Table 1 *Compounding* *Factor for 1*[1]	Table 2 *Compounding* *Factor for* *1 Per Annum*[2]	Table 3 *Sinking Fund* *Factor*[3]	Table 4 *Discount* *Factor*[4]
1	1.15	1.00	1.00	.870
etc.	—	—	—	—
19	14.23	88.21	.011	.070

[1] What an initial amount becomes when growing at compound interest.

[2] Growth of equal year-end deposits all growing at compound interest.

[3] Level deposit required each year to reach 1 by a given year.

[4] How much 1 at a future date is worth today.

Answer: (a) Go to the appendix and find the page titled "Rate 15%"; (b) go down the first column until you get to "Year 19"; (c) go to the right, under the third column and find the factor ".011"; (d) multiply that factor by $160,000; (e) the resulting figure $1,760 (.011 × $160,000) is the answer.

Example #5

Judi, age 40, has been reading a lot about retirement planning but has only recently taken the matter seriously. She wants to be a millionaire when she retires but needs to know what kind of financial sacrifices she will have to make between now and age 65 when she retires. She guesses that in order to end up with a million bucks, she will have to stick with aggressive growth mutual funds which she has heard average 14% a year. Judi would like to know how much she is going to have to save each year.

	Rate 14%			
Year	Table 1 Compounding Factor for 1[1]	Table 2 Compounding Factor for 1 Per Annum[2]	Table 3 Sinking Fund Factor[3]	Table 4 Discount Factor[4]
1	1.14	1.00	1.00	.877
etc.	—	—	—	—
25	26.46	181.87	.0055	.038

[1] What an initial amount becomes when growing at compound interest.

[2] Growth of equal year-end deposits all growing at compound interest.

[3] Level deposit required each year to reach 1 by a given year.

[4] How much 1 at a future date is worth today.

Answer: (a) Go to the appendix and find the page titled "Rate 14%"; (b) go down the first column until you get to "Year 25"; (c) go to the right, under the third column and find the factor ".0055"; (d) multiply that factor by $1,000,000; (e) the resulting figure $5,500 (.0055 × $1,000,000) is the answer.

As you can see from all five of these examples, a series of payments or savings is again involved. In a sense, Table 3 is just a different approach to arriving at the same answer you could get using Table 2. While both tables assume a disciplined investor, in Table 2 the investor knows the figure of his initial investment, and in Table 3 the investor knows the figure of his end-result.

TABLE 4: HOW MUCH A LUMP-SUM IN THE FUTURE IS WORTH TODAY

The simplest use of Table 4 is to calculate the cumulative effects of inflation. Whatever the assumed or actual historical rate of inflation, you can quickly see what it does to the purchasing power of a dollar. Table 4 can also be used when you want to know what lump-sum is needed to be invested at a certain rate of return in order to end up with a specific dollar amount in the future. This second use of Table 4 makes it similar to Table 3, except Table 3 assumes that annual savings can be made and Table 4 assumes that only a single lump-sum is involved.

Table 4 is frequently used by investors who have an existing portfolio but cannot afford to add any more money. These investors want to know if they will end up with a certain sum of money at the end of so many years. Table 4 can also be used in conjunction with Table 3 for those savers who have a lump-sum to invest (Table 4), can save a certain amount of money each year (Table 3), and want to know if a specific dollar can be reached.

There are three things you need to know in order to use Table 4: (1) the amount of money you want to end up with; (2) how many years the lump-sum needs to be left alone to grow; and (3) the actual or assumed rate of growth you are expecting from the investment. Listed below are some examples as to when you would use Table 4.

Example #1

John and Mary have $20,000 in bank CDs. They want to end up with $100,000 in the future. Their comfort level for investing is such that they are assuming an 8% rate of growth from the $20,000 once they take the money out of bank CDs. John and Mary want to figure out how many years they will have to wait to see their $20,000 grow to $500,000.

		Rate 8%		
Year	*Table 1 Compounding Factor for 1*[1]	*Table 2 Compounding Factor for 1 Per Annum*[2]	*Table 3 Sinking Fund Factor*[3]	*Table 4 Discount Factor*[4]
1	1.08	1.00	1.00	.926
etc.	—	—	—	—
21	5.03	50.42	.020	.199

[1] What an initial amount becomes when growing at compound interest.

[2] Growth of equal year-end deposits all growing at compound interest.

[3] Level deposit required each year to reach 1 by a given year.

[4] How much 1 at a future date is worth today.

Answer: First, determine what percentage of $100,000 the lump-sum figure of $20,000 represents ($20,000 ÷ $100,000 = .20). Next: (a) Go to the appendix and find the page titled "Rate 8%"; (b) go down the fifth column until you find the factor closest to .20 (which would be .199); (c) go to the left and see how many years is on the same line as .199; (d) the answer is "Year 21."

Example #2

Ben has been reading about inflation. He wants to know what $50,000 will "shrink to" (reduced purchasing power) in 20 years if inflation continues to average 4% a year.

		Rate 4%		
Year	Table 1 Compounding Factor for 1[1]	Table 2 Compounding Factor for 1 Per Annum[2]	Table 3 Sinking Fund Factor[3]	Table 4 Discount Factor[4]
1	1.04	1.00	1.00	.962
etc.	—	—	—	—
20	2.19	29.78	.034	.456

[1] What an initial amount becomes when growing at compound interest.

[2] Growth of equal year-end deposits all growing at compound interest.

[3] Level deposit required each year to reach 1 by a given year.

[4] How much 1 at a future date is worth today.

Answer: (a) Go to the appendix and find the page titled "Rate 4%"; (b) go down the first column until you get to "Year 20"; (c) go to the right, under the fifth column and find the factor ".456"; (d) multiply that factor by $50,000; (e) the resulting figure $22,800 (.456 × $50,000) is the answer.

Example #3

Susan likes guarantees and wants to know if the $33,000 she has today will be worth $50,000 in five years. She is going to invest the $33,000 in a five-year bank CD that has a locked-in rate of 5%.

		Rate 5%		
Year	Table 1 Compounding Factor for 1[1]	Table 2 Compounding Factor for 1 Per Annum[2]	Table 3 Sinking Fund Factor[3]	Table 4 Discount Factor[4]
1	1.05	1.00	1.00	.952
etc.	—	—	—	—
5	1.28	5.53	.181	.784

[1] What an initial amount becomes when growing at compound interest.

[2] Growth of equal year-end deposits all growing at compound interest.

[3] Level deposit required each year to reach 1 by a given year.

[4] How much 1 at a future date is worth today.

Answer: (a) Go to the appendix and find the page titled "Rate 5%"; (b) go down the first column until you get to "Year 5"; (c) go to the right, under the fifth column and find the factor ".784"; (d) multiply that factor by $50,000; (e) the resulting figure $39,200 (.784 × $50,000) is what Susan would have to start out with in order to end up with $50,000.

Example #4

Dan has just become a grandfather. He has just learned that if his granddaughter is going to go to Harvard, she is going to need $300,000. Dan is willing to invest whatever is necessary but he only wants to make a single investment. He wants to know how much he is going to have to invest today, assuming a 10% rate of growth, so that his granddaughter ends up with $300,000 in 18 years when she enters Harvard.

		Rate 10%		
Year	Table 1 Compounding Factor for 1[1]	Table 2 Compounding Factor for 1 Per Annum[2]	Table 3 Sinking Fund Factor[3]	Table 4 Discount Factor[4]
1	1.10	1.00	1.00	.909
etc.	—	—	—	—
18	5.56	45.60	.022	.180

[1] What an initial amount becomes when growing at compound interest.

[2] Growth of equal year-end deposits all growing at compound interest.

[3] Level deposit required each year to reach 1 by a given year.

[4] How much 1 at a future date is worth today.

Answer: (a) Go to the appendix and find the page titled "Rate 10%"; (b) go down the first column until you get to "Year 18"; (c) go to the right, under the fifth column and find the factor ".180"; (d) multiply that factor by $300,000; (e) the resulting figure $54,000 (.180 × $300,000) is how much Dan will have to set aside today in order for his granddaughter to end up with $300,000 in 18 years.

Example #5

Judi, age 65, has an impressive stock and bond portfolio that she relies on as her sole source of support. The portfolio averages 8% a year. Each year, Judi takes out 10% of whatever the portfolio is worth. She wants to know what percentage of her portfolio will be left "in today's dollars" (meaning adjusted for inflation) at the end of 10 and 20 years if she continues to withdraw 10% each year plus factors in an assumed inflation rate of 5%.

		Rate 7%		
Year	Table 1 Compounding Factor for 1[1]	Table 2 Compounding Factor for 1 Per Annum[2]	Table 3 Sinking Fund Factor[3]	Table 4 Discount Factor[4]
1	1.07	1.00	1.00	.935
etc.	—	—	—	—
10	1.97	13.82	.072	.508
etc.	—	—	—	—
20	3.87	41.00	.024	.258

[1] What an initial amount becomes when growing at compound interest.

[2] Growth of equal year-end deposits all growing at compound interest.

[3] Level deposit required each year to reach 1 by a given year.

[4] How much 1 at a future date is worth today.

Answer: The first step is to do a little math and figure out which "Rate" table will be used. If you average 8% a year but you take out 10% a year, the net effect is a loss of 2% per year; if inflation averages 5%, then the "real loss" each year is 2% + 5% (or 7%). (a) Go to the appendix and find the page titled "Rate 7%"; (b) go down the first column until you get to "Year 10"; (c) go to the right, under the fifth column and find the factor ".508"; (d) multiply that factor by 1 (we do not know the amount of her portfolio—she wants a percentage answer); (e) the resulting figure .508 (.508 × 1), or 51% (round up the .508 figure) is how much Judi will have of her current portfolio in 10 years. Repeat steps a–e to find out the value in 20 years.

All five of the examples above deal with a lump-sum. Some of the examples deal with inflation while others are concerned with whether or not a specific dollar figure will be reached. Table 4 is a simple way to see what the cumulative effects of inflation will do to a portfolio. The table can also be used if you want to determine how aggressively your current portfolio must grow in order to reach your financial goal.

Summary

This chapter has shown you how to use the four financial tables that are the foundation of all financial planning and investment software. These tables never need to be updated. The only thing that will change in the future are expected, projected, or guaranteed rates of return—meaning you will simply take the same steps but will use different "Rate" pages (or tables). With a basic hand-held calculator, you can now "look into the future" to project the cumulative effects of inflation, how much you will end up with, or how much you will need to save each year.

Now that we have laid some foundation, it is time for you to learn how to develop your own financial or investment plan. Chapter 5 shows you the five basic steps (goals, objectives, strategy, implementation, and review). The chapter is written from the perspective that you are an investment advisor and a client has come to you for some long-term planning advice. As you will see, the financial tables with which you became familiar in this chapter are used in Chapter 5.

Let's Remember This:

► What financial tables represent and how they can be easily used.

► The benefits of making annual contributions.

► How long it will take you to get $1 million (or any other amount).

▼

THE FINANCIAL PLANNING PROCESS

WHAT WE ARE GOING TO TALK ABOUT IN THIS CHAPTER:

▶ The Five Parts of a Financial or Investment Plan

▶ A Detailed Example of a Financial Plan

▶ What Type of Future Adjustments May Be Necessary

The value of having a financial plan cannot be overemphasized. Without a "road map," it is difficult to determine whether or not you are getting to where you should be going in a timely fashion. One way I explain the importance of financial planning to my clients is by using an analogy. Since most of my clients are in their late 50s or older, I tell them the story of the cruise ship.

Suppose that you were boarding a cruise ship and happened to immediately meet the captain. After some introductory remarks, you ask the captain some questions: "Captain, how long will it take us to get to where we are going?" "Captain, what means of navigation do you use?" "Captain, what do you use to fuel the ship?" "Captain, when are we leaving?" and, "Captain, where are we going?" If the captain answered "I don't know" to all of your questions, there is a pretty good chance that you would either be scared or would want to get off the ship as soon as possible.

When it comes to our financial futures, the great majority of people have no clue as to where they will end up at retirement or what investments should be used. In fact, most people spend more time planning an ocean cruise than they do their investments. Yet, financial planning is not difficult and does not have to take much time. Let us go through the steps so you can see how easy it is to plan your financial future.

The Five Components of a Financial Plan

Every financial plan should be comprised of at least five parts: (1) goals, (2) objectives, (3) strategy, (4) implementation and (5) review. Goals have to do with what you want to accomplish financially during and beyond your lifetime—a comfortable retirement, buying a home, sending a child through college, or providing for your loved ones after your death. Objectives turn goals into dollar figures.

Dollars & Sense:

You are about to learn how to draft your own financial plan by going through an example. Do not be turned off by this example because your net worth, age or goals are different than what is shown. It is easy to plug in the numbers that apply to your personal situation.

The five-step process you are about to learn is something that you can buy in a software program for anywhere between $20 and $1,000, with one important difference: Later chapters in this book will show you the shortcomings of these financial programs.

As an example, if your goal were to send a child through four years of public college, your objective would be to end up with an account for the child of $60,000 (this assumes that four years of public school plus room and board come to $15,000 per year). Once an objective and time deadline are determined, it is relatively easy to decide how much needs to be invested either as a lump-sum or on an annual basis, given an expected or known rate of return.

The third step of the financial plan is the strategy. Your strategy is to decide which investments should be used to reach your financial objective(s)—given a specific time horizon, risk level and amount of capital. Besides deciding which investments to use, you will also need to know what percentage of the entire portfolio each investment category will represent. As an example, based on your current holdings, time horizon, risk level and dollar objective, you may determine that the safest way to reach your objectives is to invest half of your portfolio in a global stock fund, a quarter in high-yield corporate bonds and the final quarter in medium-term U.S. government bonds.

Implementation is related to the third step, strategy. Implementation means actually making the investments plus deciding which vehicles are to be used. That is, are you going to use individual stocks, a growth and income mutual fund run by Mary Jones, or a slightly more aggressive growth fund managed by Ed Smith? Implementation also means deciding when the investment is to be made. Thus, you may decide to dollar-cost average the small company stock portion over a 12-month period (e.g., invest $1,000 each month into the XYZ small cap growth fund for the next 12 months). Or, you may decide to invest in long-term municipal bonds immediately.

The fifth, and final, step of the financial plan process is review. How often a portfolio is reviewed depends upon market conditions and the risk level of each investment you own. As an example, a conservative portfolio that is comprised solely of debt instruments such as money market accounts and bonds needs only to be reviewed once or twice a year—unless interest rate concerns have been such to have caused moderate price swings in the value of the bonds; in such a situation, a review may be warranted after a particularly bad or good month. A stock-oriented portfolio should be reviewed at least semi-annually if not quarterly. These more frequent reviews may bring to light new buying opportunities or the sell-off of an equity that you have been patient with for several quarters or years.

Reviewing a portfolio also means rebalancing once a year or when one of your investment categories now represents much more or less of the entire portfolio pie than planned. As an example, suppose that it was determined that half of your portfolio should be in high-yield municipal bonds and half in large cap stocks. At the end of the year, you are happy because both investment categories performed well. However, your calculations show that the stock portion did extremely well and stocks now represent 62% of the entire portfolio. You might think this is fine—keeping a winner is perhaps a good idea. But a 62% weighting in equities means you are now at a different risk level and this may not be a good idea. To get you back to the originally planned weightings, enough of the stocks must be sold off so that their proceeds can be used to buy more bonds so that bonds will once again represent 50% of the portfolio pie.

EXAMPLE 5.1—THE 5 STEPS OF INVESTMENT STRATEGY

Step	*Examples*
1. Goal(s)	Comfortable retirement, send a child to college, buy a home, etc.
2. Objective(s)	End up with $700,000 in 20 years, $100,000 in 18 years, $30,000 in 5 years, etc.
3. Strategy	Invest 25% of portfolio into each of the following: growth funds, small company growth funds, international stock funds, and individual government securities.
4. Implementation	Buy the XYZ growth fund, the ABC small company growth fund, the LMN international fund, and five to ten U.S. government bonds.
5. Review	Review the mutual fund holdings after a year; consider selling off part of the "winners" and adding to the "losers."

A SAMPLE PLAN

To see how a financial plan is developed, let us go through an example. After following the example, you will be able to draft your own plan, based on your particular circumstances. So, when reading the example that follows, keep in mind that it is unimportant that we are talking about someone who is 40 years old, but you are only 29, or that the person can save $5,000 a year, but you can save $8,000 a year. The purpose of the example is so that you understand how each step is developed or carried out.

Let us suppose you are an investment counselor and you are meeting with the client for the first time. After asking a series of questions, you discover the following information about your new client:

1. Age: 50 (single, no plans for marriage within the next several years)

2. Health: excellent

3. Employment: dentist (self-employed and his job is stable)

4. Insurance: health, major medical, and disability

5. Extraordinary Financial Events Expected: none

6. Current Holdings: $50,000 in bank CDs, $20,000 IRA account in government bonds

7. Can Comfortably Save: $10,000 a year

8. Current Income: $60,000 a year (tax bracket is 40%, state and federal combined)

9. Goal: 15 years from now, retire on $45,000 annually

10. Risk Level: moderate

11. Biases: hates penny stocks and likes mutual funds

12. Support: no children or previous spouse; parents are well-off financially

13. Client Believes Inflation Will Continue To Average: about 3% a year

At this point you have all of the information you need. You now know what the client is trying to accomplish, his time frame, risk level, current holdings, how much can be saved each year, his tax bracket, investment biases, his insurance coverage, inflation expectations, support obligations to others (none), and if there are any "extraordinary" financial events expected (i.e., an expected inheritance, purchase of a new car, etc.). Now you are ready to make some calculations (using the financial tables found in the appendix).

The client has told you that his risk level is "moderate." This means that the bank CDs and government bonds can be repositioned so that the portfolio reflects a moderate level of risk instead of its present conservative level. Since the CD money is not sheltered from taxes and the retirement account is, each of these investments needs to be looked at separately.

If the $50,000 in CDs was instead invested in growth stocks, one could project what the $50,000 would grow to in the future. Assuming a 12% rate of return (which is what the S & P 500 has averaged over the past 50 years) and a "tax efficient" portfolio of stocks (meaning that very little of the gain is taxed each year), an 11% tax deferred rate of growth is a fair projection (12% growth minus 1% for current taxes). Before going to the tables in the appendix, you still need to offset this 11% figure by inflation expectations: 3% a year (11% minus 3% for inflation = 8% real return).

Now, go to the appendix and look for the page that has "Rate 8%" at the top. Look under the first column that is titled "Table 1." This is the column you want to use whenever you have a lump-sum ($50,000 in our example) that is growing at a certain rate for a specific number of years.

Following column one down to the row that is opposite "Year 15" (you want to see if your client can comfortably retire in as little as 15 years), you will see the number 3.17. By multiplying $50,000 by 3.17 you end up with the figure $158,500—which is what $50,000 will grow to in 15 years, assuming an average annual after-inflation return of 8%.

The client also has a $20,000 conservative IRA account that can be repositioned. Since money in an IRA account grows and compounds tax deferred, whatever investment you recommend for this money will not be affected by current taxation. IRA money can also be repositioned without triggering a taxable event. Assuming the $20,000 is invested in a global stock mutual fund and that the long-term historical rate of return for such an investment has been 13%, we can see what will happen to this money after 15 years of growth. To make this calculation, the same appendix and column is used ("Table 1"), but you will have to turn to the page that has "Rate 10%" (13% minus 3% for inflation) at the top of the page. Go down the column marked "Table 1" until it is across from "Year 15" and you will see the number 4.18. This means that $20,000 growing at 10% a year for 15 years will result in a lump-sum figure of $83,600 ($20,000 × 4.18).

Finally, according to the client, $10,000 can be saved each year. Let us assume that the $10,000 savings each year is invested in a combination of utility stocks and high-yield corporate bonds that average 10% annually. Further assume that these investments are part of a variable annuity "family of funds," meaning the investment will grow and compound tax deferred (one of the features all annuities have is indefinite tax-deferred growth; it is only when money is taken out of an annuity that it becomes taxable).

Turn once more to the appendix and go to the page that has "Rate 7%" at the top (remember that although the expected growth rate was 10%, we have to knock it down to 7% in order to offset inflation). This time, you will be using a different column, the one marked "Table 2." Table 2 is used whenever the same amount of money is invested each year. Now, go down Table 2 until you are opposite "Year 15" (since we are still looking at possible retirement in 15 years). The figure, 25.13 in this case, is what $10,000 is multiplied by; the resulting number $251,300, is what an annual investment of $10,000 will grow to at the end of 15 years, assuming an average annual return of 7%. Now, let us look at our subtotal.

EXAMPLE 5.2—TOTALING UP THE GROWTH

▶ $50,000 shifted from CDs to growth stocks . . . projected growth in 15 years is $158,500

▶ $20,000 IRA account repositioned from government bonds . . . projected growth in 15 years is $83,600

▶ $10,000 invested each year in utilities and high-yield bonds . . . projected growth is $251,300

▶ subtotal above = $493,400

Your client, assuming the repositioning into new investments described above plus the expected rates of return, should end up with a lump-sum of approximately $493,400 ($158,500 + $83,600 + $251,300). During retirement, assuming that the $493,400 can be invested at 9% (given a more conservative posture 15 years from now), your client can expect an annual income of $44,406—a figure very similar to the goal of $45,000.

ADDITIONAL CONSIDERATIONS

At this point, let us pause and consider some points not previously discussed: (1) inflation will not cease during the client's retirement years; (2) Social Security benefits will most likely be in the $11,000 range ($17,160 in inflated dollars, assuming that Social Security benefits for someone like your client would currently be $11,000 a year and such benefits will inflate by 3% annually); and (3) some unforeseen events could take place during the coming years that will throw off a number of the assumptions or projections made (e.g., inflation may average 4% a year or more, there could be radical changes to the tax code, the client may find that he cannot save as much as he thought each year, investment returns turn out to be lower, a major expense arises, etc.).

EASIER THAN YOU MAY THINK

The beauty of having the financial plan is that adjustments can easily be made along the way. If more of something is needed in time, then the client can do one of several things: (1) increase the risk level so that the projected rates of return should be higher so that the growth figures above will become greater; (2) work for more than

15 years; (3) save more each year; or (4) scale back the definition of "comfortable retirement." By reviewing the plan once every year or two, realistic and relatively painless adjustments can be easily made.

Once the background information has been collected, drafting a basic financial plan for you or a client can be accomplished in about half an hour. I say "basic financial plan" because there was no insurance-needs analysis done in this plan (because it is beyond the nature of this book). As you can now see, a financial plan for an individual or couple in their accumulative years boils down to a series of numbers: to what a lump-sum figure will grow and/or to what a series of annual savings will grow—given a specific number of years, rate of return, and assumed rate of inflation.

Money Talks: There can be a huge difference between compound interest and simple interest. Compound interest means that interest is being earned on interest as well as principal. Simple interest means that only the principal is earning interest, not any previous interest payments or credits. As an example, if you had $100 earning 12% a year and such interest was compounding, the $100 would grow to $200 at the end of six years ($400 at the end of 12 years). If the same $100 were earning 12% simple interest, it would take a little over eight years for $100 to grow to $200 (and a total of 25 years to get to $400).

SUMMARY

You now know the foundation for asset allocation. Without the knowledge you have just gained, the asset allocation process is pointless since it does not look at the whole investment picture. Asset allocation attempts to get someone the best possible risk-adjusted returns, given the client's risk level. You cannot determine this until you know: (1) what the beginning point is (current holdings); (2) how much can be saved each year (the more that can be saved, the less the risk since money will not have to grow as fast); (3) any biases that need to be worked around (i.e., the client may have a speculative stock that should be sold but isn't because of a large tax consequence); (4) what the real rate needs to be (once inflation and taxes are factored in); and (5) any extraordinary events expected along the way that may increase or decrease the investor's net worth or ability to save.

The next step before getting to the actual process of asset allocation is to gain a historical perspective of different investments. It is important that you understand what can be expected from an investment, both in terms of return and risk. Without a set of realistic figures, dividing a portfolio into different asset categories is meaningless because you will not know what to expect from each of the investments selected.

LET'S REMEMBER THIS:

- ▶ A financial plan and its components.

- ▶ An example of how you would draft a financial plan.

- ▶ What kind of adjustments you can make if you come up short of your original goals.

INVESTMENTS

WHAT WE ARE GOING TO TALK ABOUT IN THIS CHAPTER:

▶ Describing the Major Investment Categories

▶ Historical Returns Covering a Wide Range of Holding Periods

▶ The Volatility of Each Investment Category

The purpose of this chapter is twofold: (1) to define a series of investments that will be used throughout the book, and (2) to provide a historical perspective detailing how a number of investments have fared over time. Even brokers and advisors should read this chapter to make sure that we are both speaking the same language when we use words like "large stocks" and "long-term government bonds." As you might suspect, there are a number of ways to define "large company stocks," just like there are different definitions for exactly what is meant by "long-term." Most of this chapter will be comprised of a series of charts showing the performance and range of returns of these different investments over various holding periods.

NO UNIVERSAL DEFINITION

There is no single correct or universal definition for most investments. Even something as simple as "stocks" can either be narrowly or broadly defined. As an example, any one of the following descriptions of stocks is correct: (1) preferred; (2) common; (3) the Standard & Poor's 500 (S & P 500); (4) all stocks on the New York Stock

Exchange (NYSE); (5) a combination of stocks listed on the NYSE, American Stock Exchange (AMEX), the regional exchanges such as the Pacific Stock Exchange, plus stocks that are part of the National Association of Securities Dealers Automated Quotation System (NASDAQ); (6) a compilation of "(5)" plus all over-the-counter stocks (OTC) not part of NASDAQ; (7) what is described in "(6)" plus penny stocks; (8) the Russell 5,000; or (9) one of the indexes comprised by Value Line. There are even more ways to describe or define stocks, particularly when you start adding foreign or global indices, but I think you get the point.

Dollars & $ense:

You are about to see a number of peformance bar charts that are rarely found in one source. Surprisingly, an "encyclopedia" of investments and their performance is difficult, if not impossible to find. Another thing that is special about these bar charts is that each one is accompanied by a risk measurement—something that is also often difficult to find out or discern.

Even though the bar charts are "time sensitive" (all results are for periods ending 12/31/95), they focus on 15-year figures. A 15-year period encompasses enough good and bad periods to be fairly representative of what you can expect in the future.

The definitions and descriptions below will be limited to those assets or investment categories that will be used in this book. This will minimize confusion and make it easier for you to refer back to this section if you later forget some of these terms. Each definition and description is followed by a bar chart that includes the average annual return and standard deviation (a form of risk management) for the last 3, 5, 10 and 15 years (all periods ending December 31, 1995).

STANDARD DEVIATION

This shows an investment's range of returns. The higher the return potential of an investment, the greater its standard deviation. Standard deviation is often used as a means of measuring an investment's risk level since every investment, including real estate, bank CDs, gold, and stocks, has a standard deviation. The lower the standard deviation, the more predictable the returns. A future chapter deals exclusively with standard deviation. However, in order to better use the bar charts that follow, a quick illustration will show you how standard deviation works.

Suppose you were considering an investment in "large company stocks" (the first bar chart below). As you can see, for the three years ending October 31, 1995, large company stocks averaged 16.2% per year. This looks like a very appealing investment since this performance figure does not give you any indication as to the amount of risk that was, or could have been, taken.

Dollars & Sense: All of the bar charts presented in this chapter, except two, are from neutral sources. The "Residential Real Estate" and "Art and Collectibles" are considered to be tainted because their respective sources represent entities that are considered self-serving.

The bar right next to 16.2% represents this investment's standard deviation for the past three years (15.4%). This means that large company stocks had an average annual return that fluctuated between 0.8% (16.2% − 15.4%) and 31.6% (16.2% + 15.4%) most of the time (every two out of three years). This is important for you to know as an investor so that if you make such an investment, you have a pretty good idea of the ups and downs (on an annual basis) that you will most likely experience. Rarely, if ever, does an investment have an "average" return.

Large Company Stocks   Also known as "the stock market," the typical stock in this category has a market capitalization of approximately $18 billion. Market capitalization can be defined as the total value of all of a corporation's outstanding shares of stock. Popular indicators of the stock market include the S & P 500 (500 different stocks) and the Dow Jones Industrial Average (30 different stocks). Over the years, the Dow and the S & P 500 have been very similar in their returns.

Large Company Stocks

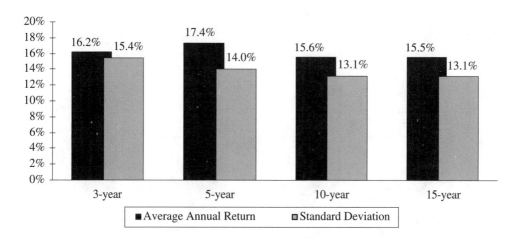

Small Company Stocks   There are approximately 3,200 stocks listed on the New York Stock Exchange (NYSE). "Small stocks" represent the bottom 20% of the stocks on the NYSE as measured by market capitalization. The roughly 640 stocks that make up this list change each year as either new stocks are added to the NYSE or existing stocks are removed from the list as they grow in size. A popular index used to gauge small stock performance is the Russell 2,000.

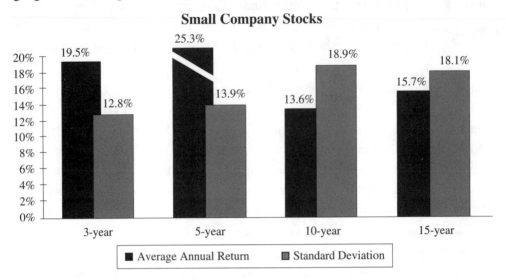

Small Company Stocks

Long-Term Government Bonds Bonds issued by the U.S. government that have a remaining maturity of over ten years. Even though the category or description "long-term" includes bonds with remaining maturities of 10 to 30 years, the table below represents government securities with a 20-year remaining maturity.

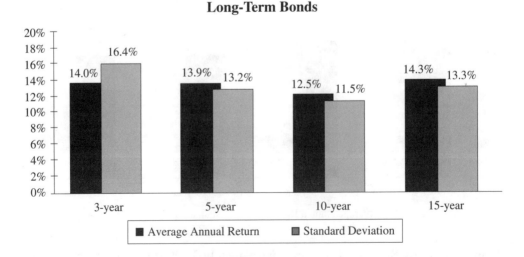

Long-Term Bonds

Intermediate-Term Government Bonds Bonds issued by the U.S. government that have a *remaining* maturity of five to ten years. Assuming the same coupon rate, a

30-year bond issued 25 years ago is not any more or less volatile, or valuable, than a five-year government note that was just issued—both securities have a remaining maturity of five years. The table below shows the performance of government bonds with a remaining maturity of five years.

Intermediate-Term Bonds

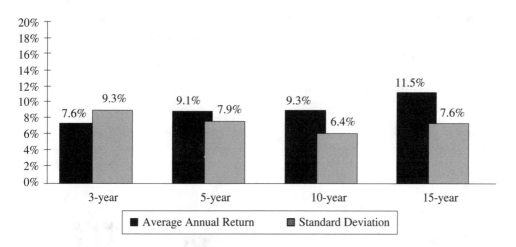

U.S. Treasury Bills Government-issued debt with original maturities of 3, 6, and 12 months. The return from T-bills is very similar to that found with short-term bank CDs and money market accounts. The figures shown below represent T-bills that have a remaining maturity of just one month.

U.S. Treasury Bills

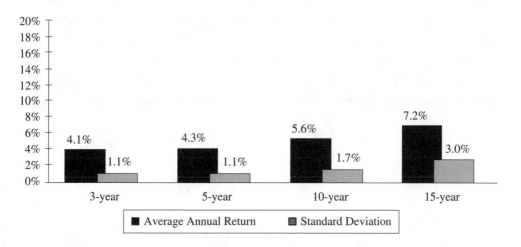

Certificates of Deposit (CDs)   Receipts for having deposited funds at either a bank or a savings and loan. In return for depositing funds, the issuer of the CD agrees to repay the amount of the deposit plus interest on a specified date. CDs have maturities that range from several days to 10 years. The rate of interest (or yield) received by the depositor is determined by the current level of interest rates minus whatever profit margin the issuer wants to keep for itself. The liquidity of CDs is determined by the agreement (contract) signed by the depositor and the financial institution. There is usually a penalty if the depositor wishes to cash in his CD prior to its originally-agreed upon maturity.

Certificates of Deposit (CDs)

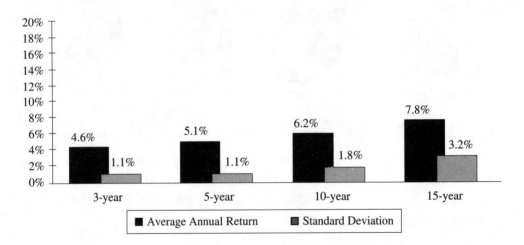

Money Market Funds   A pooled account, often a mutual fund, that invests in securities that mature in less than one year (the typical maturity is less than 50 days). These funds or accounts are usually comprised of one or more of the following instruments: Treasury bills, certificates of deposit (CDs), commercial paper, Euro-dollar CDs and notes. There are four different categories of money market funds: all-purpose, government-backed, federally tax-free and doubly tax-exempt.

Money Market Funds

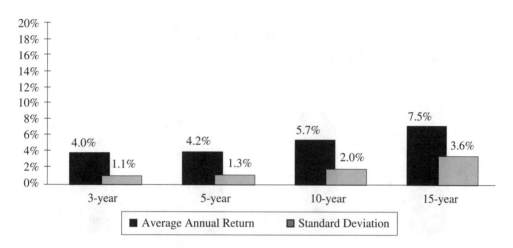

High-Yield Corporate Bond Funds   Funds that invest in corporate bonds rated below investment grade or "bank quality." High-yield bonds are considered speculative grade, which consists of a rating of BBB or lower (Standard & Poor's) or Baa or lower (Moody's). Because of their lower credit quality, these bonds usually offer a higher yield to compensate for the greater default risk posed by their issuer. The overall default rate of high-yield bonds in recent years has been around 1%.

High-Yield Bonds

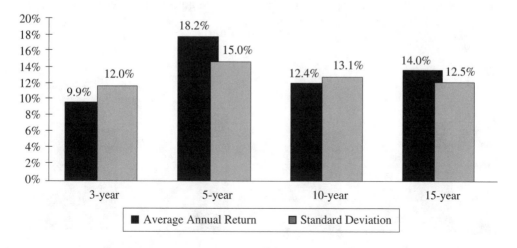

Convertible Securities Funds   Mutual funds that invest in debt instruments or preferred stock of a corporation. These may be exchanged for a specified number of shares of the common stock of the same corporation at a specified price as defined by the corporation upon the issuance of the security.

Convertible Securities Funds

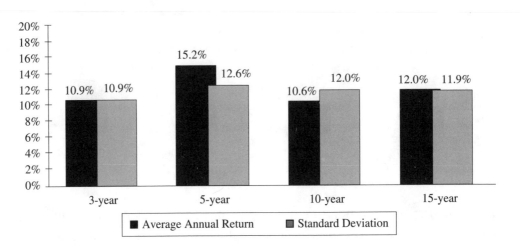

International Bond Funds   Mutual funds that invest in debt instruments issued by foreign entities, mainly other governments, that are denominated in that country's currency. Besides the interest rate risk normally found with domestic bonds, foreign bonds pose additional risks of currency fluctuation as well as any potential default risk with foreign governments. However, investors in international bonds benefit from diversification of their debt portfolio as well as often getting a higher yield.

International Bonds

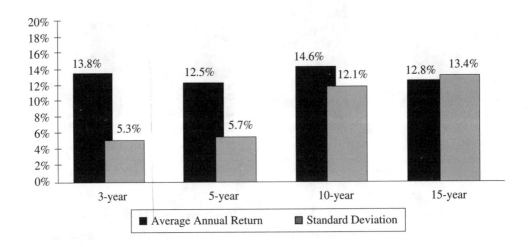

Global Bond Funds   Mutual funds that invest in both domestic and foreign debt instruments. The typical global bond fund has somewhere between 30% and 70% of its holdings in domestic bonds and the balance in foreign (also known as "international") bonds. Normally, these kinds of global funds have less risk than a similar fund that invests only in U.S. or foreign securities.

Global Bonds

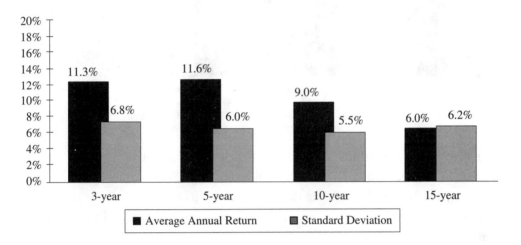

Foreign Stock Funds   Funds that invest in international equity securities, meaning equities from any country other than the United States. Investing in foreign stocks allows the equity investor to diversify his portfolio and to take advantage of growth opportunities that might be greater than those found in the domestic market. Again, as with international bond funds, there are currency risks when investing in international securities, although some funds hedge their exposure to minimize currency fluctuations.

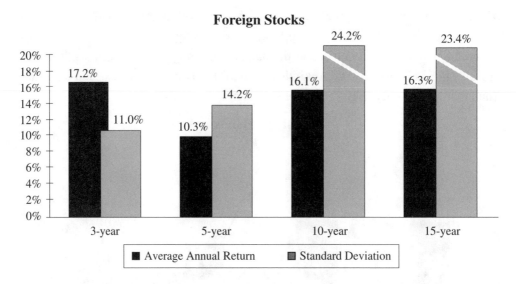

Foreign Stocks

Emerging Markets Funds Mutual funds that invest in countries whose growth potential far exceeds those of the industrialized nations. Such markets pose a greater risk environment for investors, but the potential payoffs can be equally as rewarding. Emerging markets are found in the Pacific Basin, Latin America, Africa and Eastern Europe.

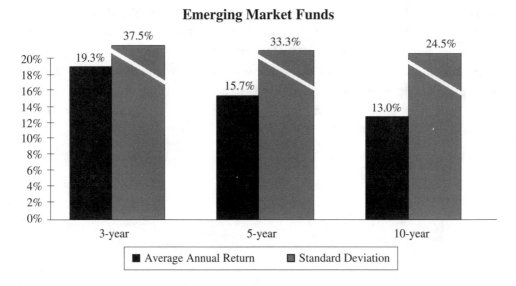

Emerging Market Funds

Global Stock Funds Mutual funds that invest in both domestic and foreign equity securities. The portfolio weighting for U.S. stocks usually ranges from 30% up to 70%, with the balance being in overseas equities. Most, if not all, of the foreign stocks are from economically mature economies; emerging markets stocks are a small, or non-existent, part of these funds.

Global Stocks

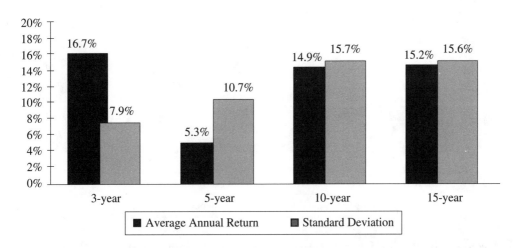

Equity-Income Funds Mutual funds that focus on the current income component of total return. Capital appreciation is a secondary concern (but normally ends up representing a larger part of the fund's total return). These funds invest at least 65% of their assets in equity securities with above-average yields. These tend to be the most conservative type of stock fund.

Equity-Income Funds

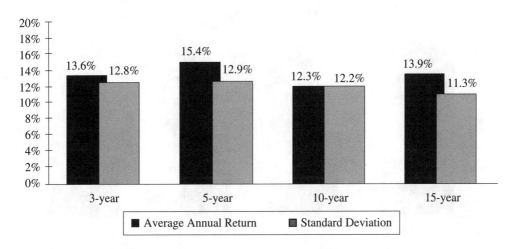

Gold There are several ways to own gold: bullion, coins and indirectly (a gold mining stock or a mutual fund or variable life product that invests in the bullion and/or mining stocks). Most of the time, bullion is much less volatile than shares of a gold mining company. The table below shows how bullion has performed.

Gold

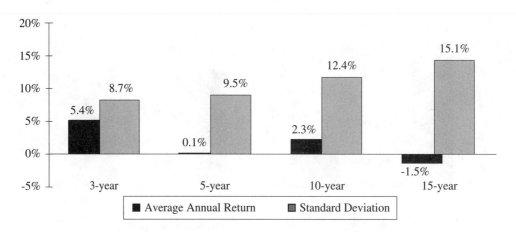

Precious Metals Funds   Funds that purchase metals in one or more of the following ways: bullion, South African gold stocks and non-South African mining stocks. The proportion and type of metal held by a fund can have a great impact on its performance and volatility. Outright ownership of gold bullion is almost always less volatile than owning stock in a gold mining company. Gold has traditionally been looked to as a hedge against inflation or global disaster. These sector funds represent one of the most, if not the most, volatile category of mutual funds.

Precious Metals Funds

	3-year	5-year	10-year	15-year
Average Annual Return	24.7%	10.8%	10.4%	6.7%
Standard Deviation	42.1%	41.3%	32.7%	31.3%

Real Estate Investment Trusts (REITs)   Publicly traded securities that must invest at least 75% of their assets in real asset or derive 75% of their gross income from rent on real property or from interest on mortgages. Initially authorized by Congress in 1960, REITs were specifically designed to provide small investors with a tradable interest in a pool of properties or mortgages. Equity REITs are the most popular REIT vehicle (and have also been the better long-term performer). They provide the potential for appreciation, high dividends and moderate risk.

Real Estate Investment Trusts (Equity)

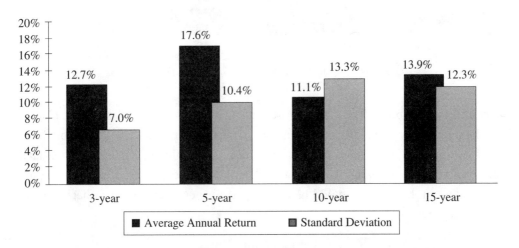

Residential Real Estate   The most popular form of housing in the U.S. remains the single-family detached house, although condominiums have contributed to the demand in the housing market. Pricing of residential real estate is primarily a function of housing demand, which is based on several factors, including demographic trends, interest rates, per capita income, the state of the economy and tax issues (as the Tax Reform Act of 1986 clearly demonstrated). Risk level can largely be dependent upon the size of one's mortgage in relation to the owner's equity. Because the debt-to-equity ratio can vary by quite a bit, the risk level of residential real estate can range from conservative to very aggressive.

Residential Real Estate

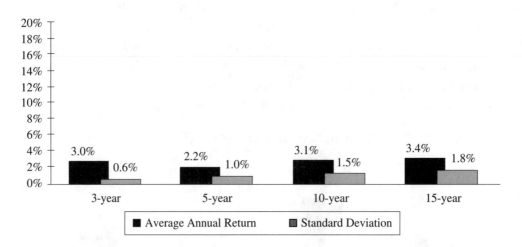

Art and Collectibles   These are investments that have a pure intrinsic value placed on them (which is essentially the price those in the marketplace are willing to bid for). This intrinsic value is based more on abstract, intangible benefits rather than any material cash-flow potential. Since these markets are considered highly illiquid, investment in these areas should be considered for personal benefit rather than for portfolio growth.

Art and Collectibles

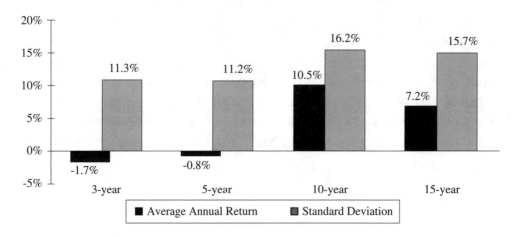

Growth Stocks   Stocks that possess high earnings growth or growth potential. Investors are usually willing to pay a premium for growth stocks in the form of a high price multiple in the hopes that these companies will meet or exceed their earnings forecasts.

Growth Stocks

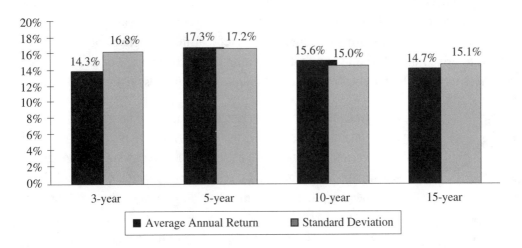

Value Stocks Stocks whose prices trade at low price multiples (also referred to as low p/e ratios) because either they or the industries their companies operate in have temporarily become out of favor with investors. Many seek opportunities in the rebound of these shares since they trade close to their intrinsic values (thus minimizing the downside risk).

Value Stocks

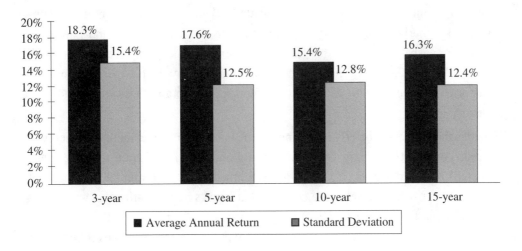

Summary

We now have a common language from which to work with when it comes to describing the different investments that will be covered throughout the book. Perhaps more importantly, and certainly more interesting, is that you now know the historical returns for various investments. One of the chief learning objectives of this chapter was to drive home the point of how lengthening the holding period of an investment makes its overall returns less volatile and therefore usually less risky.

Money Talks: One's "holding period" refers to how long you plan to keep the investment before selling it. The financial advisor knows that you may have to sell part or all of your portfolio if an emergency arises, but since such occurences are rare, any anticipated holding period does not, and should not, take into account the possibility of a financial emergency (the issues of marketability and liquidity cover emergencies). Usually, expected holding periods coincide with a specfic event (i.e., retirement, a child entering college, a target date to pay off a loan or a mortgage) or a round number (e.g., "If this investment acts like its supposed to, I plan on keeping it for at least 10 years.").

The next step is understanding the different kinds of risks associated with different investments. Once these risks are known, we can then find ways to combat them. The next few chapters will examine the risks most commonly associated with stocks, bonds, and cash. Chapter 8 looks at stocks and their ups and downs. Chapter 9 covers what happens to bonds when interest rates rise and fall. Chapter 10 deals with money market accounts (comprised of "cash equivalents") and the effects of inflation. These three risks, market risk (for stocks), interest rate risk (for bonds), and purchasing power (for cash), will most likely be the three biggest risks your investments will be exposed to; which risk(s) and how much risk will be involved depend upon which categories of investments are included in your portfolio and the weighting of such category(s).

Besides the three risks briefly mentioned in the paragraph above, there are other types of risk your portfolio may be subject to (again, depending upon the category(s) selected). As an example, if you own foreign securities or a mutual fund, variable annuity, unit trust, or variable life contract that invests in international stocks, bonds, or money market instruments, there is a currency risk (or reward, depending upon what happens to the currencies represented by these foreign securities in relation to the U.S. dollar). Another example is limited parternships. Even the few that turn out decently are subject to marketability risk (the ability to sell your partnership units to someone else). There is also a real question as to how much liquidity risk there is in limited partnerships (assuming you find a buyer, how many cents on the dollar you can expect to get). Finally, in the case of emerging markets, there is also political risk (what could happen to your investment if the foreign country decides to privatize the company or industry or what could happen to the value if there is political unrest).

EXAMPLE 6.1—THE DIFFERENT RISKS INVESTMENTS ARE SUBJECT TO

Investment Category	*Type(s) of Risk*
Common Stocks	market
Utility Stocks	market, interest rate
Penny Stocks	market, marketability, liquidity
Foreign Stocks	market, currency
Emerging Markets Stocks	market, currency, marketability, liquidity, political
High-Quality Bonds	interest rate
High-Yield Bonds	interest rate, market, liquidity
Cash Equivalents	purchasing power
Real Estate	market, marketability, liquidity
Gold and Other Metals	market, purchasing power
Rare Coins and Stamps	market, marketability, liquidity
Foreign Bonds	interest rate, currency
Limited Partnerships	market and/or interest rate, marketability, liquidity

---

Before we get into these three categories, let us first look at a form of risk measurement that every investment shares: standard deviation. Although standard deviation is a term commonly used in statistics, it is not difficult to understand. The term is another way of qualifying an investment's range of returns, usually over the past 36 months. Moreover, most of the investment vehicles you would even consider making a part of your portfolio have published standard deviation figures.

As you will see in Chapter 7, standard deviation is one of the best ways of seeing the historical extremes of an investment's (or entire portfolio's) return. Standard deviation provides some guidelines for what you can expect (there are no guarantees) from an investment or portfolio in the future, based on its ups and downs in the past.

LET'S REMEMBER THIS:

▶ A wide range of generic investments.

▶ The historical returns of all of these categories over the past 3, 5, 10, and 15 years.

▶ The risk level or volatility of each investment category and the effects of time.

▼

DEFINING AND MEASURING RISK

WHAT WE ARE GOING TO TALK ABOUT IN THIS CHAPTER:

▶ Some of the Differences Between Conservative, Moderate, and Aggressive

▶ A Risk Test

▶ Standard Deviation and Ranges of Returns for Selected Investments

For most people, "risk" is characterized by how much of one's investment could be lost. "Low risk" connotates a loss of probably somewhere in the neighborhood of 1 to 5%. "Moderate risk" may be translated to something like a possible loss of 6 to 10%, and "large risk" may bring visions of a loss of something over 10 to 15%. One of the problems of defining risk is that people have different perceptions of what risk is, as well as precisely defining the difference between a small, moderate or large loss.

Someone who drives only a few miles a day probably doesn't consider freeway driving much of a risk in their life. A truckdriver who is on the road several hours a day may view driving as the riskiest part of his life. Similarly, someone who has lived through the Great Depression may constantly worry about another crash in the stock market, while the typical mutual fund investor who entered the market in 1990 may firmly believe that there will never be another crash. Keeping all perspectives in mind, let us look at a way of measuring investment risk that is not only more universal, but is also more exacting.

Risk refers to how much your portfolio could fall over a given period of time. Few investors are worried about better-than-expected gains. It is downward, not upward, volatility that scares people. The greater the drop in value, the greater the risk. The element of time is also important because some investors are more patient than others.

You and Risk

The level of patience may have to do with one's personality, but it may also have to do with general market conditions (e.g., the investor who becomes frustrated with a certain stock that is not increasing in value even though the overall stock market is constantly hitting new highs), or one's time horizon (e.g., a lump-sum of money is needed in a few years in order to send Junior to college). As you can see, risk has to do with loss, the degree of loss, and the expected period of recovery.

A conservative investor does not care that his portfolio will recover within a year—his concern is his most recent monthly statement, which shows his holdings have dropped by 2%. The conservative investor is not placated by the broker who assures him that the loss will be recovered within a few months. Instead, the conservative investor might be thinking that at this rate (-2% per month), he'll have a huge loss (-2% a month $\times$ 12 months) at the end of a year.

The moderate investor is not particularly concerned with any reasonable loss (e.g., perhaps something in the 1 to 10% range) as long as the loss is made up within a year or so. The aggressive investor is willing to accept a greater loss than the moderate investor and is also willing to be more patient in return for the expectation of a higher overall return.

Risk Tests

There are a number of "risk tests" you can take. These are usually brief questionnaires that help you or your advisor determine what kinds of investments you should be in; the questionnaires are often compiled by brokerage firms or mutual fund companies. Unfortunately, there is no single set of questions or series of exams that can accurately measure risk. In some ways, defining one's risk level is like trying to define love—people have different viewpoints depending upon how they were raised, their past relationships, as well as what they have read or heard about the topic.

A broker or investor who has just attended an upbeat seminar about the future of the stock market may look at things differently than you or me. Someone who has just read a book titled *The Coming Stock Market Crash* may also look at investments differently—at least for a short period of time. It is these experiences, recent readings, and listening to the financial "gurus" that all help to shape our definition of risk as well as what investments we feel most comfortable with. Thus, how you respond to a risk questionnaire tomorrow may be very different than how you would respond to a similar questionnaire right after the stock market had climbed or dropped 500 points.

EXAMPLE 7.1—A RISK QUIZ

Answer the questions below and add up your score to get an idea of how comfortable you tend to be with investment risk.

1. An investment in your portfolio decreases in value by 20% a month after you buy it. What would you do?

    a) Hold it and hope it will regain its value.

    b) Sell it and avoid any further declines.

2. Which investment makes you most comfortable?

    a) Money market funds.

    b) Common stocks.

    c) High-quality bonds.

3. As a contestant on a game show, which would you choose (in cash)?

    a) A 50% chance at winning $5,000.

    b) A 20% chance at winning $25,000.

4. One month after you buy it, an investment increases in value by 25%. What would you do?

    a) Hold it and hope for further increases.

    b) Sell it.

continues

Example 7.1—A Risk Quiz (Continued)

5. You inherit $5,000. What would you be most likely to do with the money?

    a) Add it to a low-risk investment you already have.

    b) Put it in an investment more aggressive than anything you currently own.

    c) Add it to your bank account.

6. For which raffle would you be most likely to buy a ticket?

    a) First prize is $150 and tickets cost $1 each.

    b) First prize is $750 and tickets cost $5 each.

    c) First prize is $1,500 and tickets cost $10 each.

Scoring:

Total your score based on the point values below.

1. a-3 b-1   **4.** a-3 b-1

2. a-1 b-3 c-2   **5.** a-2 b-3 c-1

3. a-1 b-2 c-3   **6.** a-1 b-2 c-3

If you scored:

9 points or less—You may be uncomfortable with investment risk.

10–14 points—You are most likely comfortable taking some investment risk.

15 points or more—You are probably an aggressive investor.

Range of Returns

One way to make the defining of risk more precise is to look at an investment's standard deviation, also known as its "range of returns." Historically, every investment has had a range of returns. As you might imagine, the range of returns for short-term bonds is much narrower than the range of returns for common stocks. You never see a short-term U.S. government bond drop 10% in value, even over the course of a year or two. Yet, there are thousands of examples of common stocks that have dropped 10% during a day or week.

**Dollars &
Sense:** If all this talk about risk tests and standard deviation just seems like too much, look at a chart I use (see p. 105). This chart presents risk and return in a real-world context.

Because short-term U.S. government bonds fluctuate less in value than common stocks, these bonds are less volatile and, therefore, less risky. And, since standard deviation is simply a measurement of volatility, short-term bonds have a smaller standard deviation than common stocks. To get a better idea as to what standard deviation actually means using numbers, let us go through the formula that determines an investment's standard deviation.

PERFORMANCE AND VOLATILITY

Usually, the first piece of information provided on an investment's performance is its average annual return. This is the expected return (but by no means guaranteed unless you are dealing with certain fixed-rate annuities, bank CDs or life insurance contracts) on the investment based on its historical performance over a certain period. The second piece of information that should be provided is how much fluctuation has occured between the investment's average annual rate of return and the annual return for any given year. Knowing the volatility of an investment's performance is just as important as knowing how well it has performed—this fluctuation in investment performance is a measure of how risky the investment is; the risk in this case is the uncertainty of an investment's performance. One quantitative measure of this risk is the standard deviation.

AN INVESTMENT'S STANDARD DEVIATION

Calculating the standard deviation of an investment's performance is somewhat complicated, for it involves squaring the differences between the average annual return and all the actual annual returns observed, adding these differences up and then taking the square root of the summation. It's interpretation can be just as complicated as it assumes a normal distribution of series. But what standard deviation can tell you is the probability of how volatile that investment's performance has been over a certain period. Let's look at a simple example:

Suppose over a 50-year period the average annual return of an investment came out to be 10%. Now let's suppose that the calculated standard deviation over this period is 12%. Again assuming a normal distribution of series (performance figures), the standard deviation shows the range of performance observed for 67% of the years in this period (two out of every three years). The range in this instance is 10% (the historical average annual return) plus or minus 12% (one standard deviation), which translates into returns that range between -2% to +22% (for every two out of three years). This means that over the past 50 years, this investment has produced annual returns between -2% and 22% two out of every three years.

If you want an even more precise view of how volatile the investment returns had been, add and subtract another 12% off the average annual return (remember: you are using 12% only for this example, each investment has its own standard deviation). This will produce a range that will explain the volatility of the performance 95% of the time (19 out of 20 years). In this case, that range would be -14% (10% − 12% − 12%) to 34% (10% + 12% + 12%).

When determining an investment's standard deviation, or range of returns, there are two additional points to keep in mind. First, the lower the standard deviation, the more predictable or accurate the actual range of returns will be. Second, a single standard deviation shows expected returns 67% of the time (two out of every three years). For more predictability, two standard deviations need to be used.

Common Stocks: Standard Deviation and Performance

The chart below shows the performance of the S & P 500 (the stock market) and its volatility from the end of 1926 to the end of 1995. The bars represent total returns and the black shaded area shows the standard deviation. Each tick mark represents a 10-year period of time. Notice how overall stock market volatility has actually decreased over the past 70 years. A number of incorrect articles and commentaries in recent months and years have left readers, viewers and listeners with the impression that stock market volatility has been increasing.

Standard Deviation for Selected Investments

The table below shows the three-year annualized return (ending 12/31/95) standard deviation for a number of different investments. The range of returns for two out of three years is given ("1 Standard Unit") as well as the expected range of returns for 19 out of 20 years ("2 Standard Units").

10-Year Rolling Returns and Standard Deviations of the S & P 500 (1926-1995)

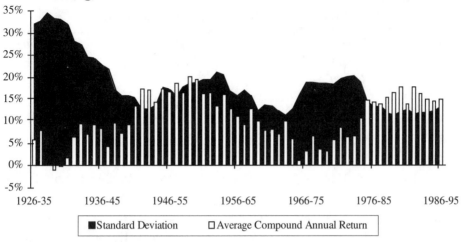

In the table below, the first column lists the investment category. The second column shows the average annual return for the investment using data from the last three calendar years, ending December 31, 1995. The third column, "Standard Deviation," shows the investment's standard deviation for the most recent 36 months. The fourth column, "1 Standard Unit," illustrates the expected range of returns for every two out of three years. The fifth column, "2 Standard Units," illustrates the expected range of returns for every 19 out of 20 years. Two standard deviations are not frequently used because even though they are more "accurate," they normally encompass too large a range of returns.

Returns and Standard Deviation for Selected Investments (Three Years Ending 12/31/95)

Investment Category	3-Year Annualized Return	Standard Deviation	1 Standard Unit	2 Standard Units
Money market accounts	3.99%	1.15%	+2.8% to +5.1%	+1.7% to +6.3%
Tax-free municipal bonds	8.77%	13.72%	-5.0% to +22.5%	-18.7% to +36.2%
Intermediate-term government bonds	7.22%	9.31%	-2.1% to +16.5%	-11.4% to +25.8%
Long-term government bonds	12.82%	16.37%	-3.6% to +29.2%	-19.9% to +45.6%

continues

Returns and Standard Deviation for Selected Investments
(Three Years Ending 12/31/95) [Continued]

Investment Category	3-Year Annualized Return	Standard Deviation	1 Standard Unit	2 Standard Units
Foreign government bonds	13.66%	5.33%	+8.3% to +19.0%	+3.0% to +24.3%
High-yield corporate bonds	9.21%	11.95%	-2.7% to +21.2%	-14.7% to +33.1%
Real estate investment trusts	12.48%	6.97%	+5.5% to +19.4%	-1.5% to +26.4%
Utility stocks	7.14%	19.30%	-12.2% to +26.4%	-31.4% to +45.7%
Balanced mutual funds	10.47%	11.27%	-0.8% to +21.7%	-12.1% to +33.0%
Equity-income mutual funds	12.92%	12.83%	+0.1% to +25.8%	-12.7% to +38.6%
Globally balanced mutual funds	11.18%	11.27%	-0.1% to +22.4%	-11.4% to +33.7%
Growth mutual funds	12.67%	13.50%	-0.8% to +26.2%	-14.3% to +39.7%
Global equity funds	13.79%	14.08%	-0.3% to +27.9%	-14.4% to +41.9%
Foreign equity funds	13.29%	18.65%	-5.4% to +31.9%	-24.0% to +50.6%
Small company stock funds	15.04%	13.11%	+1.9% to +28.1%	-11.2% to +41.3%
Aggressive growth funds	15.01%	15.08%	-0.1% to +30.1%	-15.2% to +45.2%
Emerging markets funds	14.04%	37.48%	-23.4% to +51.5%	-60.9% to +89.0%
Natural resources funds	12.02%	10.84%	+1.2% to +22.9%	-9.7% to +33.7%
Precious metals funds	18.26%	42.15%	-23.9% to +60.4%	-66.0% to +102.6%

SUMMARY

You now have a very good grounding in investment return, risk and range of returns. Some of the information may still seem unncessary for your particular situation, but I can assure you that having this kind of foundation is quite important. The more you understand about an investment, particularly what kinds of losses it can sometimes sustain, the less likely you will be taken advantage of by some mutual fund advertisement, stockbroker, or financial planner.

Dollars & Sense:

For more information about determining your risk level, consider contacting one or more of the following mutual fund companies. These companies provide a wide assortment of risk tests brochures, worksheets and software (that is either free or sold for a nominal charge).

Rowe Price (800) 638-5660

Oppenheimer (800) 525-7048

Putnam (800) 345-2228

Franklin / Templeton (800) 342-5236

Money Talks:

Although not frequently cited, the proper definition of "standard deviation" is variance or volatility of return from the investment's average annual rate of return. Most financial writers believe that standard deviation is synonymous with risk and although this may be true most of the time, it is not always the case. As an example, several years ago, a number of foreign equity mutual funds had some fantastic returns while experiencing few negative months. These funds were dubbed "high risk" because they had a large standard deviation—not from the negative months, which were modest in size and degree, but from some positive months' returns that were nothing short of fantastic.

Let's Remember This:

▶ One way to determine your risk level.

▶ Defining and applying standard deviation.

▶ Ranges of returns and standard deviations for a number of different investment categories.

▼

Stock Market Risk

Although standard deviation is a somewhat universal means of measuring or quantifying risk, beta is a yardstick for measuring U.S. stock market risk. More specifically, beta compares a stock's volatility to that of the S & P 500 (500 of the largest companies in the country). The S & P 500 always has a beta of 1.00. This is true regardless of whether or not the stock market is moving up, down, or sideways. It does not make any difference that the Dow or the S & P 500 is hitting all-time highs, the economy is experiencing robust growth or extreme recession, or that interest rates are climbing or falling—beta for the S & P 500 always remains at 1.00.

A stock's beta is calculated by comparing its price at the end of the month to that of the S & P 500 Index. A total of 36 months are used; at the end of every quarter, the then most recent 36 months are used. Thus, a stock's beta is updated quarterly.

Using beta to measure a stock's volatility in relation to the overall market can often be misleading since a stock's beta can be exaggerated or downplayed by just a handfull of months' price movements. However, beta becomes a very good gauge when it is computed for a portfolio of stocks, particularly with a large portfolio such as a mutual fund, variable annuity, or variable life contract. With so many stocks, there will be a "cancelling out" effect—most of the "exaggerated" months for certain stocks in the portfolio will cancel out those months when certain stocks had lower-than-typical volatility. In short, beta can often be a misleading figure when it covers one or just a couple of stocks; it becomes a much more reliable indicator when it represents a large portfolio of stocks.

Dollars & Sense: Despite its limitations, beta remains the best measurement of U.S. stock market-related risk. Still, this kind of risk can be small in comparison to other things that can positively or negatively affect the entire market or select securities.

Market Beta Is Always 1.00

Any stock, mutual fund, variable annuity or variable life contract that has a beta greater than 1.00 is expected to be more volatile than the S & P 500. Similarily, any individual stock, or portfolio of stocks, that has a beta less than 1.00 will usually be less volatile than the overall market (meaning the S & P 500). A beta of 1.00 means that if the S & P 500 moves up, say 8%, your stock portfolio should also move up about 8% in value during the approximate same period of time. If the S & P 500 were to fall by, say 5%, a portfolio with a beta of 1.00 should also be expected to fall about 5%. One of the best known examples of a portfolio with a beta that always remains at 1.00 is the Vanguard 500 Index Portfolio. This mutual fund owns shares of every one of the 500 companies in the S & P 500.

Most portfolios have a beta that is greater or less than 1.00. If a portfolio has a beta of .90, then it is expected to rise or fall 90% of whatever the S & P 500 does. A beta of 1.20 is expected to rise or fall 20% more than the overall market. Some additional examples of beta are shown in the table below.

EXAMPLE 8.1—BETA

Portfolio Beta	Portfolio Value	Value After S & P Falls 7%	Value After S & P Rises 8%
1.00	$10,000	$9,300 (100% of 7%)	$10,800 (100% of 8%)
0.95	$10,000	$9,335 (95% of 7%)	$10,730 (95% of 8%)
0.70	$10,000	$9,510 (70% of 7%)	$10,560 (70% of 8%)
0.50	$10,000	$9,650 (50% of 7%)	$10,400 (50% of 8%)
1.10	$10,000	$9,230 (110% of 7%)	$10,880 (110% of 8%)
1.20	$10,000	$9,160 (120% of 7%)	$10,960 (120% of 8%)
1.50	$10,000	$8,950 (150% of 7%)	$11,400 (150% of 8%)

SYSTEMATIC VS. UNSYSTEMATIC RISK

Beta measures stock market risk, also known as "systematic risk." There are two types of risk associated with U.S. stocks: systematic and unsystematic risk. Systematic risk is that part of a security's risk that is common to all securities in the same investment category. In the case of stocks, systematic risk is synonymous with market risk and is measured by beta. Since systematic risk is a common thread of all investments in a broad category, it cannot be eliminated by diversification within that same category.

Unsystematic risk represents the risk component that is unique or special to a specific security. As an example, Coca-Cola has a unique formula for their syrup, Disney has unique management, IBM has global name recognition, and Ford Motor Company has specially-designed automobiles and trucks. Unsystematic risk can be reduced by diversification within the same general category (e.g., common stocks, convertible securities, government bonds, tax-free bonds, real estate, etc.) and, to a lesser degree, within the same industry group (e.g., buying GM when you already own Ford, or Apple Computer Co. when you already own IBM).

EXAMPLE 8.2—SYSTEMATIC RISK (30% OF THE RISK OF INVESTING IN COMMON STOCKS) AND UNSYSTEMATIC RISK (THE OTHER 70% OF THE RISK OF INVESTING IN STOCKS)

Type of Risk	*Examples*
Systematic Risk	Stock market crash.
	Bear market.
	Drop in market due to interest rate concerns.
Unsystematic Risk	Ford introduces a new line of cars.
	IBM brings in new management.
	Pepsi changes its marketing strategy.
	General Foods announces it will buy back $1 billion of its own stock.
	Intel says its newest chip will be ready for shipping in a month.
	Sears quarterly profits are higher than analysts predicted.
	Johnson & Johnson decides to pull out of South America.
	XYZ and ABC plan a joint venture.

When it comes to investing in common stocks, it is estimated that systematic risk represents 30% of the risk pie and unsystematic risk equals the other 70% of the pie. So, the great news is that well over half the risk of investing in common stocks can be eliminated just by investing in several different stocks. The other 30% of the "risk pie" can be reduced by investing in things other than common stocks.

As you can now see, a stock or portfolio that has a low beta is not an assurance that moderate losses are still not possible. On October 19th, 1987, the day of the crash, it did not matter much whether or not a stock (or portfolio of stocks) had a low, average, or high beta—the losses were great across the board.

Beta Shortcomings

As previously mentioned, beta measures a stock's market risk. More specifically, it is to be used for domestic (U.S.) equities. Even though you may come across beta figures for foreign stocks, foreign bonds, and domestic bonds, such figures are almost meaningless. As an example, the beta for gold mining stocks (most of which are located outside of the United States) is very low, yet these stocks are about twice as volatile as small company stocks. In fact, metals funds have twice the volatility (as measured by standard deviation) of aggressive growth mutual funds. To say that beta is some kind of measurement for government or high-quality corporate bonds is almost like saying that seat belt safety relates to safety around the home—there is no real relationship between the two.

How You Should Use Beta

You do not need to compute a domestic stock or equity portfolio's beta because a number of sources already do it for you. In the case of individual stocks, brokerage firm research will often include beta. Value Line and Standard & Poor's also include this as part of their reports. To find out the beta of a specific mutual fund, you can get reports from CDA/Weisenberger, Lipper Analytical Services, Morningstar or Value Line. In the case of variable annuity and variable life equity subaccounts, Morningstar has a separate publication that covers these products.

Beta can be a useful tool when you are constructing a domestic equity portfolio. It is a means whereby you can decrease the market-related risk of that part of your portfolio. By selecting individual stocks, mutual funds, or variable subaccounts that have a low beta (anything less than 1.00), you will be increasing the likelihood that there will be less of a loss during extended market downturns. Keep in mind that beta is only a useful tool when there is an apples to apples comparison; that is, beta should only be used for U.S. stocks and portfolios of U.S. stocks.

EXAMPLE 8.3—A SAMPLING OF BETAS (MUTUAL FUNDS ONLY)

Name of Security	Beta
Aggressive Growth Mutual Funds	1.00
Growth Mutual Funds	0.90
Growth and Income Mutual Funds	0.90
Energy and Natural Resources Funds	0.90
Technology Stock Mutual Funds	1.10
Utility Mutual Funds	0.70
Gold Funds	0.65
Fidelity Magellan Fund	1.04
Fidelity Low-Priced Stock Fund	0.71
Fidelity Contrafund	0.92
20th Century Growth Fund	1.05
Harbor Value Fund	0.98

The table above shows how using beta alone can be a misleading means of measuring risk. As an example, gold funds have a beta of 0.65, yet they typically have twice the volatility of aggressive growth funds. There can also be a false sense of security with a low beta stock or mutual fund, the feeling that things can't get too bad if there is a stock market crash or extended correction: Such thinking is often wrong.

SUMMARY

This brief chapter has introduced you to beta. You now know how beta can be a useful tool when you are trying to get a handle on a stock's (or a portfolio of stocks) risk. You have also learned how beta can be misused: (1) it only deals with systematic risk; (2) it has little meaning when used to measure the market risk of foreign securities or U.S. bonds; (3) a low beta does not ensure that a stock will not fall substantially when the overall market collapses; and (4) beta, or systematic risk, cannot be reduced by diversification within the U.S. stock market (but unsystematic risk can be greatly reduced by such diversification).

The next chapter covers the greatest risk faced by high-quality bonds: interest rate changes or the belief that rates may change in the near future. As you will discover, there is an inverse relationship between bond prices and interest rates (meaning that when one goes up, the other goes down). Since debt instruments such as high-quality corporate and municipal bonds, as well as U.S. government securities, play an important role in the marketplace, as well as in most peoples' portfolios, it is important that you understand what causes interest rate changes and what these changes can do to the value of your bond portfolio.

Money Talks:

A statistic you may find more useful than beta is alpha. The difference between beta and alpha is that alpha can be used for a wider range of investments, not just domestic stocks. Alpha does not rely on a single benchmark figure such as the S & P 500 (which always has a beta of 1.00), but instead looks at an investment's historical return and risk level.

Let's Remember This:

- ▶ What beta means and how it is used.

- ▶ Systematic and unsystematic risk and what you can (and can't) do about it.

- ▶ The negatives of using beta.

BOND MARKET RISK

WHAT WE ARE GOING TO TALK ABOUT IN THIS CHAPTER:

▶ What Interest Rate Risk Means and How It Can Affect You

▶ Calculating Yield-to-Call and Yield-to-Maturity

▶ Describing Duration and the Time Value of Money

The biggest fear that owners of high-quality domestic bonds have is that interest rates will go up or that there is a belief that rates might go up sometime within the next few months. But, just like market "risk" and common stocks, interest rate "risk" is a two-way street. When interest rates fall or there is at least a moderate sentiment that rates may fall, bond prices increase.

When you read about "interest rates" falling or rising, more often than not the writer or commentator is referring to the prime rate (what banks use in pricing their commercial loans to their best and most creditworthy customers) or to the 30-year U.S. government bond (which is actively traded and quoted throughout the day). There is certainly a wide range of other interest rate benchmarks available, but it is one of these two that most affect the price of a bond or other debt instrument that has more than just a couple of years left until it matures.

Most people do not know that when interest rates go up, bond values go down or that when interest rates fall, bond values increase. And the majority of the people who do understand this relationship do not understand why. The reason why bond prices fall when interest rates go up is because of competition; the same thing is true when bond prices rise. It is this "market comparison" or "market adjustment" that causes bond prices to change.

Following the Price Movement of a 10-Year Bond

If you owned a 10-year bond issued by the U.S. government that you paid $1,000 for and had a coupon rate of 8%, do you think you would be able to sell it for $1,000 a month from now if the government issued new 10-year bonds that had a coupon rate of 9%? Phrased another way, if you had a $1,000 to invest, what would you rather own something that pays you $80 a year (8%) or something that is just as safe but pays $90 a year (9%)? Obviously, you would rather get 9% a year on your money instead of 8% if the safety level were identical and the maturity date was virtually identical.

Continuing with the example in the paragraph above, if you did own an 8% bond and wanted to sell it, there is a price the marketplace will pay for such a security, even though new bonds with virtually the same maturity (tenars) are yielding 9%. The discounted price of your bond will have to be low enough to attract buyers but not so low that the new yield (to the next buyer) is higher than necessary. Let's go through a couple of examples to see what I mean.

Example 9.1—Selling a Bond at a Discount

An 8% 10-year bond that pays out $80 a year in interest can compete against a 9% 10-year bond that pays out $90 a year. The 8% bond's selling price will have to be discounted in order to make it more appealing. If the bond were sold for $950, then the new owner would receive a current yield of 8.4% ($80 ÷ $950 = 8.4%). At first glance, this is not as appealing as paying $1,000 and buying a brand new 10-year bond that pays $90 a year (8.4% vs. 9%). However, the yield on the 8% bond would actually be higher than 8.4% because if someone were to pay $950 for this bond they would receive $1,000 for it upon maturity in a little less than 10 years.

In order to properly value this discount (or you could call it a "windfall" of $50), the difference between the discounted price and the face value (a $50 difference) needs to be prorated over the life of the bond (10 years). Fifty dollars prorated over 10 years comes to $5 a year. So, if someone were to buy your original 8% bond (that you paid $1,000 for) at the asking price of $950, the new owner would receive $80 a year plus an additional $5 "on paper." When you add any paper increases to the current yield you end up with what is known as yield-to-maturity. You cannot call such paper increases "current yield" because part of such yield is not actually realized until the bond is redeemed upon maturity for its full face value of $1,000.

The actual formula for calculating a discounted bond's yield-to-maturity is as follows:

(coupon rate + prorated discount) ÷ [(the bond's face value +
the discounted selling price) ÷ 2] = yield-to-maturity

Plugging the numbers from our example into this formula will give us the bond's yield-to-maturity:

($80 + $5) ÷ [($1,000 + 950) ÷ 2] = $85 ÷ $975 = 8.71% yield-to-maturity

As you can see, an 8.71% yield-to-maturity is still not as attractive as a 9% yield-to-maturity (the 9% bond has a current yield and yield-to-maturity of 9% since the bond's current value is the same as its original purchase price). Let us see what happens if we lower the price of the 8% bond to $900. Using the same formula, we get the following yield-to-maturity (note: you will see $10 below instead of $5 because we are now prorating a $100 discount over ten years instead of a $50 discount over 10 years):

($80 + $10) ÷ [($1,000 + 900) ÷ 2] = $90 ÷ $950 = 9.47% yield-to-maturity

A 9.47% yield-to-maturity is too much. This means that we will have to try some number between $950 (since a $50 discount is not enough) and $900 (since a $100 discount is more than necessary).

SUPPOSE INTEREST RATES FALL

Let us now look at a more positive set of circumstances by changing the facts of this example. Let us suppose you bought a 10-year 8% government bond a couple of months ago for $1,000. Today you pick up the paper and discover that new 10-year government bonds that sell for $1,000 each have a yield of 7%. You suspect your $80 per year bond is worth more (a premium) than a new bond that pays $70 a year. Before telephoning your broker, you remember the yield-to-maturity formula and make some of your own calculations.

EXAMPLE 9.2—SELLING A BOND AT A PREMIUM

An 8% 10-year bond that pays out $80 a year in interest can be "adjusted" so that it can be fairly compared against a 7% 10-year bond that pays out $70 a year. The 8% bond's selling price will have to be raised in order to make it more like the 7% bond. If the bond were sold for $1,100, then the new owner would receive a current yield of 7.3% ($80 ÷ $1,100 = 7.3%). At first glance this certainly looks better than a brand new 10-year bond that pays $70 a year (7.3% vs. 7.0%). However, the yield on the 8% bond is actually lower than 7.3% once the premium is factored in.

In order to properly value this premium (or you could call it a "penalty" of $100 since whoever pays $1,100 for the bond will only get back $1,000 when the bond matures), the difference between the premium price and the face value (a $100 difference) needs to be prorated over the life of the bond (ten years).

One hundred dollars prorated over ten years comes to $10 a year. So, if someone were to buy your original 8% bond (that you paid $1,000 for) at the asking price of $1,100, the new owner would receive $80 a year minus a "paper loss" of $10 per year. When you subtract any paper losses to the current yield you end up with what is known as yield-to-maturity. You cannot call such paper losses "current yield" because the yearly decrease in value of $10 is not actually realized until the bond matures and is redeemed for $1,000.

The actual formula for calculating a premium bond's yield-to-maturity is as follows:

$$\text{(coupon rate} - \text{prorated discount)} \div [\text{(the bond's face value} + \text{the discounted selling price)} \div 2] = \text{yield-to-maturity}$$

Plugging the numbers from our example into this formula will give us the bond's yield-to-maturity:

$$(\$80 - \$10) \div [(\$1,000 + \$1,100) \div 2] = \$70 \div \$1,050 = 6.66\% \text{ yield-to-maturity}$$

As you can see, an asking price of $1,100 is too much because no one wants a yield-to-maturity of 6.66% when they can get 7%. This means that the premium (or asking price) will have to be trimmed. Let's see what happens if you were to ask $1,060 for your 8% bond (we will be prorating $60 over 10 years). Using the same formula, we get the following yield-to-maturity:

($80 − $6) ÷ [($1,000 + $1,060) ÷ 2] = $74 ÷ $1,030 = 7.18% yield-to-maturity

A 7.18% yield-to-maturity is a little generous. This means that we will have to try a number that is just a little more than $1,060 so that the prorated premium brings the yield-to-maturity down to an even 7.00% so that it is fairly priced against new bonds that also have a 7% current yield and 7% yield-to-maturity.

These two formulas are to be used as a guideline; neither formula is exact. To find out the exact value of a government, municipal, or corporate bond you should contact at least three brokerage firms and get some quotes. You will find that there is usually a difference between these quotes. Do not get these quotes just for the sake of finding out what your bonds are worth on a given day. This would be pointless since bond values often change daily. Instead, get competitive bids the same day you plan on selling the bonds. Whether you are buying or selling bonds, you will want to go with the brokerage firm that will give you the best price (the highest price if you are selling and the lowest price if you are buying).

An Alternative

You may not want to memorize or even reference the two formulas above. Instead, you can refer to the table below. This table gives you a quick gauge as to what happens to a bond's value when interest rates change. Three different government securities are shown: 5-year U.S. Treasury Note, 10-year U.S. Treasury bond, and a 30-year U.S. Treasury bond. It is assumed that each of these three securities has a 7% coupon rate at the time of an interest rate change (the times would be different since 5-, 10-, and 30-year government paper would never all have the same coupon rate). The purpose of showing three different maturing securities is to show you how maturity impacts the value of a marketable debt instrument when interest rates rise by one, two, or three points (8%, 9%, and 10% respectively) or fall by one, two, or three points (6%, 5%, and 4% respectively).

There are a couple of noteworthy things to point out about the table below. First, a rate decrease (which causes bond prices to increase) has more of an impact than an interest rate increase. As an example, the five-year note (or it could be a bond with a remaining maturity of five years) increases by $43 when rates fall 1%, but only $41 when rates rise. In the case of the 30-year bond, a 1% decrease (interest rates fall from 7% to 6%) causes the bond to appreciate $138, but a 1% increase in rates (from 7% to 8%) causes the bond to only drop $113. In short, this is a pretty good risk-reward trade-off.

The second interesting part of a rate change is that additional cuts or increases (from 1% to 2%) are slightly magnified if rates are falling but less magnified when rates increase. As an example, the 30-year bond appreciates $309 when rates fall by two full percentage points (which is more than $138 × 2) but depreciates $206 when rates increase by two full points (which is less than $113 × 2). (Note: the $138 figure represents a one point drop and the $113 figure represents a one point increase.) The same slight magnification occurs when rates fall three full points and the same "less magnification" takes place when interest rates increase by three points.

Keep in mind that the losses or gains shown below are "paper" (similar to a stock going up or down in value but not sold); they become real (or "realized" for tax purposes) only when the security is sold. Part or all of these losses or gains can be eaten away in a relatively short period of time if interest rates change or as the bond gets closer to maturity (when it is redeemed for full face value, $1,000).

What Happens to a Bond's Value When Interest Rates Change

	4%	5%	6%	7%	8%	9%	10%
5-Year Treasury Note	$1,135	$1,088	$1,043	$1,000	$959	$921	$884
10-Year Treasury Bond	$1,245	$1,156	$4,074	$1,000	$932	$870	$813
30-Year Treasury Bond	$1,521	$1,309	$1,138	$1,000	$887	$794	$716

An 8% 10-year bond that pays out $80 a year in interest can be "adjusted" so that it can be fairly compared against a 7% 10-year bond that pays out $70 a year. The 8% bond's selling price will have to be raised in order to make it more like the 7% bond. If the 8% bond were sold for $1,100 then the new owner would receive a current yield of 7.3% ($80 ÷ $1,100 = 7.3%). At first glance this certainly looks better than a brand new 10-year bond that pays $70 a year (7.3% vs. 7%). However, the owner of the new 8% bond needs to keep in mind that he is not going to receive his purchase price when the bond matures. The $1,100 bond will be redeemed for $1,000; the $100 premium needs to be prorated over the life of the bond (thereby reducing its true yield).

**Dollars &
$ense:**
A rough guide to determining a bond's volatility is to simply remember that when interest rates move a full point, a long-term bond can be expected to drop or appreciate about 11%; an intermediate-term bond will rise or fall about half that amount (approximately 6%). This rule of thumb is not as accurate as the table above (which is based on duration), but it is much easier to remember.

WHAT MAKES SOME BONDS MORE VOLATILE THAN OTHERS

As far as interest rates are concerned, a bond's volatility is determined by two things: its coupon rate and the remaining maturity of the bond. A bond's coupon rate is always part of the bond's description. As an example, if someone wanted to sell you some bonds for $10,000 they would tell you the issuer (e.g., GM, IBM, the state of California, the U.S. government, GNMA, etc.), the maturity date of the bond (when interest payments cease and the face value of the bond is paid off to the owner) and its coupon rate (e.g., 6%, 6.25%, 8%, 9.125%, etc.).

You would want to know the issuer of the bond if you were concerned with safety and marketability. An IBM bond is easier to sell than one called Joe's Computer Company. A bond issued by the U.S. government has more appeal than a bond issued by General Motors, even though there is virtually no chance that GM will ever default on one of their bonds.

The maturity date is important to know for a couple of reasons. First, if you were interested in IBM (or some other well-known corporate name) bonds, you would soon discover that IBM has several different outstanding bonds. The only distinction between some of these bonds might be the maturity date or the coupon rate. As an example, IBM could have an 8% bond that matures on 12/31/98 and a different 8% bond that matures on 6/1/02 (June 1st, 2002). Or, IBM could have two different bonds that both mature on 12/31/99 but one has a 7.5% coupon and the other has a 7.125% coupon rate.

The second reason the maturity date is important has to do with volatility. The longer the maturity of the bond, the greater its volatility (see table under the section above titled "An Alternative"). A 30-year U.S. government bond is much more sensitive to interest rate changes (for better or worse) than a 10-year U.S. government bond. Since there are literally thousands of different bonds available for you to buy, you may wish to own bonds that have a maturity date that coincides with a specific event in your life (e.g., retirement, a child about to enter college, you want to buy a home in four years, etc.).

Don't Try to Predict Interest Rates

No one has been very good at predicting interest rates. There are lots of people who claim to be able to make such predictions, but if someone had such skills, believe me, they would not need any clients and they would not have to work for anyone else. With such skills you could make a fortune trading in your own account. Even though no one is any better at predicting interest rate movements than they are at predicting what the stock market will do next, this does not stop lots of investors from thinking they know what is going to happen. This kind of foolish thinking is based on a "gut reaction," listening to a convincing speaker or reading some article, or relying on some formula that the foolish thinker believes no one has ever thought of before or is known by a select few.

Whatever the case may be, if you feel that you know what interest rates are going to do during the next several months or couple of years, you can buy bonds whose maturity date coincides with your belief. If you feel interest rates are headed upward, buy bonds that are going to mature in two years or less. Then, when the bonds mature, you can buy higher yielding bonds (assuming your predictions are correct). If you believe interest rates are going to fall, you will want to buy long-term bonds (those with a remaining maturity of 15 to 30 years). If interest rates do fall, long-term bonds will appreciate more than intermediate- or short-term bonds. Finally, if you are uncertain as to what interest rates will do (an opinion or belief we should all share), buy intermediate-term bonds (those with a remaining maturity of 6 to 10 years). This middle-of-the-road approach means that if rates do fall you will make some money (at least on paper); if rates go up, you will lose some money, but only about half of what you would have lost on paper if you owned long-term bonds instead.

The second determinant of value in regard to interest rate changes is the coupon rate. The higher the coupon rate, the lower the volatility. A 6% bond is more volatile than a 9% or 10% bond. The ultimate in volatility is zero-coupon bonds. These bonds pay no current interest but instead "credit" the investor's account with what is known as accreted interest. The accreted interest is realized when the bond is sold or upon maturity. Zero-coupon bonds always sell at a price below face value (also known as redemption value) because the difference between the purchase and redemption price represents accreted interest.

YIELD-TO-CALL VS. YIELD-TO-MATURITY

So far we have looked at a bond's current yield, maturity date and what affects the value of the underlying bond (your principal). There is another measure of value: yield-to-call. Most bonds have what is known as a call feature. A call feature allows the issuer to force you to sell them back the bond before its maturity date. Call features are very common with most municipal bonds and a number of corporate bonds. The U.S. government does not issue any bonds that have a call date; all securities issued by the federal government are non-callable.

Whenever you buy a corporate or municipal bond, find out if it has a call feature and what the provisions of the call feature are; the provisions have to do with the selling price and the date when the bonds could be called away.

EXAMPLE 9.4—BONDS WITH A CALL FEATURE

Your broker has just phoned you with some information about a bond you find appealing. The broker has told you that the bond's issuer is General Motors, the bond has an 8% coupon rate, is being offered for $1,000 and the bond matures on 12/31/20 (in the year 2020). Being a savvy investor, you ask the broker if this GM bond has a call feature and if so what its provisions are. The broker tells you that the bond does have a call feature and the provisions are as follows: GM can call this bond away (meaning they can force you to sell it back to them) anytime after 2004 and that the call price is 101 (which translates into a dollar figure of 101% of face value, which works out to 101% of $1,000 or $1,010.

You decide to buy the bond for the following reasons: (a) you feel confident that GM will be around for a long time and that they will pay their bills (which include paying you interest on the bond); (b) you believe an 8% yield is attractive now and will most likely be attractive in the coming years; (c) you are assured that for at least the next several years (until the year 2004), GM must pay you interest; and (d) if GM does decide to call away your bonds you will make a slight profit (you are paying $1,000 for a bond that GM will have to pay you $1,010 for if they want to retire the bond before its maturity date in the year 2020).

The example above is straightforward, but this is not always the case. Look at the next example to see how complex the decision can be.

Example 9.5—Bonds With a Call Feature: A Dificult Decision

Your broker has just phoned you with some information about a bond you initially find appealing. The broker has told you that the bond's issuer is General Motors, the bond has an 11% coupon rate, is being offered for $1,200 and the bond matures on 12/31/20 (in the year 2020). The bond does have a call feature and the provisions are as follows: (1) GM can call this bond away anytime after 2004 and the call price is 101 ($1,010).

Despite a very tempting coupon rate of 11%, deciding whether or not to buy this bond is tricky for a couple of reasons. First, a purchase price of $1,200 means that your current yield would be 9.16% ($110 ÷ $1,200) and not 11% (it would only be 11% if you could buy the bond for $1,000). Second, the yield-to-maturity will be even less than 9.16% since the $200 premium you would be paying needs to be amortized over the bond's remaining life, which we will say is 25 years for sake of illustration (remember: when any bond matures, you will receive the face value, which is $1,000, not your purchase price, which may be more or less than $1,000). Using the formula we learned earlier, the yield-to-maturity for this bond would be:

$$(\$110 - \$8) \div [(\$1,000 + \$1,200) \div 2] = \$102 \div \$1,100 = 9.3\%$$

The $110 represents what GM is paying each year on the bond. The $8 represents the $200 premium prorated over 25 years ($200 ÷ 25 = $8).

Since the bond has a call feature, you will want to know the worst case situation, what the yield will be if the bond is called away at the earliest possible date, which is the year 2004 in this example (we will use eight years as the number of years between your purchase date and the year 2004). Calculating a bond's yield-to-call is the same as yield-to-maturity except you use the earliest call date (year 2004 in our example) instead of the bond's maturity date (year 2025). As you may have already figured out, any premium paid will now be prorated over a shorter period of time, thereby lowering the bond's yield over its "lifetime."

For our example, the $200 premium is to be prorated over eight years ($200 ÷ 8 = $25 per year). So, the formula looks like this:

$$(\$110 - \$25) \div [(\$1,000 + \$1,200) \div 2] = \$85 \div \$1,100 = 7.7\%$$

By changing the "maturity" date from 25 down to 8 years, the yield over time drops from 9.3% down to 7.7%. So, if the bond is called away by the issuer, the yield-to-call would be what the investor would end up with as an overall annualized return.

If you do not follow some or even all of these examples about yield-to-maturity or yield-to-call, don't worry. It is valuable for you to just understand what causes a bond's volatility, why, and how much harm (or benefit if interest rates fall) can be caused. Your broker will be able to tell you what these different yields are, but it is important to make sure you ask these kinds of questions before buying any kind of bond. Even though U.S. government bonds do not have a call feature, they frequently trade at a premium (some price over $1,000 per bond) or a discount (some price under $1,000 per bond).

Look Beyond a High Yield

Investors are often tempted by bonds that have higher than normal yields. What is "normal" depends upon the general level of interest rates and what kind of bond we are talking about. People are naturally attracted to the higher yield but often do not know why they are being offered such a "good deal." The truth is that the deal may be good or bad whether the yield is high or low. A high yield can work out to be a good deal if your goal is current income and you do not mind that whatever premium you pay now will be completely lost over time. The premium investor may rather receive more now than later. Someone 85 years old would probably rather have more now than later. The 85-year-old can rightfully figure that a $20, $100, $200, or even $400 premium that is amortized (and eventually lost) over the next 20 years (assuming that is the bond's remaining life) is no big deal because it is not very likely the 85-year-old will live to be 105.

On the other hand, a bond that pays a low yield may be attractive to an investor looking for some current income and some gain of principal. This kind of investor looks forward to the bond's maturity date when he cashes in the bond for $1,000. His profit will be the difference between the purchase price discount and full face value plus all of the interest payments received along the way.

Even though you may be confused about bond yields and pricing, there is one more concept that you should have a general understanding about: duration.

Duration and the Time Value of Money

Duration is how bond fund managers and sophisticated investors view their bond holdings. Duration looks at a bond's coupon rate (how much does it pay each year) plus the bond's remaining maturity. Even though it shares a number of the same traits as the formulas we looked at earlier, duration is more sophisticated because it considers (and factors in) the time value of money. Before getting to duration, let me talk a little about the time value of money.

Would you rather receive $1 today or $1.05 in one year? Which is a better deal depends upon what you think inflation will average during the next year plus what kind of yield you think you could safely get if the $1 were invested in something like a one-year T-bill, one-year CD or money market fund. We know that inflation is probably going to continue, at some level, for many years. So, if inflation were to average 3% during the next 12 months plus we felt that a 5% return on a very conservative one-year investment was a fair assumption, you and I would rather have $1 today instead of $1.05 in a year. If I changed the facts somewhat and quoted $1 today or $1.10 in a year, the $1.10 in a year would be the wiser choice— assuming that inflation and a risk-free rate of return were each in the 3 to 5% range.

This is what the time value of money is all about. Do you want X now or X plus Y in the future? Getting back to bonds and measuring volatility, the equation to determine a bond's duration (how sensitive the bond is to interest rate changes) looks at all of the bond's cash flows (the semi-annual interest payments) plus its redemption value (which is almost always $1,000 per bond) plus the number of years until maturity. The number of years of interest payments and the number of years until maturity (which would both be the same number) are important for discounting purposes (e.g., $1 today may be worth the same as $1.08 in a year or $1.16 in two years or $1.24 in three years).

A more precise definition of duration (as it appears in a book by Barron's) is: "A weighted-average term-to-maturity of the bond's cash flows, the weights being the present value of each cash flow as a percentage of the bond's full price." As far as how this relates to a bond's price change due to interest rate movements, duration represents the percentage change in the price of the bond that would take place if the general level of interest rates were to increase or decrease by exactly 1%. So, if a bond has a duration of seven, this means that if interest rates were to change by one full percentage point, the bond would change in value by approximately 7%. Thus, if the bond were worth $1,000 before the rate change, it would be worth $1,070 if interest rates fell 1% and $930 if interest rates increased by 1%. The higher the duration, the longer the maturity of the bond (or bond portfolio).

So, if a mutual fund or variable annuity representative says that the XYZ bond portfolio (which could be government, municipal or corporate bonds) has a duration of nine, you can safely assume that the bonds in the portfolio have a long maturity. More to the point, you can assume that if interest rates change 1%, the bond will change in value by 9%.

Since duration is a more exacting way of determining a bond's potential volatility and it is information that you do not have to calculate, there is no reason you should not be using it. Almost every mutual fund that contains bonds will quote you the duration of the bond portfolio right over the phone if you ask. A number of publications, such as Morningstar, also include the duration of bond portfolios in mutual funds and variable annuities.

Money Talks:

The use of duration has become more widespread in recent years but the term is still not widely used by the investing public. What turns people off to the concept of duration is that the formula for duration is based on the time value of money (i.e., a dollar today is worth more than a dollar tomorrow or next week). Duration discounts the future cash flows (the semi-annual interest payments of bonds) plus the eventual redemption price (face value) of a debt instrument and shows such cumulative discounts as a present value.

Although you will probably never learn how to compute a bond's duration (and there is little reason why you should), simply understanding that whatever the figure might be is important, say someone tells you bond X has a duration of seven years, you know that "seven" (or whatever the number is) represents the percentage of change the debt instrument will have if interest rates change by a full percentage point (or half that number if rates change by half a point).

THE COMPONENTS OF TOTAL RETURN

According to the Lehman Brothers Municipal Bond Index (dated 12/31/94), over the last 10 years, 87% of the total return realized by investing in a portfolio of long-term, tax-exempt bonds was the result of income that had been reinvested; 13% was from the bonds' price appreciation.

In a similar study by Lehman Brothers, over the same five-year period (12/31/89 to 12/31/94), 100% of the total returns realized by investing in a diversified portfolio of bonds with varying maturities and issuers was the result of income that had been reinvested. "Price appreciation" in the bonds themselves actually had a -1% impact on total returns. Over a 10-year period, 97% of total returns resulted from reinvested income and 3% was the result of price appreciation of the bonds.

Summary

This is probably the most difficult chapter in the book. A fair number of new phrases and formulas concerning bonds and bond funds were introduced and examined. Even though you may not feel comfortable with some or all of these concepts, you should at least have a pretty good idea as to what causes a bond's price to move up and down and to what degree. You now know a lot more about interest rate risk than most bond investors. A 1996 study shows that a high percentage of people who buy government bond funds from savings institutions such as banks do not realize that the value of their principal can, and will, fluctuate. Apparently, the word "government" or "U.S. government" connotates a type of safety (stability of principal) that simply does not exist. You now know that a government bond's face value is only guaranteed if the bond is held until maturity.

The next chapter deals with inflation, also known as purchasing power risk. This is the type of risk most closely associated with what a number of financial writers call "risk-free" investments. As you will see, "risk-free" investments such as money market funds, bank CDs, and U.S. Treasury bills (T-bills) would only be risk-free if we lived on a planet that did not have income taxes or inflation.

Dollars & Sense: Whenever you buy an individual bond, unit trust (which is a fixed portfolio of securities), bond fund or any other kind of bond portfolio, always ask your broker what the yield-to-call and yield-to-maturity are. Investors often buy bonds based on an appealing yield, only to later find out (after it is too late), that the true yield (once the bond is called away) is much less than they bargained for.

Let's Remember This:

- ▶ Interest rate risk.

- ▶ Calculating the true yield of a callable bond or any bond for which you pay a premium or discount.

- ▶ How duration is used to calculate interest rate risk.

▼

Money Market Funds and Risk

What We Are Going to Talk About in This Chapter:

- ► Income Taxes, Inflation and Money Market Returns
- ► The Rule of 72
- ► The Benefits of Fixed-Income Investments

A money market account is a portfolio of short-term debt instruments of very high quality with a maturity that averages 90 days or less. A large number of cash equivalents (i.e., bank CDs, commercial paper, and T-bills) are included in a money market account or fund in order to reduce risk. Regulations require that money market accounts be almost exclusively comprised of only the most highly rated "paper" (instruments). This requirement protects investors against savings institutions and mutual fund companies trying to attract more customers by offering higher yields (higher than what should be expected from such a conservative investment). The average maturity is kept to 90 days or less so that investors do not have to worry about changing interest rates affecting the value of the portfolio. The vast majority of money market funds have an average maturity that ranges from 30 to 60 days. No matter what the maturity in one of these accounts, instruments are coming due every day or week and are immediately replaced with new paper (such as new CDs, T-bills, etc.).

Your Initial Investment

When you invest in a money market fund, you own a very small part of each instrument in the portfolio. The money market fund you invest your $1,000 in might have $1 billion in assets; your $1,000 investment means that you own 1,000/1,000,000,000 of each piece of paper in the portfolio. The overall return from all of those instruments represents your (and everyone else who owns shares in that money market account) gross return or yield. If $25 million dollars worth of paper matures tomorrow, the portfolio management will immediately buy new paper worth $25 million to replace the debt instrument that has just matured.

If the maturing paper was yielding 5% and the new paper yields 5.2%, the overall yield of the portfolio will increase, but only by an insignificant amount, for two reasons. First, $25 million represents just 2.5% of a $1 billion portfolio. Second, if the value of 2.5% of a portfolio changes by 0.2%, an overall yield that was 5% will not even increase to 5.01%.

When you first invest in a money market fund, you get the exact same rate of return as someone who has been in the same money market account for several months or years (both yields will be identical from your first day forward, although the older investor may have received a slightly different yield the day, week, or month before you entered since the fund's yield may change a little every day or so). You also get the same rate of return whether you invest $100 or $1 billion. Everyone in the fund owns a piece of everything in the portfolio, some investors just own a bigger chunk of each piece.

A Constant $1 Per Share

Money market funds are always sold for $1.00 a share; if you have $1,000 to invest in a money market account, you will end up with exactly 1,000 shares. The price per share of a money market fund never changes, not even after several months or years. The interest you earn in a money market fund, which is similar to the kinds of returns you would get from a T-bill or bank CD, is credited to your account in the form of additional shares. So, even though you may start out with 1,000 shares, at the end of several days you will have 1,001 shares. At the end of a year, your 1,000 shares will have grown to 1,050 (assuming the account averages 5% for the year), 1,060 (if your yield is 6%), etc. There is no minimum or maximum guaranteed rate of return with money market accounts. The return you get depends upon short-term interest rates in general.

Making Additions and Withdrawals

You can add or take money out of a money market account at any time. These accounts earn interest every day. You do not have to leave the money until the end of a week, month, or quarter to get what you are entitled to. Part or all of the account can be liquidated with a phone call, by written instruction, or by writing a check (that is linked to the money market fund).

When you make a withdrawal from a money market account, the portfolio's manager will try to match your request with brand new money that is just entering the fund (one or more new investors). If the outflows (redemptions) are greater than the inflows (new purchases) for any given day, management will sell off part of one of the instruments in the portfolio if necessary. This kind of sale is not very common but it is always an option management has.

Features

Money market accounts provide a number of features and benefits not found with other investments: (1) a price per share that remains constant; (2) free check-writing privileges; (3) free replacement checks; (4) interest that compounds daily; and (5) the option of going into different types of money market funds.

Dollars & Sense: If check-writing privileges are important to you, find out if the money market account or fund you are thinking about buying into charges on a per check basis (only a few funds have such a charge) or has a minimum amount for each check written (typically $100 to $250). These types of restrictions are quite common; the management company wants to keep expenses to a minimum in order to provide you, one of its shareholders, with the highest possible yield.

Variety

There are three kinds or types of money market accounts. The most common and popular is a "general purpose" money market fund. These funds have no tax benefits but almost always offer a higher yield than the two other kinds of money market accounts. A "federal" or "government only" money market fund is comprised only of paper issued or backed by the U.S. government. These kinds of accounts are the ultimate in safety and may be exempt from state income taxes. "Tax-free" money market accounts are comprised of short-term paper issued by municipalities (i.e., tax anticipation notes and bond anticipation notes). These accounts yield less than government or general purpose money market accounts on a pre-tax basis, but provide a better after-tax return to investors in a high state and federal income bracket. Tax-free money market funds are exempt from federal income taxes and may be exempt from state income taxes, depending upon whether or not the instruments in the portfolio were issued by a municipality in your state.

Dollars & $ense: Money market yields are just like bank CD yields, they can vary all over the board. Phone several mutual funds, including Alger, Fidelity Spartan and Vanguard, and ask them what the highest yielding money market fund is that they have; find out if such a fund is "temporarily" waiving part or all of its current expenses. If it is, consider using another money market fund that is not using such a gimmick to attract new money.

Inflation and Money Market Funds

As we have already learned, there are several kinds of risk associated with any investment you can think of; conventional wisdom thinks of risk as the chances of losing part or all of one's principal. Such thinking is correct but too narrow in its definition of risk. In the previous chapters we have seen how the volatility of an investment is measured (standard deviation), the biggest risk associated with common stocks (market risk) and high-quality bonds (interest rate risk). This chapter is the third part of the triad. It covers the risk of inflation or how increases in the prices of goods and services you and I use have an effect on the real rate of return from our investments.

There are a number of definitions of inflation. A classic definition of inflation is: "Too much money chasing too few goods" or "A rise in the prices of goods and services." One of my favorite descriptions of inflation is one that uses an analogy. It is an analogy that I believe gives a better description of what causes inflation and why. The setting for the analogy is a desert island.

Suppose you just moved to a small island and discovered that only two items were produced on the island: television sets and coconuts. After being on the island a couple of days, you decide to buy a television and you learn that the island's currency is coconuts. The island produces roughly 100 coconuts a year and a television set, which takes six months to manufacture on the island, costs 50 coconuts. Since there is no other means of exchange or barter, you decide to start growing coconuts as soon as possible because you want to start watching television.

After a year of carefully cultivating your coconut trees, you end up with a bumper crop. Your trees produce 50 coconuts. This means that the island's production of coconuts has increased by 50%, from 100 to 150. You are excited because you remember that a television set manufactured on the island cost 50 coconuts last year and the year before. You assume that the price of televisions has remained at 50 coconuts. You gather up your 50 coconuts and head down to the television store. As you start to pay for the television, the store manager interrupts you by saying, "I'm sorry, but the cost of a television is now 75 coconuts and you are the reason why television sets for everyone this year will be 75 coconuts. I must raise the price of my televisions by 50% because you have flooded the market with our currency. In fact, the amount of currency has increased by 50%. No longer are there 100 coconuts out there; there are now 150 coconuts."

The sudden price increase may not seem fair to you, but you begin to understand why. The economy you stepped into was evenly balanced. A year's worth of growth by the coconut growers on the island was just enough to buy two television sets. A year's worth of manufacturing also produced exactly two television sets. Now, a year after you have been on the island, the equation has changed. A year's worth of coconuts (100 plus your 50) would be able to buy a year and a half's worth of television production. With the introduction of your coconut crop, television sets are now cheaper— unless the manufacturers raise prices. In a sense, it is just like living in a larger economy that uses paper currency and you arrive on the scene with a printing press that increases the amount of currency by 50%.

As you can see by the island analogy, currency, whether it is U.S. dollars or Japanese yen, is simply a commodity. The rarer the currency is, the more valuable it becomes; or, looked at another way, the less money they print the scarcer it becomes. A lot of a currency's worth is its perceived value. The same thing is true with diamonds. The supply of diamonds is great, but a cartel has successfully controlled the flow of new diamonds into the marketplace by limiting the supply each year. If the market were flooded with diamonds tomorrow, it would only take a few days or weeks for the word to get out and the price of diamonds would plummet.

WHAT CAUSES INFLATION

Inflation is actually caused by two things: the amount of currency that has been printed and the availability of that currency. The U.S. Treasury Department could let the printing presses run wild, but if all of the production were stored in secure warehouses, inflation would not change. For it is the amount of times that a dollar bill changes hands that really causes inflation.

If everyone had a lot of cash but was not spending it, retailers would have to slash the prices of their goods and services in order to attract purchasers. You and I might not be interested in buying a second or third new car if the price tag of our favorite vehicle were $25,000, but if the price dropped to some ridiculous figure such as $12,000, we would become much more tempted to make that additional purchase.

At the other extreme, let us suppose that there was not a lot of currency available, but everyone you and I knew loved to buy things. I dip into my savings account and go out and buy a new car for $25,000. The person I buy the car from takes my $25,000 and buys another car for $22,000 to replace the one he sold me. The $22,000 check that he sends to the car factory is used to buy steel and electronic equipment for the car and to pay for the labor used in assembling the car. The workers are paid a salary and they take part of their salary and buy groceries, television sets and clothing. The things they buy enable other people to keep their retail businesses, maintain their employees and pay these employees a salary, part of which is used by the employees to go out and buy things.

As it turns out, my $25,000 auto purchase has had a rippling effect in the economy. My purchase helped the salesman who sold me the car. The salesman in turn ordered a replacement car which means that there is now work (and money) for the people involved in auto production, advertising and shipping. These workers in turn brought money to the local shops in their area, helping employment even more. A lot of people are happy and benefit whenever someone like you or me buys a car, television set, or bag of groceries. This multiplier effect benefits society in a lot of ways, but someone along the line must be disciplined.

If everyone spends every dime they earn, then there is no money available for capital formation. New companies cannot be created because no one has a savings account that the bank can tap to make a loan. The people who want to start new companies (and hire workers who will pay taxes and also buy things) cannot go to a securities underwriter because no one has any money to invest in stocks or bonds—no matter how tempting the proposition. No one has stocks, bonds, or bank accounts because no one is saving for the future. Everyone is simply consuming as soon as they cash their paychecks.

Fortunately, such a society does not exist, at least not on earth. A number of people do not consume every dollar they earn. Instead, they deposit some of it in a bank account, perhaps out of convenience or for an emergency. Other people take part of their earnings and buy things like stocks, bonds, and real estate with the hope that they will get a higher return on these investments than they will at the bank. But even the money at the bank can be lent out to help create additional wealth. The local barber may go to her banker and request a loan so that she can open a second barber shop across town in the hopes of making more money. Those that buy stocks and bonds create a marketplace for existing and new securities to flourish. Stock prices go up when more and more dollars (yen, francs, pounds, etc.) start chasing after the existing supply of stocks. Think what would happen to the price of IBM or General Motors stock if suddenly tomorrow everyone wanted to own at least 100 shares.

THE DECEPTION OF INFLATION

Back in the very early 1980s, when interest rates seemed to keep going up, investors were overjoyed with the returns they were getting on money market accounts. For the 1981 calendar year, some of these accounts had a yield that averaged about 12% for the year. Getting 12% on a "risk-free" investment such as a money market fund seems like a great deal until you factor in income taxes and inflation. Back in the early 1980s, the top marginal income tax bracket (state and federal combined) was 60% in some states. If you start off with 12% and pay 60% of your yield in income taxes, you will net 4.8%. An after-tax return of almost 5% still sounds pretty good until you factor in the effects of inflation. For the 1981 calendar year, inflation was 12%. So, if you have an after-tax return of close to 5% and then subtract 12% for inflation, your real return becomes -7%. Suddenly, the original return of 12% doesn't seem so good.

What I have just described goes on today, but at much lower rates. Overall tax rates have dropped for most people and interest rates on cash equivalents plus the rate of inflation has dropped dramatically. Still, the picture is not that appealing. For the 1996 calendar year, it looks like a year's yield in a money market account will come to around 5%. Assuming a top combined income tax bracket of 45%, an investor will still keep 55% of 5% (55% of 5% = 2.75%). As long as inflation comes in at less than 2.75% for the year, the money market investor will still have a real positive return. If inflation turns out to be something over 2.75% for the year, then this "risk-free" investment has been damaged by the effects of inflation. The example below will provide you with a historical perspective as to what happens to a risk-free investment once its returns have been adjusted for income taxes and inflation.

	Why "Risk-Free" Investments are Losers		
Year	*Money Market Return*	*Return After Taxes*	*After-Tax & Inflation-Adjusted Return*
1976	5.3%	2.9%	-1.8%
1977	5.0%	2.8%	-3.8%
1978	7.2%	4.0%	-4.7%
1979	11.1%	6.1%	-6.4%
1980	12.8%	7.0%	-4.8%
1981	16.8%	9.2%	0.3%
1982	12.2%	6.7%	2.7%
1983	8.6%	4.7%	0.9%
1984	10.0%	5.5%	1.5%
1985	7.7%	4.2%	0.4%
1986	6.3%	3.5%	2.3%
1987	6.1%	3.4%	-1.0%
1988	7.1%	3.9%	-0.5%
1989	8.9%	4.9%	0.2%
1990	7.8%	4.3%	-1.7%
1991	5.7%	3.1%	0.1%
1992	3.4%	1.9%	-1.0%
1993	2.7%	1.5%	-1.2%
1994	3.8%	2.1%	-0.6%
1995	5.5%	3.0%	0.3%

The kind of returns you see in the table above are very similar to what would have happened had you invested in money market accounts and short-term bank CDs.

THE RULE OF 72

If you want to see the cumulative effects of inflation, use the rule of 72. This will show you how many years it takes for a dollar (or ten billion dollars) to lose half of its purchasing power. Simply divide the assumed, projected or historical rate of inflation into the number 72. The resulting number is the number of years it takes to halve the buying power of a sum of money.

EXAMPLE 10.1—USING THE RULE OF 72

Let us suppose that you believe the overall rate of inflation is going to increase in the future. Based on your assumptions, you now feel that inflation will average 6% a year in the future. By dividing 6 into 72 you can see that $1 will be worth only 50 cents in 12 years (meaning it will only be able to buy what 50 cents buys today). At the end of the second 12-year period, the 50 cents will only have the same purchasing power as 25 cents in today's dollars.

The rule of 72 can be used no matter what the assumed or actual rate of inflation. It is a quick and easy way to see how long it takes to halve the value of a dollar, yen, franc or any other currency that is subjected to the rate of inflation you are using in the equation (X divided into 72).

The rule of 72 can also be used in a more positive manner. The rule of 72 can show you how long it takes an investment, any investment, to double in value. The only thing you need to plug into the formula is the assumed, actual, or projected rate of return (total return, meaning any growth of principal plus any dividends or interest payments made along the way). So, if you have a portfolio worth $39,000 and you believe that the overall rate of return (sometimes referred to as a "blended rate") for this portfolio will continue to average 8%, $39,000 will grow to $78,000 in nine years ($72 \div 8 = 9$). If the investor's time horizon is stretched out and the same rate of return applies, $78,000 will grow to $156,000 at the end of the second nine-year period.

A FIXED-INCOME'S WORST LONG-TERM ENEMY: LOSS OF PURCHASING POWER

Most years, the rate of inflation is not that noticeable. Hearing that GM, Ford or Toyota has raised the price of their cars by 3% does not seem like a big deal, but such increases year-in and year-out turn into a big deal after a number of years. In the mid-1970s, a fully-loaded Cadillac cost about $7,000. Today, a new fully-loaded Cadillac costs over $40,000. Think what your investment portfolio must do as far as growth just to keep pace with inflation.

Traditionally, fixed-income investments such as cash equivalents and bonds have not been a good hedge against inflation. Historically and conceptually, it is easy to see why. Conceptually, a fixed-income makes sense if you live in a world of fixed costs. In other words, a world that does not have inflation or increasing tax rates. Historically, it is also easy to see why fixed-income investments do not make a lot of sense for most people.

Suppose you just retired with a nest egg of $300,000. You invest the entire $300,000 in U.S. government bonds that pay 7% and mature in 15 years. You receive $21,000 (7% of $300,000) for each of the next 15 years. At the end of 15 years your bonds mature for $300,000. During these years, the purchasing power of your $21,000 is likely to slowly decline each year (note: the last time we did not have inflation was 1954). Over a 15-year period, if inflation were to average just what it has averaged over the past 50 to 60 years, your cumulative purchasing power would drop between 40 and 50%. Imagine what will happen to your purchasing power during the second 15 years, assuming you can buy new bonds that have a similar yield (it will drop by another 40 to 50%).

When You Get Older

What I have just described in the paragraph above happens to millions of Americans each year. And there are obviously millions more that retire with far less than $300,000. Instead of being their "golden years," their lives are constantly at the mercy of interest rates and inflation. Think how you would feel if you knew today that during each of the next 15 years your standard of living was going to drop and at the end of those 15 years you had to look forward to an even bleaker future.

As we get older our options for investing and employment become more limited. You and I know that the job prospects for a man or woman who is 60 or 70 are not nearly as great as they are for someone in their 30s, 40s, or 50s. Similarly, the older you get, the less time your portfolio has to recover from a large loss that could occur in the stock market or in real estate (which can be much more volatile than stocks).

Example 10.2—How Real Estate Can Be the Scariest Investment You Ever Make

You already own your own home and have some money to invest. You decide to buy real estate because: (1) its overall track record looks pretty good; (2) people have to live somewhere; and

(3) they ain't makin' any more of the stuff. You take your $100,000 and buy a $1 million office building that is fully leased by a very high quality tenant, let's say a division of AT&T. Although you have taken on a $900,000 mortgage to buy this $1,000,000 property, you are not concerned because AT&T isn't going anywhere (at least not for the next five years because of their lease) and their rent payments not only pay for the mortgage, but you are also able to pocket $500 each month.

At this point, things look great. AT&T is paying your entire mortgage, your banker loves you because you have such a high-quality tenant, and you are netting an extra $500 a month from the rent payments.

Fast-forward to five years from now. AT&T decides not to renew the mortgage. Suddenly you have a $1,000,000 building that is costing you about $9,000 a month (your mortgage payment). You decide to sell the building but discover that even if AT&T had renewed their lease, the rental market is soft and a renegotiated lease would have only brought in $6,000 a month. You also discover that because of the relatively high vacancy factor in the city, buildings, including yours, are not worth as much as they used to be.

You end up selling the building for $930,000, but after paying a selling commission and closing costs, you end up netting $870,000. Netting $870,000 doesn't seem so bad until you remember that you still owe the bank about $900,000. After taking out a pad of paper and pencil, you realize that you have not only lost 100% of your original investment (the $100,000) but you have also lost $30,000 (the difference between the mortgage and the net proceeds from the sale of the building).

Losing a 100% or more of your investment is tough to swallow. But it could have been much worse. The example I have just described assumes that the building has only lost 7% of its value ($1,000,000 down to $930,000). Consider how bad the loss would have been if you had bought the building in California in 1988 or 1989 and then sold it in 1993, 1994, 1995 or 1996. There is a good chance that your loss would have been several hundred thousand dollars. Or phrased another way, it would have probably been a loss of 300 to 500%. How do you explain to your spouse or friend that you have not only lost all of your money, but you also owe the bank another $200,000 to $400,000?

THE BENEFITS OF FIXED-INCOME INVESTMENTS

Although most categories of fixed-income investments have not been a particularly good hedge against the long-term effects of inflation, there are a number of reasons why you should consider making them part of your portfolio. These reasons include: (1) easy to understand; (2) known rate of return; (3) specific maturity date; (4) controllable volatility; and (5) a way to diversify your holdings. Let us briefly look at each of these points.

When you buy a bond, you know what your interest rate will be and when the bond will mature. You can also find out the quality of the bond, as measured by a rating service such as Fitch, Moody's or Standard and Poor's. When you invest in a bond fund or bond subaccount (in the case of a variable annuity or variable life contract), you can find out the average maturity or duration as well as the quality breakdown (e.g., 35% rated AAA, 24% rated AA and 41% rated A) of the portfolio. The bonds in a mutual fund, variable annuity and variable life contract "never" mature since management is constantly buying and selling new bonds. There is only one mutual fund company, Benham, and one variable annuity contract, offered by Franklin, that has "target" portfolios (meaning they are comprised of bonds that mature on a specific date and that date will not change).

Individual bonds have a specific rate of return. There are what are known as "adjustable-rate" securities whose interest rates can be adjusted upward or downward (depending on the general level of interest rates), but these kinds of bonds and funds are not very popular and have not performed as well as originally expected. When you buy a mutual fund or variable product that includes a bond portfolio, the initial yield you are quoted will change as new bonds are added to the portfolio (due to new money coming in or as a replacement for old bonds maturing or sold off). And, as previously mentioned, the same thing is true with money market accounts—their yield also changes. Still, the current yield from any kind of debt instrument is always much more predictable than the return from a stock or other investment.

The maturity date of an individual bond is also known at the time of purchase. If you hold the bond until it matures, you can be assured that you will receive interest payments every six months (unless it is a zero-coupon bond which pays no current interest, the investor instead gets accreted interest) plus full face value. The face value of a bond is almost always $1,000. So, whether or not the full face value is more, less, or the same as your purchase price depends upon whether or not you bought the bond for a discount (some dollar amount less than $1,000 per bond), a premium (you paid more than $1,000) or its face value.

Since bonds have different maturity dates, you have the ability to control the volatility of your bonds (the fluctuation in value of your principal from the time of purchase until you sell the bond or it matures, whichever comes first). Short-term bonds (those with a remaining maturity of five years or less) have $1/3$ to $1/2$ less volatility than medium or intermediate-term bonds (those with a remaining maturity of 10 years or less) are $1/3$ to $1/2$ less volatile than long-term bonds (those with a remaining maturity of more than 10 years).

When it comes to portfolio diversification and risk reduction, nothing beats cash equivalents such as money market funds. This kind of account loves increasing interest rates; bond and real estate owners hate increasing rates and stock investors often dislike rising interest rates. As interest rates increase, so do the yields on money market funds. Next to cash equivalents, the best way to reduce portfolio risk is to add short-term bonds. These kinds of bonds are quite stable and will fluctuate very little, even when your long-term bonds are suffering (or perhaps increasing in value if interest rates are dropping) or your stock holdings are going through a rough time.

LIVING WITH A DEBT PORTFOLIO IN A WORLD OF INFLATION

Ultra-conservative and very old investors should have most, if not all, of their holdings in debt instruments—despite what I have said about the cumulative effects of inflation. There are a couple of ways to combat the effects of inflation even if 100% of your portfolio is in debt instruments. These ways include: (1) reinvestment; (2) including high-yield bonds; and (3) including foreign bonds.

Toward the beginning of the chapter, I talked about someone retiring with $300,000 who invested the entire amount in 7% U.S. government bonds. When the bonds matured in 15 years and were replaced with new bonds, the investor's purchasing power had cumulatively dropped by close to 50%; at the end of the second 15-year period, another 40 to 50% drop in purchasing power would take place (assuming inflation averages 4 to 5%). This means that at the end of his first 15 years in retirement, this person was going to have to live on half of his original income (the dollar amount may not have changed, but its purchasing power sure did). By the end of the second 15-year period, the investor would have to adjust once again and begin to live on only 25% of his original income (50% of 50%). However, it did not have to be this way.

By reinvesting part of your income, a conservative investor can offset part or all of the effects of inflation. If you receive 7% but only spend 5%, you can reinvest the remaining 2% into more bonds or money market accounts. If inflation averages 4% and you are reinvesting 2%, you halve the effects of inflation. At a 4% rate of inflation, it takes about 18 years for the purchasing power of a dollar to drop by half.

If you reduce the rate of inflation to 2%, it now takes over 36 years for one's purchasing power to be diminished by 50%.

Why High-Yield Bonds Are Good

High-yield bonds are another way you can help beat off the effects of inflation on a portfolio of debt instruments. High-yield bonds are bonds whose credit rating is anything less than "investment grade," also known as "bank quality." This would include a bond rated by Standard & Poor's that was less than BAA (investment grade being AAA, AA, A, and BBB rated issues). In the case of Moody's, something less than investment grade would be bonds rated below Baa (investment grade being Aaa, Aa, A, and Baa rated issues).

If you stick with bonds (or bond funds and variable annuity subaccounts) that invest in securities rated just below investment grade, such as bonds rated BB or B, you should have nothing to worry about. Just this one or two grade difference often provides a yield difference of another 1 to 3%. So, instead of getting 7% from a government bond, a high-yield bond will give you an 8 to 11% return. And since bonds have a higher coupon rate (yield), this means they have a shorter duration, which means they have less interest rate risk. Furthermore, the typical high-yield bond has a shorter maturity, particularly in a mutual fund, than a government or high-quality corporate bond. The shorter maturity helps to greatly reduce volatility due to interest rate changes (also known as interest rate risk).

The track record of high-yield bonds is pretty impressive. They have outperformed government and high-quality corporate bonds over the past 3, 5, 10 and 15 years. They also have a tendency to beat these other kinds of bonds on a yearly basis.

Even though high-yield bonds are debt instruments, they are often categorized as a hybrid, since they act somewhat like a bond and somewhat like a stock. High-yield bonds are like other kinds of bonds in that they do react negatively to interest rate changes or fears, but they will not act as negatively. These hybrids act somewhat like stocks because they tend to appreciate in value when there is good economic news (government and other high-quality bonds almost always react negatively to positive economic news since such news is often viewed as inflationary). When the economy is good or simply recovering, there is less likelihood that a corporation will have financial difficulty (unable to pay its bills, which include paying interest on bonds).

Another way to live with debt instruments is to include foreign bonds as part of the portfolio. These are bonds issued by governments or corporations outside of the United

States. Foreign bonds have the same kinds of risk (or reward) as domestic bonds but there is also a currency risk. If the currency of the foreign bond decreases in value against the U.S. dollar, then the price of the foreign bond will go down (all other things being equal). If the currency appreciates against the U.S. dollar, the foreign bond will appreciate in value (your principal will increase), again all other things being equal or remaining the same.

Foreign, also known as international, bonds add diversification to a portfolio because sometimes their values fluctuate differently than their U.S. counterparts. When the Federal Reserve is trying to cool down the economy (by raising interest rates, which causes domestic bonds to fall in value), the United Kingdom, Japan, Germany, Canada, or other countries may be trying to stimulate their economies (by lowering interest rates, which would cause that country's bonds to appreciate) or maintain current economic policy (leave rates alone which means that the bonds would maintain their current value). There are also a number of stable economies around the world that offer higher yields than can be found with their domestic counterparts. High-quality foreign bonds have outperformed high-quality U.S. bonds over the past 3, 5, 10 and 15 years.

Money Talks: A money market fund is virtually the same as a money market account you might have at a bank. Such accounts at banks may be insured by FDIC but such insurance is of little importance or value. Since all money market funds and accounts, by definition and regulation, can only include short-term debt instruments whose ratings fall within the two highest categories, the odds of you losing any money (or any interest you were due) are several thousand to one.

SUMMARY

This ends our discussion of market, interest rate and purchasing power risk. Now that you are familiar with the major kinds of risks that affect investments, you are ready to start constructing a portfolio. In an earlier chapter we went over the process of setting goals and objectives as well as how a basic investment plan is structured. Before you can properly set up a portfolio, you need to know about correlation coefficients. This somewhat odd sounding phrase describes how two or more investment categories "interact" with each other—meaning when investment ABC goes down, what is the likelihood (and to what degree) that investment XYZ will also go down, stay the same or increase in value?

Ideally, the categories represented in your portfolio should not all be sensitive to the same things. That is, you do not want your entire portfolio to drop in value when interest rates change, the stock market goes down, inflation becomes out of hand or a foreign currency drops in value in relation to the U.S. dollar. As strange as it may sound, you want different parts of your portfolio to react to different things, which will sometimes result in positive returns and sometimes result in negative returns or flat returns.

Dollars & Sense: For liquidity purposes, consider a short-term bond fund, one whose bonds have an average maturity of one to two years or less. These kinds of funds have very low volatility, often allow you to write checks against your account (for free) and may have a yield advantage of .5 to 1% over a traditional money market fund (and perhaps up to a 2% or 3% advantage over a bank's money market account.

Let's Remember This:

▶ The effects of income taxes and inflation on money market yields.

▶ A quick formula to figure out how long it takes money to double.

▶ Some of the benefits of fixed-income investments.

CHAPTER 11

INTERNATIONAL INVESTING

WHAT WE ARE GOING TO TALK ABOUT IN THIS CHAPTER:

- ▶ How Currency Can Affect Your Foreign Investment Returns
- ▶ The Best-Performing Foreign Stock Markets vs. the U.S. Stock Markets
- ▶ The Best-Performing Global Bond Markets

There is a perception that investing in foreign, also known as international, stocks and bonds is much riskier than investing in their U.S. counterparts. International investing is riskier, but only by a modest amount. When you invest in foreign stocks or bonds, you take on the same risks you do with similar domestic investments, plus there is a currency risk. This means that you are not only investing in international securities, you are also "investing" in that country's currency. If that currency appreciates against the U.S. dollar, then your returns in that foreign security become even higher (or whatever loss there is in the security may be partially or more than offset by the currency gain). Similarly, if that foreign currency depreciates (loses value) against the U.S. dollar, then your returns are lowered (or your losses are increased if the security has dropped in value). Let us go through an example.

Suppose you are interested in a Japanese stock or a mutual fund that invests only in Japanese stocks. We will call this investment Japan, Inc. When you invest in Japan, Inc., your dollars are converted to yen which are used to purchase Japan, Inc. You do not see this conversion taking place, but it happens. To put it in a different perspective, when a citizen of Mexico, Canada, Japan or any other foreign country buys U.S.

stocks, their respective currency must first be converted to U.S. dollars. The Mexican investor may get a confirmation (statement) showing that X number of shares of a U.S. stock were purchased for Y number of pesos, but the number of pesos being charged to the client's account is based on the exchange rate (the number of pesos it takes to equal a dollar) at the time the trade is entered by the client's brokerage firm. When our Mexican investor sells his shares of the U.S. stock, the sale takes place in U.S. dollars, which are then converted to pesos and then credited to the investor's account.

Getting back to our U.S. investor who wants to own shares of Japan, Inc. (a mutual fund or individual stock or bond), let us see how the currency risk might affect the investor by presenting a chronological table.

EXAMPLE 11.1—THE SECURITY STAYS FLAT, BUT THE YEN INCREASES IN VALUE

Investor Buys Japanese Security

Date & Transaction	Price of Japan, Inc.	Exchange Rate	What the U.S. Investor Sees	Net Profit or Loss
6/1/96 buy 1 share of Japan, Inc.	700 yen	100 yen = $1	$7	——
9/1/97 sell 1 share of Japan, Inc.	700 yen	50 yen = $1	$14	$7 profit

In this first example, the yen has appreciated in value by 50% from the date of purchase to the date of sale (what happens between the buy and sell dates is unimportant—it's what the yen is worth on the date of sale that's important). Japan, Inc. is selling for exactly what it was purchased for, 700 yen. However, since it now takes half as many yen to equal a dollar, the currency exchange will produce twice as many dollars.

Example 11.2—The Security Stays Flat, But the Yen Decreases in Value

Investor Buys Japanese Security

Date & Transaction	Price of Japan, Inc.	Exchange Rate	What the U.S. Investor Sees	Net Profit or Loss
6/1/96 buy 1 share of Japan, Inc.	700 yen	100 yen = $1	$7	——
9/1/97 sell 1 share of Japan, Inc.	700 yen	150 yen = $1	$4.67	$2.33 loss

In the second example, the yen has depreciated in value by 50% from the date of purchase to the date of sale. Japan, Inc. is selling for exactly what it was purchased for, 700 yen. However, since it now takes 50% more yen to equal a dollar, the currency exchange will result in fewer dollars.

Example 11.3—The Security Increases and the Yen Decreases in Value

Investor Buys Japanese Security

Date & Transaction	Price of Japan, Inc.	Exchange Rate	What the U.S. Investor Sees	Net Profit or Loss
6/1/96 buy 1 share of Japan, Inc.	700 yen	100 yen = $1	$7	——
9/1/97 sell 1 share of Japan, Inc.	1,400 yen	150 yen = $1	$9.33	$2.33 profit

In the final example, the price of Japan, Inc. has doubled in terms of yen. Unfortunately for our U.S. investor, the yen has lost value in relation to the dollar; so it takes more yen to equal one dollar, thereby eating into the profits (which should have been

100%). Once the sale takes place and the proceeds, 1,400 yen, are converted into U.S. dollars, the profit drops from $7 ($14 × $7) to $2.33 ($9.33 × $7). If our investor had been living in Japan all along (meaning he was using the yen as his currency before, during and after the sale of Japan, Inc.), he would have made a 100% profit (from 700 to 1,400 yen).

As you can see from the three examples above, "currency risk" should really be called "currency gamble" since there is about a 50/50 chance that a country's currency will appreciate (or depreciate) against the dollar over a given period of time.

Other Issues Besides Currency

The examples above are quite extreme, but I wanted to use large round numbers so you would more easily understand what was going on. Normally, over the course of a year or even two years, the dollar appreciates or depreciates modestly against a given currency. Most of the time when you invest in foreign securities either directly (buying individual stocks or bonds) or indirectly (buying shares of a mutual fund or units of a variable annuity that invests in foreign stocks and/or bonds), your biggest risk (or reward) will be how the security fares in terms of its local currency. Oftentimes, currency movements are negligible compared to the ups and downs of the market.

There are actually a couple of reasons why international (or foreign) securities are more volatile than their U.S. counterparts. First, U.S. stock markets are the most efficient in the world and they are also the most highly regulated. Second, the amount of research devoted to U.S. stocks is greater than the resources devoted to foreign security analysis. Part of the reason for the difference in spending is that the U.S. stock market is much bigger than the number two market, Japan, and quite a bit bigger than numbers three, four, and five (U.K., Germany and France). Third, transaction costs are generally less with U.S. securities. If you pay less in fees and commissions, then your security(s) does not have to increase as much before you break even.

The Real Value of Foreign Securities

Overseas securities become our friends when they are combined with U.S. stocks and/or bonds. This is because foreign stocks and U.S. (domestic) stocks often do not move up and down in value at the same time and to the same degree. The same thing is true, but to a somewhat larger degree, when it comes to international bonds and domestic bonds. When the U.S. (the Fed) is trying to curb inflation (or the fear of inflation), interest rates often go up (meaning bond prices drop). At the same time, somewhere else in the world, another country's government may be trying to stimulate growth by lowering their interest rates (meaning that country's bonds are going up in value).

Since 1970, there has not been a three-year period when a portfolio of 30% foreign stocks and 70% U.S. stocks wasn't safer than a portfolio of 100% U.S. stocks. This means that when you combine domestic and foreign securities, you are decreasing your risk level. Moreover, more often than not, return levels increase when international and U.S. equities are in the same portfolio. According to a Stanford University study, a global portfolio (global means U.S. and foreign securities) can have up to 51% less risk than a U.S. portfolio. Not only is there less risk, there is also greater return potential. The bar chart below shows how U.S. stocks (as measured by the S & P 500) have fared against the best performing stock market for each of the past 10 years.

U.S. vs. Foreign Stocks (1986–1995)

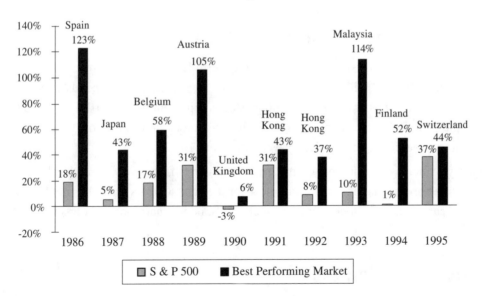

Not only have foreign stocks outperformed U.S. stocks, the same is true when it comes to government bonds. In the past, international government bonds have done better than domestic bonds. The table below shows the top performing bond markets for each of the past ten years (1986 to 1995).

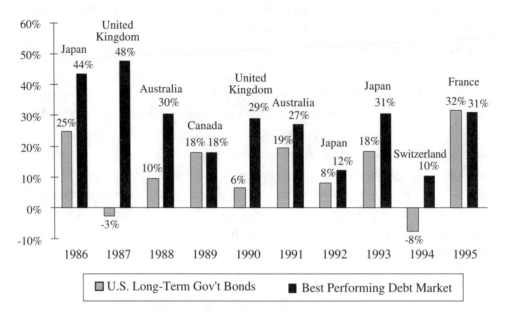

Best Performing Bond Markets Around the World (1986–1995)

□ U.S. Long-Term Gov't Bonds   ■ Best Performing Debt Market

The Benefits of Global Diversification Revisited

A portfolio limited to just U.S. stocks and long-term U.S. bonds should perform well most of the time and with only a modest amount of risk (the risk depends upon the maturity of the bonds and what percentage stocks represent in the portfolio). In fact, over the past 50 years, the chances of both U.S. stocks and long-term U.S. bonds declining in value the same calendar year are about 1 in 12.

When you increase the number of investment categories from two to four, the chances of a loss are even smaller. As an example, over the past 20 years, there has not been a single year when U.S. stocks, foreign stocks, U.S. bonds, and foreign bonds were all negative.

Beware of Certain Advisors

Some financial planners and brokers will tell you to stay away from any kind of foreign security. These statements are made out of ignorance. The number of studies that support the enhanced risk-reward characteristics of a global (vs. domestic only) portfolio are numerous. In fact, I have never seen a study, report, or article that even remotely suggests that adding foreign securities to a domestic-only portfolio is a bad idea for any reason.

Money Talks: Although the words "international" and "foreign" are interchangeable, the word "global" is not. A global portfolio includes U.S. securities whereas a foreign (or international) fund does not. A global portfolio will usually have less risk than a foreign portfolio because the U.S. stock market is more stable than most, if not all, other markets around the world. Being the biggest and the most efficient has its advantages.

SUMMARY

In the next chapter you will learn how to measure the relationship between the performance of two or more different investments. This concept, known as "correlation," is very useful if you want to construct a portfolio containing investments that do not have the tendency to move up and down together at the same time. Understanding correlation and correlation coefficients is really the only way to make sure that you have proper diversification.

LET'S REMEMBER THIS:

► Why and how currency movements can benefit your returns.

► How foreign securities can reduce your portfolio's risk level.

► A year-by-year comparison of the best-performing stock markets versus U.S. returns.

▼

How Investments Relate to Each Other

What We Are Going to Talk About in This Chapter:

► What Correlation Means and How It Can Benefit Investors

► Why You Do Not Want to Simply Pick the Best Past Investment

► A Correlation Matrix Showing the Relationship Between Several Investments

As previously mentioned, there are three components to asset allocation: (1) historical returns, (2) standard deviation and (3) correlation coefficient. The first two components have been covered in previous chapters. Correlation coefficient refers to how two or more investments react during the approximately same period of time. Phrased another way, we want to know what is likely to happen to investment X when investment Y goes up, down or remains relatively unchanged.

Looking at the stock market, you know that there are periods of time when most stocks are increasing or decreasing in value. As stock investors, you and I are not concerned when stocks are going up; we do become anxious, fearful, nervous or uncertain as to what we should be doing when our stocks are dropping in value. Our anxiety is greatly reduced if we know that other parts of our portfolio are either increasing in value or at least maintaining their values.

Example 12.1—Correlation of Investments

When Two or More Investments	They Are
react in a similar fashion	positively correlated
react in a dissimilar fashion	negatively correlated
react in a random fashion	randomly correlated

When two or more investments tend to move in the same direction during the same approximate period of time, there is a positive correlation. If these two investments tend to move in opposite directions (e.g., when X goes up, Y goes down and vice versa), there is a negative correlation. When two or more investments move in a nonpredictive fashion, they are said to be randomly correlated. To better understand the concept of correlation, let us go through an example.

You've Just Moved to an Island

Let us suppose that you just moved to a large island and want to invest in one or more of the local businesses. After doing some research, you discover that the people who inhabit the island love to eat. You further discover that when the weather is sunny, most of the island people go to the store, buy charcoal, and then barbeque. When it rains (and no one barbeques), the islanders cook inside, using their propane cookers.

There are only three companies on the island to invest in: The Charcoal Company, Propane People and Swimsuits, Etc. The Charcoal Company and Propane People are negatively correlated because when charcoal sales are up, propane sales are down and vice versa. Charcoal and swimsuits are positively correlated because when it is sunny, people go out and buy swimsuits and they also buy charcoal. What should you invest in?

An aggressive investor would choose just one of these three companies in the hopes of making "a killing." The conservative investor would probably choose the company that was the safest (i.e., the company whose product was the cheapest to advertise, produce, store, distribute and sell) even though the potential profit would be smaller. The smart investor would invest equally in both The Charcoal Company and Propane People.

The smart investor is willing to accept a little less return as a trade-off for also accepting much less risk. The smart investor is accepting less risk than the conservative investor because the conservative investor is only investing in one company. Even though that one company looks safe, all sorts of unpredictable things could happen to it in the future (e.g., a scandal, unforeseen competition, a fire at the manufacturing plant, etc.). The smart investor could experience the same thing but only half his money would be at risk (the other half would be with a different company).

There is no strong reason for the smart investor to invest in charcoal and swimsuits since these companies are positively correlated. Investing in both of these companies is a little safer than just investing in one of them but not nearly as safe as investing in two companies that prosper at exactly different times (negative correlation).

So far our island investing example has covered three companies: two that are positively correlated (they tend to move up and down in value at approximately the same time) and two negatively correlated businesses (when one company's sales are up, the other's are down). What has not been covered so far in this example is random correlation. Let us suppose we had a fourth company on the island the grew and sold food. Since the islanders eat the same amount of food whether it is rainy or sunny outside, the food company would be randomly correlated to charcoal and propane sales.

EXAMPLE 12.2—CORRELATION OF INVESTMENTS ON A HYPOTHETICAL ISLAND

Company Names	*They Are*
Charcoal Company and Swimsuits, Etc.	positively correlated
Charcoal Company and Propane People	negatively correlated
Charcoal Company and the food company	randomly correlated
Propane People and the food company	randomly correlated

Adding the food company to the aggressive or conservative portfolio would reduce overall volatility during certain periods—we just do not know in advance when those periods will be (it will happen in a random fashion). The success of food sales is not dependent on the success of charcoal or propane. The aggressive investor's portfolio will become less risky for two reasons: risk is spread out and "random correlation" means that during some periods, when one company is doing well, so will the other. It also means that during other periods, when one company is doing poorly, so is the other.

The Real World

Unfortunately, investing is not as simple as our island illustration. The fact is that there are few companies, industry groups, or entire categories of investments that are negatively correlated. There are lots of examples of positively correlated businesses (e.g., IBM, Dell Computer and Compaq are just three hardware computer companies; GM, Ford and Chrysler are also highly correlated because all three of these companies are heavily dependent upon auto sales). There are also lots of examples of companies that are randomly correlated (e.g., computer chip maker Intel's sales are not related at all to clothes manufacturer Levi Strauss).

As a risk-conscious investor, one of your goals is to make sure your portfolio includes investments that are positively correlated (easy to do), randomly correlated (fairly easy to do) and negatively correlated (difficult to do but not impossible). If your investment advisor is unfamiliar with correlation coefficients, have him or her read this chapter.

Example 12.3—Performance-Related News

The Announcement	The Consequence
The economy is performing better than expected.	Long-term U.S. government bonds drop 3% in value and high-quality corporate bonds drop 2.5% (positive correlation).
The Fed cuts interest rates.	Government bonds increase by 2% but stocks fall 1% (negative correlation).
The Fed cuts interest rates.	Government bonds increase by 2% and stocks climb 3% (positive correlation).
GM reports disappointing earnings.	GM stock falls and so does Ford and Chrysler stock (positive correlation).
GM reports disappointing earnings for four straight quarters.	GM stock falls each time, but Ford stock goes up 1 point the first time, remains unchanged the second and third time, and drops the fourth time (random correlation).
The Fed cuts interest rates.	Bonds stage a rally but money market fund yields drop .5 % over the next three months (negative correlation).
The U.S. trade deficit with Japan widens and is expected to worsen.	Export stocks fall but Toyota and Nissan rise (negative correlation).

The Formula for Calculating a Correlation Coefficient

Determining the correlation coefficient of two investments can be calculated using the following formula:

$$\text{Correlation } (X,Y) = \text{Cov}(X,Y)/\sigma x \sigma y$$

X = Asset 1

Y = Asset 2

Cov(X,Y) = covariance of asset 1 to asset 2

σXσy = product of the standard deviations of assets 1 and 2

Each additional investment (i.e., adding a third, fourth, fifth, etc.) compounds the formula, making it very difficult to use without a computer program. Fortunately, a number of investment advisors and stockbrokers now use or have access to modern portfolio theory (MPT) software that includes correlation coefficients for several dozen different investment categories. Some software programs include specific investments (e.g., the XYZ growth fund instead of the general category "growth funds") and therefore include several hundred different possibilities.

What is a Meaningful Correlation

Like other things in life, there are degrees or shades of a correlation coefficient, sometimes referred to as important, significant or meaningful. A positive correlation is anything that is +0.01 or higher (+1.00 being a perfect correlation, meaning two investments that move virtually identically with each other during good, bad or neutral periods). A positive correlation is meaningful if it falls between +0.3 to +1.0. A negative correlation is anything that is -0.01 or lower (-1.00 being a perfect negative correlation). A random correlation is anything between -0.3 and +0.3. There is no such thing as a "meaningful random correlation"; by its very definition, random means that there is simply no relationship between the performance of two or more investments.

EXAMPLE 12.4—DEGREES OF CORRELATION AND LIKELY RESULTS

▶ The correlation between ABC and XYZ is +1.00. This means that if ABC goes up 4%, XYZ should also go up about 4%. If ABC drops 2%, XYZ should also drop about 2%.

▶ The correlation between DEF and GHI is +0.50. This means that if DEF goes up 4%, GHI should go up about 2%. If DEF drops 2%, GHI should drop about 1%.

▶ The correlation between JKL and MNO is +0.20. This means that if JKL goes up 4%, MNO should go up 0.8% (.20 × 4%). However, since the correlation is random (it is below +0.3), there is a fair chance that MNO may remain neutral, go up a little, or go down a little. If JKL drops 2%, MNO should also drop (since the correlation is positive), but since it is random, there is a fair or pretty good chance than MNO will remain level, go down a little, or go up a little.

▶ The correlation between PQR and STU is -0.40 (a slightly significant negative correlation). This means that if PQR goes up 4%, STU should go down about 1.6%. If PQR drops 2%, XYZ should increase about 0.8% (.4 × 2%).

▶ The correlation between VWX and YZA is -0.70. This means that if VWX goes up 4%, YZA should drop about 2.8% (.7 × 4%). If VWX drops 2%, YZA should climb about 1.4%.

A CORRELATION COEFFICIENT MATRIX

The table, or matrix, below shows the correlation between a series of two different investments. Some of these relations are fairly obvious, such as the high positive correlation between the S & P 500 and small stocks (0.80); however, there are certainly some surprises. For example, despite all of the hype the financial press has given to the difference between "growth" and "value" stocks, the correlation between these two is extremely high (0.90). Such a high correlation should cause one to greatly question how effectively such diversification by using both categories can actually reduce risk (very little, it appears). Notice also that the relationship between long-term (shown as "LT") government bonds and intermediate-term government bonds (shown as "IT") to the S & P 500 is very close to random. Again, this is something that is contrary to what we have been led to believe over the past couple of years.

All of correlations below were based on monthly data for each of the investments shown covering the last 15 years, ending December 31, 1995.

How Investment Categories Interact With Each Other: Correlation Coefficients

	S & P 500	Small Stocks	LT Gov't Bonds	IT Gov't Bonds	T-Bills	Inflation	Growth	Value	EAFE	REIT-Equity
S&P 500	1.00	—	—	—	—	—	—	—	—	—
Small Stocks	0.80	1.00	—	—	—	—	—	—	—	—
LT Gov't Bonds	0.41	0.22	1.00	—	—	—	—	—	—	—
IT Gov't Bonds	0.36	0.17	0.92	1.00	—	—	—	—	—	—
T-Bills	-0.08	-0.09	0.05	0.15	1.00	—	—	—	—	—
Inflation	-0.22	-0.19	-0.25	-0.17	0.44	1.00				
Growth	0.98	0.78	0.40	0.34	-0.08	-0.22	1.00	—	—	—
Value	0.97	0.79	0.40	0.36	-0.08	-0.20	0.90	1.00	—	—
EAFE	0.45	0.36	0.22	0.22	-0.09	-0.30	0.42	0.45	1.00	—
REIT-Equity	0.61	0.68	0.30	0.31	-0.07	-0.23	0.56	0.63	0.36	1.00

SUMMARY

In this chapter we have learned about correlation coefficients, the relationship between two or more investments. No single investment has a correlation coefficient; there must be at least two assets before a correlation can be determined. The purpose of determining the correlation coefficient of two or more different investments is to determine what is most likely to happen to our overall portfolio if one investment goes up, down or remains neutral. By including assets in our portfolio that are randomly or negatively correlated, overall risk can be reduced.

Money Talks: Correlation coefficients, the relationship between the price movement of two or more investments, is normally calculated based on an extensive period of time. Investors, or more likely advisors, are concerned with these relationships as a means of guiding the construction of a portfolio that will hopefully have either less risk or better risk-adjusted rewards.

We are almost finished with the asset allocation process. One of the final steps is to design a portfolio that is either on the efficient frontier or near it. The efficient frontier is a series of portfolios, ranging from ultra conservative to extremely risky, and everything between. What is special about each of these portfolios is that they each represent an excellent trade-off between risk and return potential. There is no universal portfolio that fits every investor; your efficient frontier depends upon your risk level. True, your return potential may be higher or lower than that of your neighbor's, but so is your tolerance for risk.

As you will see, the efficient frontier is a series of portfolios at different risk levels, all connected by a line that is somewhat shaped like a boomerang. Once you have determined your risk level, with the proper software it is easy to construct a portfolio that will get you a very good or excellent risk-adjusted reward.

 Dollars & Sense: Understanding the relationship between two or more investments is only important if you want to reduce your portfolio's risk level. Sometimes, maintaining your current risk exposure can result in increased returns by properly utilizing investments whose correlation is random or negative.

LET'S REMEMBER THIS:

- ▶ The benefits of random and negative correlations.
- ▶ Why picking the "best" or "most conservative" investment can be the wrong choice.
- ▶ The relationship (correlation) of several different investment categories.

Optimizing Your Portfolio

What We Are Going to Talk About in This Chapter:

- ▶ Defining the Efficient Frontier
- ▶ Why There Is No Best Portfolio
- ▶ Global Portfolios and Their Enhanced Risk-Reward Characteristics

An eight-cylinder car will run on seven cylinders, but the ride will be smoother and the gas mileage better if all eight cylinders are running correctly. The same thing is true when it comes to investing. There are a number of ways to structure a portfolio that is conservative, moderate, aggressive or somewhere between. Several of these ways will produce the overall desired trade-off of risk and return. But in the case of portfolio design, there is a way to get an extra cylinder's worth without paying anything extra. And it all has to do with the efficient frontier.

The efficient frontier is a line that runs between a horizontal axis (which measures standard deviation) and a vertical axis (which measures performance). The two axes are at 90 degrees to each other. Conceptually, since we have always been told that risk is commensurate with return, one would think that the line representing the efficient frontier would be at 45 degrees, equidistant from the risk axis and the return axis.

Fortunately for us, the line is curved, allowing us to construct a portfolio that could provide us with higher returns and no increase in risk or similar returns to what we are now doing but with less risk.

The graph below (Example 13.1) shows two efficient frontiers; the lower curved line represents a domestic-only portfolio and the upper curved line is a global portfolio (U.S. and foreign securities). How each of the numbered (one through five) or lettered (A through C) portfolios is weighted is shown in the table that follows the graph. Without even looking at these weightings, it is obvious by the position of the two curved lines that the global portfolio has better returns at different risk levels (as represented by the standard deviation axis).

Focusing just on the global line for a moment, you can see that there is little difference in return potential for number 3 versus number 4, yet the risk level increases by quite a bit—from 12 to 16%. This does not mean that you should not consider

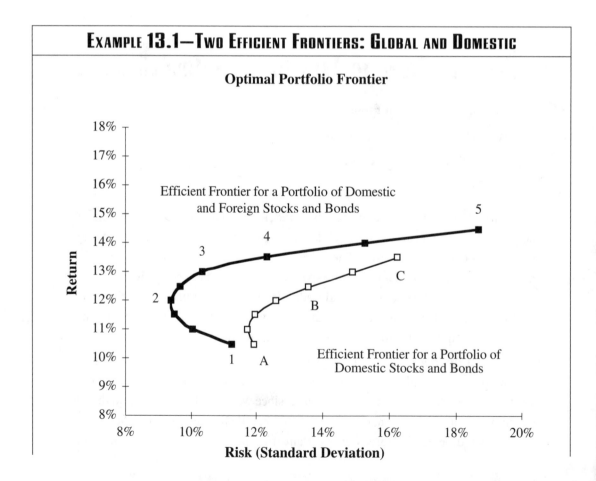

EXAMPLE 13.1—TWO EFFICIENT FRONTIERS: GLOBAL AND DOMESTIC

Optimal Portfolio Frontier

Efficient Frontier for a Portfolio of Domestic and Foreign Stocks and Bonds

Efficient Frontier for a Portfolio of Domestic Stocks and Bonds

Return

Risk (Standard Deviation)

Portfolio	U.S. Stocks	U.S. Bonds	Foreign Stocks	Foreign Bonds
1	—	89%	—	11%
2	19%	34%	—	47%
3	40%	—	—	60%
4	38%	—	23%	39%
5	28%	—	72%	—
A	8%	92%	—	—
B	55%	45%	—	—
C	100%	—	—	—

portfolio number 4 or even portfolio number 5. These riskier portfolios may be the right choice for a more aggressive investor. However, it is clear that on a risk-adjusted return basis, portfolios 1 through 3 are a much better trade-off.

The highest return potential would be with portfolio number 5, a mix of 28% U.S. stocks (the S & P 500) and 72% foreign stocks (the EAFE Index). The lowest expected return is a pure domestic portfolio, letter A, a mix of 8% U.S. stocks and 92% U.S. government bonds. Keep in mind that all of the portfolios shown above are considered to be very efficient—each is on an efficient frontier.

No Relationship Between the Past and the Future

Putting together a portfolio using the efficient frontier is based on historical data. Obviously, it is highly unlikely that an investment or series of investments (a portfolio) will perform in the future exactly how it acted in the past. Studies have clearly shown that there is no relationship between past, present and future returns. The correlation of two investments can also change over time (e.g., there are times when bond and stock prices have been highly correlated and other times when the relationship has been quite random). Finally, the standard deviation of an investment can, and does, change. These are the three components used to determine an efficient portfolio: historical returns, correlation coefficients and standard deviation.

In the late 1970s and early 1980s, when money market yields were quite high by any standard, there was little need to venture into stocks or long-term bonds. Why try and get a 10 to 20% return in stocks or bonds when you could get a double-digit return in a money market account without any of the risks associated with stocks or bonds? Because of this incredible risk-reward relationship (virtually no risk and very high returns) for money market accounts and bank CDs, these instruments suddenly became the investment of choice. Cash equivalents ended up being a large percentage of most efficient portfolios. Yet few financial experts would dispute the fact that such cash equivalents (bank CDs, commercial paper, T-bills, etc.) are a bad investment, particularly on an after-tax and after-inflation basis.

At the other end of the spectrum, there have been periods when gold mining stocks (which are even more volatile than bullion itself) have experienced phenomenal appreciation. And despite their always high standard deviation (risk level), such investments became a meaningful part of a number of efficient portfolios in the past. Yet, when viewed during more "normal" periods, it is obvious that there are other alternatives to metals and gold mining stocks, alternatives that exhibit similar or better correlations with other more mainstream investments plus have had better return characteristics over most periods of time.

The efficient frontier, and those portfolios that fall close to the frontier (that curved line), should be used as a framework for developing a portfolio that you feel comfortable with—one that includes investment categories you feel like you understand or perhaps categories that have not been so wildly volatile. An efficient frontier portfolio will not solve all of your problems, but it will provide a certain amount of peace of mind, provided you are not tempted by portfolios or individual investments that have had high returns without any regard for risk.

Fully Appreciating Risk

Risk realization is a critical part of any investment program. If you end up taking on too much risk, you may panic after the first downturn in the market, bailing out and swearing that you will never go into stocks again. This would be a grave mistake if your time horizon is more than just a few years. When things seem to be going well for stocks, make sure that you translate standard deviation numbers into real terms. If you have $100,000 invested in something that has an expected return of 15% a year and a standard deviation of 26%, this means that at the end of a year there is a 66 to 67% chance that your portfolio will suffer up to a $26,000 loss or enjoy up to a $26,000 gain. What happens the other third of the time could be more extreme than making or losing $26,000.

Before making the plunge, ask yourself (using the example above) how you would feel if you lost $26,000 or so in one year. Ask yourself how long it took you to save that money on an after-tax basis (if these are nonqualified dollars). And also ask yourself if such a loss is going to cause you to shift your long-term investment strategy. If such a loss would cause a change in your long-term strategy, you are probably entering dangerous waters that should be avoided. You may be much better off with an expected return of say 10% and a standard deviation of 8% (or whatever numbers you find tolerable).

Las Vegas wants you to use chips so that when you lose, they will not seem like real money. The same analogy can be true when it comes to investing and those advisors you listen or subscribe to; they may not take the time to translate a percentage figure into a dollar figure. Charts and graphs are much less painful than seeing a stack of greenbacks being eaten up by market losses.

Why Not One Extreme or the Other

We now know that the purpose of proper diversification is to reduce risk. Diversification will not maximize returns. Its purpose is to improve the risk-return trade-off. Despite these statements, there are still investors who want to maximize returns even if it means maximizing risk. Depending upon their time horizon, this may not be a bad course of action; in fact, a patient, aggressive investor can be well rewarded for taking on such risk. However, if you are income oriented, then such a portfolio would be a mistake.

With maximum returns come maximum losses. Even if the investor had a 20- to 30-year time horizon (perhaps a couple that is in their early 60s), an early loss could cause permanent damage. Starting off with $500,000 and taking out $45,000 (9% of $500,000) a year is fine with a mostly stock-oriented portfolio. Such a portfolio might look something like this: 25% high-yield bonds, 25% foreign stocks, 10% foreign bonds and 40% U.S. stocks. Such a portfolio should have long-term returns that average about 11% a year (9% spent by the investor and 2 to 3% reinvested to offset inflation).

If, during the first or second year, the $500,000 drops by $100,000 and you are still taking out $45,000 a year from a portfolio that is now worth $400,000, you may be in danger later on—you may be asking too much. If instead, the $500,000 experiences a couple of good years, then there is a "cushion" to protect against part or all of a decline.

One Extreme (Aggressive)

Looking at the past half-century, the clear winner has been small company stocks. There are a number of mutual funds that specialize in small and aggressive growth stocks. The long-term, and often short-term, results can be very tantilizing. Since performance charts often do not mention the kind of volatility involved, investors are naturally attracted to such a portfolio. The dips and drops in a chart covering the past 10 or even 50 years would not give the investor a true feeling of what it is like to experience a loss. Looking at a chart that shows ups and downs is quite a bit different than actually experiencing such volatility.

Assuming the investor is still interested in maximizing returns by going 100% into something like small company stocks, such a strategy could be appropriate if all of the following are correct:

▶ The holding period will be for at least ten years.

▶ You will maintain this position even when other investments are doing better.

▶ You have the patience to see two or even three years of consecutive negative returns.

A better way to go, even if all three of these bullet points are correct, are to utilize the efficient frontier and come up with a portfolio that has historically had slightly higher returns than small company stocks but with about 10% less risk (the risk level would still be high, however). Such a portfolio would be comprised of approximately 80 to 85% small company stocks and 15 to 20% international stocks. The table below shows some periods when small stocks underperformed the less risky S & P 500.

Extended Periods When the S & P 500 Outperformed Small Company Stocks	
Period of Years	*Number of Years*
1946 to 1964	19 out of 19 years
1969 to 1976	8 out of 8 years
1982 to 1995	14 out of 14 years

Over the past half century, 1946 to 1995, a $10,000 investment in the S & P 500 grew to $2.81 million while $10,000 invested in small company stocks grew to $6.4 million. Over the past 20 years, 1976 to 1995, a $10,000 investment in the S & P 500 grew to $152,000 while $10,000 invested in small company stocks grew to $357,000.

Even though small stocks have done much better than "big stocks" (as measured by the S & P 500) over the past 50 years, the table above shows that small stocks had to have had some tremendous years to outdistance the S & P 500. The big question is whether or not the investor had the patience to wait for those few, but spectacular, years.

THE OTHER EXTREME (CONSERVATIVE)

The other extreme would be to consider investing 100% of the portfolio in cash equivalents such as money market accounts, bank CDs and U.S. T-bills. Such a strategy would result in very good risk-adjusted returns, but the returns themselves would not be enough for $500,000 that was being tapped each year for $45,000. Cash equivalents have a current yield of approximately 5% (or $25,000 a year if $500,000 is invested). As you can see, if you are taking out $45,000 a year from this hypothetical $500,000 portfolio but only putting back in $25,000 a year on average, there will be some serious cumulative depletion after just a handful of years.

An investment in cash equivalents makes sense for an investor interested in maximizing safety but with the understanding that returns are being minimized. By utilizing correlation coefficients, a portfolio comprised of 90% cash equivalents and 10% stocks has less risk than a portfolio of just cash. Historically, the 90/10 split also produces slightly higher returns.

The reason that a portfolio with 90% in cash and 10% in stocks has less risk than one with 100% in cash is that things like money market accounts, bank CDs and T-bills have fluctuating rates of return—either on a daily basis or when the instrument matures and is rolled over into a new CD or T-bill. The all-cash investor is at the mercy of interest rates and the Federal Reserve. Some years the return will be high, other years it will be low. The table below gives some examples of how much income can fluctuate over time when it is solely in cash equivalents.

T-Bill Yields for Selected Years ("in dollars" refers to earnings on $100,000)					
Year	*Yield*	*In Dollars*	*Year*	*Yield*	*In Dollars*
1971	4.4%	$4,400	1987	5.5%	$5,500
1974	8.0%	$8,000	1989	8.4%	$8,400
1976	5.1%	$5,100	1991	5.6%	$5,600

continues

T-Bill Yields for Selected Years
("in dollars" refers to earnings on $100,000) [Continued]

Year	Yield	In Dollars		Year	Yield	In Dollars
1979	10.4%	$10,400		1993	2.9%	$2,900
1980	11.2%	$11,200		1994	3.9%	$3,900
1981	14.7%	$14,700		1995	5.65%	$5,600
1985	7.7%	$7,700				

Notice that our hypothetical $100,000 investor saw his level of income jump by almost 100% from 1971 through 1975 only to drop off by about 60% in 1976. From 1981 (when the $100,000 investment threw off $14,700 in income) to 1987, the level of income dropped by about 70%; and from 1989 to 1993 the drop was similar in percentage terms (from $8,400 to $2,900). So, as you can see, the returns from things like T-bills and money market accounts can fluctuate substantially over just a few years.

The other reason a 90/10 split is usually better than a 100% commitment to cash is that money market and stock market returns are often negatively correlated. The stock market likes low yields (less competition) whereas money market funds hate low interest rates. So, when yields on money market funds are falling, there is a good chance that stock market returns are either doing well or skyrocketing.

Historically, cash equivalents such as T-bills have provided very predictable returns over short periods of time. However, as the table above shows, the yields (or returns) can vary widely over the course of just a couple of years. Surprisingly, if the investor's main objective is safety, then a 90/10 mix (90% T-bills and 10% S & P 500) has been a safer way to go.

When you seek to maximize returns you are obviously subjecting yourself to market risk. On the other hand, cash equivalents are sometimes referred to as "risk-free" investments. This is true as it relates to market risk, but is certainly not true once you expand the definition of risk and include such things as inflation and income taxes. With stocks you know that they are either going to go up, go down or remain level. With inflation and income taxes it is a one-way street—income taxes will probably be with us indefinitely and the last time inflation was negative was back in the early 1950s (and that was only for one year). Stocks give you a fighting chance, whereas inflation and taxes are not likely to drop to zero.

The table below shows what a money market fund would have to yield in 1995 (approximately $15,000) to maintain the same purchasing power as it did in 1976 (approximately $5,000).

Income Risk from Money Market Accounts

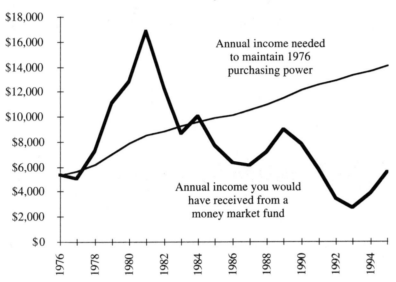

Summary

Constructing or determining the efficient frontier is very difficult without the use of software. Fortunately, there are a number of vendors that provide such software at a cost that ranges from less than $100 up to several thousand dollars. Your financial advisor may already have such software.

Being on or near the efficient frontier does not guarantee a successful portolio, but it almost always guarantees that such information will help you in getting superior risk-adjusted returns, no matter how conservative or aggressive.

Money Talks:

The efficient frontier is determined by looking at historical information (past returns, standard deviation and correlation coefficients). The efficiency of such frontiers becomes highly questionable if the data used includes periods of time when performance figures of "risk-free" investments (e.g., money market funds, bank CDs, T-bills, etc.) have been particularly high (such as the early 1980s). Like other formulas or measurements, calculating an efficient frontier is a useful tool if it is properly understood and the user has a historical perspective and common sense.

Let's Remember This:

- ► What an efficient frontier is.
- ► The reason why there is no best portfolio.
- ► How a global portfolio can provide you with less risk and better returns.

▼

Maintaining Your Comfort Level

What We Are Going to Talk About in This Chapter:

- ▶ How Inactivity Can Alter Your Portfolio's Risk Level
- ▶ When Rebalancing Should Take Place
- ▶ Differences Between Rebalancing and Reallocating

Rebalancing involves selling off part of one or more investments and buying more of one or more other categories represented in the portfolio. The purpose of rebalancing is to get the portfolio back to the originally agreed-upon weightings in the categories selected. This means there will be times when part of X is sold off and the proceeds are used to buy more of Y. "X" represents those investments that have performed better than other parts of the portfolio, and "Y" represents those investments that have been underperformers (when compared to the other components of the portfolio).

The great thing about rebalancing is that it represents a disciplined approach to investing. After something has performed well, part of it is sold off and the sale proceeds are used to buy more of whatever has underperformed. This strategy of buy low and sell high is what investors should always be doing, but rarely do, either because of ignorance, neglect, fear or greed.

When rebalancing takes place inside a qualified retirement plan, a variable annuity or variable life insurance contract, no tax events are triggered. The monies or investments maintain their tax-deferred status. When rebalancing takes place in other types of accounts, a taxable event will take place. The "taxable event" may result in a net capital gain or a net capital loss (any and all gains from any sales are first netted out against any and all losses that might have taken place when the "losers" were partially sold off). Whether the net results are a gain or a loss, do not lose sight of the fact that paying taxes means that you have made a profit—something that is much better than avoiding some taxes—but suffered a larger loss in your portfolio (or changed the risk level by not making any changes in the portfolio). Too often investors look at the tax ramifications and not at the benefits of selling something for a profit (instead of maybe waiting and watching it drop in value later).

The real purpose of rebalancing is that we want to stay true to our investment strategy. At some point, a risk level was agreed upon. Not rebalancing the portfolio periodically or even sporadically means that you are now accepting a different risk level. Usually that new risk level is higher. No one minds increasing their risk when times are good because it is difficult to ever see those good times end. When the bad times hit, and they always do, it is then that we wish we had heeded our original strategy and risk level.

What Often Happens

Once you have determined the proper mix for your portfolio and the investment strategy has been implemented, what next? If you do nothing, the equity part of your portfolio, which would include things such as growth stocks, international stock funds and real estate, will, over time, end up representing a larger portion of your portfolio than was originally planned. Using a simple example, suppose that based upon your risk level, time horizon and tax bracket, it was decided that your portfolio should be half in common stocks and half in tax-free bonds. After a year, you notice that the stock portion now represents 55% of your total, while the municipal bond portion equals 45%. The change in weightings occurred because stocks did better than bonds during the first year (which happens more often than not).

A mix of 55/45 is not dramatically different than a 50/50 mix so you decide to do nothing. After all, if stocks are doing this well, why not take advantage of the extra weighting in equities. After the second year, which turns out to be another good year for stocks, your portfolio mix is now 62/38. You are not concerned, in fact you are happy. Even though your portfolio weighting is now approaching two-thirds in favor of equities and one-third in debt, returns have been better than expected. Similar results take place in the third year; stocks do well and bonds do pretty well. The portfolio mix is now 70/30 in favor of equities. Again you do nothing because it doesn't make sense to fight a winning strategy.

The fourth year sees a turnabout. Stocks end up going through three bad quarters, losing a fifth of their value. Bonds have eked out a total return of 5% during these three quarters. As you review the portfolio, you find out that your losses are greater than expected because there is now a sizeable difference between your agreed-upon risk level and your new risk level. After some calculations you discover that 70% of your portfolio has dropped 20% and the remaining 30% (which is in bonds) has gained 5%. The final calculation shows that your overall loss is 12.5% (70% × -20% = -14% plus 30% × 5% = +1.5% for a total of -12.5%).

A loss of 12.5% is not a huge loss for most people, but it is for conservative investors. There is also a potential "chilling affect" for the conservative as well as moderate risk taker. After experiencing a 12.5% loss, such investors may be reluctant to do one or more of the following: (1) load up even more heavily on stocks since they are now at a 20% discount; (2) stay with stocks even at a 50% exposure—the 20% loss could turn into a 50% decline according to some financial gurus; or (3) stay with the long-term game plan.

Had the portfolio maintained a constant 50/50 mix (by rebalancing the portfolio once a year), a certain amount of the gains in years two and three would have been missed since stocks would represent just 50% of the portfolio at the beginning of each year. However, the losses would have also been reduced. With a 50/50 split, the portfolio would have lost only 7.5% (50% × -20% = -10% plus 50% × 5% = +2.5% for a total of -7.5%) compared to the 12.5% loss it actually experienced. Perhaps the biggest benefit to rebalancing is that by maintaining a consistent level of risk, the investor is more likely to stay the course and realize good, long-term results.

How Often You Should Rebalance

As described above, rebalancing is necessary since different investments grow at different rates. It is also important when withdrawals are made. By making distributions from just one or two of several investment categories, there is a greater likelihood that the agreed-upon weightings will get out of whack. How often rebalancing should take place is a hotly debated question.

One school of thought is that rebalancing should take place whenever an asset category increases or decreases by more than 5% from its original weighting. This would mean that a simple 50/50 portfolio would be rebalancing whenever one of the two asset categories ended up equalling 55% or more or 45% or less (a 5% change). A portfolio that had 10% in high-yield bonds would be rebalanced if the high-yield bonds ever equalled as little as 9% of the entire portfolio or as much as 11%. As you can see, a 5% change in any investment category, particularly when there are several categories represented in the portfolio, will cause a fair amount of buying and selling.

Another view is that rebalancing should take place quarterly, even if some or all of the adjustments are minor. The thinking behind this view is that allocations cannot become very distorted if they are checked (and perhaps changed) every three months.

According to all of the studies I have seen, annual rebalancing results in not only less frequent buying and selling (thereby saving time, possible commissions or fees, bid-ask spreads when dealing with individual securities, plus possible tax consequences whenever a sale is made), but results in slightly better performance. Therefore, I recommend that you review your portfolio quarterly, but only rebalance it once a year.

The disadvantage of annual rebalancing is that if a negative trend continues, losses could end up being greater than if a change were made when there is a 5% change or if quarterly rebalancing were done. The advantage of annual rebalancing is that when there are positive trends, overall returns will be higher. The other advantage of less frequent rebalancing is that oftentimes, once the markets have experienced a particularly good or bad quarter or two, things change and what used to look bad is suddenly a darling. But most importantly, neutral studies show that there is a performance advantage with annual rebalancings.

INVESTOR CONTINUES TO BE RELUCTANT TO REBALANCE

What textbooks recommend versus what happens in the real world are often different because of the human element. We all know we should do certain things (e.g., save money each year, avoid high risk investments, lose weight, exercise at least five times a week, etc.), but still resist. If you cannot get the majority of people to exercise and change their diets, which would most likely result in a longer life, what chance do financial advisors have when they recommend a course of action that cannot be sold based on a life or death threat?

I bring up these things because there is a good chance you are going to fight any rebalancing (or simply ignore the issue altogether) until after the fact—after one or more of your assets has taken a beating and your reaction is based on fear or frustration. More often than not, such a knee-jerk reaction would be the wrong thing to do; instead of selling a fundamentally good asset after it has dropped, you should be buying more of it.

Without rebalancing, the portfolio will take on a risk profile that may not be appropriate for the investor. The euphoria that is associated with good or great performance can be at odds with common sense and the original asset mix. By overweighting the current winners, the investor may later find that the better performers were peaking. The table below shows how difficult it is to predict next year's winner.

The Best Performing Investment Category (1976–1995)				
Year	U.S. Stocks	U.S. Bonds	Foreign Stocks	Foreign Bonds	Money Market Funds
1976	24%	✓	–	–	–
1977	–	–	–	39%	✓
1978	–	–	33%	✓	–
1979	18%	✓	–	–	–
1980	32%	✓	–	–	–
1981	–	–	–	17%	✓
1982	–	40%	✓	–	–
1983	–	–	24%	✓	–
1984	–	15%	✓	–	–
1985	–	–	56%	✓	–
1986	–	–	69%	✓	–
1987	–	–	–	35%	✓
1988	–	–	28%	✓	–
1989	31%	✓	–	–	–
1990	–	–	–	15%	✓
1991	31%	✓	–	–	–
1992	–	8%	✓	–	–
1993	–	–	33%	✓	–
1994	–	–	8%	✓	–
1995	37%	✓	–	–	–

As you can see, predicting what will be the next winner is difficult, even when there are only a handful of choices. Imagine how difficult it would be to choose next quarter's or next year's winner if there were a dozen different choices (e.g., gold, aggressive growth stocks, high-yield bonds, real estate, etc.).

Before even thinking about changing the investment strategy, which in this case means letting the better performers in the portfolio represent more of the whole than they should, answer the following questions:

- ► Have your financial goals changed?

- ► Has your time horizon changed?

- ► Has your risk level changed?

If the answer to all of these questions is "no" then it is important that the portfolio be rebalanced on a regular basis. The frequency of the rebalancing may depend upon your personality, convenience or study you find credible. Whatever the reason, make sure you rebalance.

Rebalancing vs. Reallocation

We now know that rebalancing is a process wherein some of the portfolio's assets are partially sold off, and the proceeds are used to purchase more shares or units of other assets. The purpose of rebalancing is to bring the current asset mix back in line with the original allocation (e.g., 20% value stocks, 20% growth stocks, 30% foreign stocks, 10% emerging markets and 20% high-yield bonds).

Reallocation is more radical than rebalancing. Reallocation looks at the original asset mix, finds shortcomings in the original mix and then makes changes that reflect the new strategy. The "new strategy" may be based on one or more of the following:

Asset Projections Have Changed	*There Have Been Unexpected Expenses*
the investor's time horizon has changed	the investor has received a gift or inheritance
the investor's risk level has changed	job security has increased or decreased
lifestyle changes (e.g., marriage, divorce, etc.)	retirement age has changed

Asset Projections Have Changed	*There Have Been Unexpected Expenses*
more or less money can be saved each year	tax laws have changed
investment savvy has increased	new investments have been introduced
the investor's needs have changed	the investor's attitude has changed

There are a number of legitimate reasons why reallocation may be appropriate. The advisor's concern should be that the reason is not based on recent market activity. The following questions may be useful in determining whether or not reallocation is necessary.

► Have one or more of the major financial objectives been achieved?

► Have the major objectives been reprioritized?

► Have any of the major financial objectives been changed?

► Has your opinion about any investment category changed based on its performance over the past one to two years?

► How have you reacted to some of the performance figures you have seen over the past several quarters?

► Do you have any fear or concern that your goals will no longer be met based on your current holdings?

► Has your need for current income changed?

ASSET ALLOCATION REVISITED

Never lose sight of the purpose of asset allocation, no matter how often you rebalance or reallocate. Such diversification does not maximize returns. (How can it? There can only be one winner each year and your money is being divided up among several investments.) The other point to keep in mind about diversification is that it does not ensure that there will not be a loss. True, there may still be losses even with proper diversification, but such losses will be small in comparison with the temptation of sticking with an aggressive portfolio.

Asset allocation and the efficient frontier are part science and part art. Any thought out portfolio is based upon projected returns, risk and correlations. It is highly unlikely, in fact it is almost an impossibility, that an investment's or portfolio's risk level, expected return or correlation to other investments will end up being what we expected. Yet, there is a very powerful conclusion to be reached by this uncertainty.

Unfortunately, there is no scientific means of measuring an investor's risk level. One's declared risk level at any moment in time can be largely influenced by one or more of the following factors: (1) the person's mood; (2) how closely the person follows the ups and downs of the market; (3) how the markets have performed over the past several days or weeks; (4) information the investor has recently received from books, articles, seminars, or advisors; and (5) the source of the monies about to be invested (e.g., gift money may be more aggressively invested than money earned at $8 an hour chopping wood).

SUMMARY

By incorporating several different investment categories into your portfolio, the following will happen: (1) some investments will perform about as expected, if not over the next few years, over the next 5 to 10 years; (2) other investments will be disappointing, falling short of the mark; and (3) a couple of investments will do better than expected. The same thing can be said about the risk level of individual investments as well as their correlation to other investments. Pooled accounts (sometimes referred to as packaged products) such as mutual funds, variable annuities and variable life insurance greatly increase the likelihood that the projections concerning risk, return and correlation will turn out to be more accurate than a portfolio comprised of a couple of dozen individual stocks and/or bonds plus one or two pieces of real estate.

To make sure the investor "stays the course," it is important that the proposed portfolio be back tested during several different market conditions. Even though such conditions are unlikely to have the exact same effects in the future, the investor can at least get a good idea as to what happens to the whole portfolio when the markets are moving up, down or remaining flat.

Money Talks: U.S. investors have a strong tendency to reallocate (look at new categories of investments) instead of rebalance (use just those categories that you and your advisor originally selected). More often than not, reallocation leads to even more disappointment as the investor continues the path of chasing last year's winners. The reason that we are so "radical" when it comes to investing is that we lack patience—an understandable trait for citizens who live in the most progressive, innovative and richest country in the world.

LET'S REMEMBER THIS:

- ▶ Rebalancing a portfolio.
- ▶ Why people are reluctant to rebalance.
- ▶ Why reallocating is too extreme an alternative to rebalancing.

RISK AND REWARD TRADE-OFFS

Even though I have been an investment advisor for over 15 years, I have yet to find a "risk test" that I thought was excellent or even very good. In order to better determine how I should position a new client's money, several years ago I came up with what I believe to be a more straightforward way of determining someone's risk level.

Unlike other "tests" or graphs, the table I came up with estimates the loss potential at different levels of risk plus provides the reader with a realistic measurement for how long it will take to recover from such a loss. Having used the table (shown later in this chapter) now for a number of years, I can tell you that it has worked exceedingly well. My clients know what kinds of losses are to be expected and how long such a losing streak may last.

I devised this table by looking at historical data from a number of different sources. I wanted to make sure that I included performance and risk figures that were reflective of general market conditions, not simply the most recent 3-, 5-, or 10-year period. I did not rely exclusively on figures from the last several years because some of these numbers would be difficult, if not impossible, to duplicate or exceed during the next 5 to 15 years. Let me give you a couple of examples to show you what I mean.

The 1980s represented the best decade ever for high-quality corporate bonds and U.S. government securities. Looking back, it is no surprise that debt instruments did so well during this period. From the middle of 1981 until the end of 1989, interest rates basically fell. Some years, interest rates fell a lot. From a brief high of 21.5%, the prime interest rate fell to below 7% by the end of President Reagan's second term.

The price of a barrel of oil fell from more than $35 to below $10 (despite the cumulative effects of inflation over this period).

The gains enjoyed by high-quality bonds cannot be duplicated during the 1990s unless the prime interest rate falls by about 14 points. This means that the prime would currently have to fall to a negative number (which is impossible) or the prime interest rate would have to skyrocket by 10 to 15 points and then plummet by a similar amount, all during the balance of the 1990s. Moreover, even if this did happen, to duplicate the total returns that bonds enjoyed during the 1980s, you would have to buy bonds after, or toward the end of, the huge increase in rates.

What this means is that any software package or program that is projecting future rates of returns on bonds is incorrect if it only includes bond data for the last 10 to 15 years. A number of studies have shown that the long-term results of bonds are going to be almost identical to the bond's coupon rate (meaning that any appreciation due to a drop in interest rates or any depreciation due to a rise in rates will cancel each other out over time). So, if long-term U.S. government bonds currently yield 7%, you can expect your total return from such bonds to be 7%—assuming you own these, or similar, bonds for several years.

Surprisingly, the 1980s was not the best decade ever for stocks, but it was the third best decade this century. Although it is doubtful that stocks will have the same average annualized returns for the 1990s that they did in the 1980s, it is certainly not impossible. In fact, looking at the first half of the 1990s, there is a pretty good chance that the 1990s will be similar to the 1980s for stocks. However, it is more likely, based on long-term historical figures going back several decades, that stocks will probably not do quite as well in the 1990s as they did in the 1980s. Again, this is another shortcoming of some programs that make projections in a vacuum (meaning there is no human element that takes a level-headed and historical approach to market data).

In the case of real estate, the correlation of past results to future results is murky. A good case can be made that real estate will soon see some boom years. However, a good case can also be made that real estate returns will continue to be quite modest for at least the next couple of years.

Cash equivalents will most likely not repeat their 1980s performance. Even though rates fell quite a bit, interest rates as a whole for the 1980s were extremely high by

U.S. standards. But, when interest rates were high in the early 1980s, money market funds were the best deal in town: no risk and fat yields. MPT software programs that focus on this period of time will give cash equivalents too large of a weighting in moderate and even aggressive portfolios.

The table I have come up with takes these and other points into consideration. What is shown below are fair expectations if your time horizon is 5 to 10 years or longer. Shorter term time periods can end up with returns that are significantly higher or lower (or even negative) than those figures shown below.

HOW TO USE THE TABLE

Assume that all investments fall on a risk spectrum (or ruler) that ranges from 10 to 100, the higher the number, the greater the risk. To give you some reference points, look at the following three examples for levels and descriptions:

A risk level of 10 = bank CDs that mature in two years or less, money market accounts, U.S. Treasury bills, and high-quality bonds maturing in two years or less.

A risk level of 50 = U.S. blue chip stocks such as IBM, McDonalds, GE, and GM.

A risk level of 100 = gambling, the lottery, uncovered options, commodities.

As you might suspect, the higher the risk level, the greater the potential return. Up to a point, each step of risk (e.g., going from a 10 to a 20) is a fair trade-off. An extra step of risk means that your return, assuming a holding period of at least five years, should also increase by a step. However, once you go above a 70 on that scale of 10 to 100, the trade-off is not fair or even—for every step of risk you take above a 70 your return potential will only increase a half or a third of a step. In other words, risk levels of 80, 90, and 100 do not represent good or equitable risk-adjusted returns (you are not being properly compensated for the added amounts of risk).

Listed below are sample portfolios, based on risk levels of 10 (very conservative) through 80 (quite risky). It is not recommended that anyone go above a 70 due to the relationship of risk and reward at such levels.

Return, Risk, Loss Potential and Recovery

Risk Level	Annual Return	Frequency of Loss	Range of Loss	Recovery Time
10	5-6%	no chance of loss *	—	—
20	8%	1 in 12	0 to -3%	6 months
30	10%	1 in 10	0 to -6%	9 months
40	12%	1 in 8	0 to -7%	10 months
50	14%	1 in 7	0 to -9%	14 months
60	16%	1 in 6	0 to -12%	16 months
70	17%	1 in 5	0 to -16%	22 months
80	18%	1 in 4	0 to -20%	25 months

*There could be a real loss due to the effects of inflation and income taxes (e.g., if you are in the 33% tax bracket and get a 6% return, your after-tax return drops to 4%; if inflation were to average 5% for that same year, the net real return would be -1%).

NOTES (DEFINITIONS):

annual return—What you should expect, on a compound basis, at the given risk level; it is very important for you to remember that these returns or ranges will not be experienced each year, but instead, over any given 4- to 6-year period of time.

frequency of loss—How often, on an annual basis, will your overall portfolio show a loss (e.g., a "1 in 8" loss means that you will sustain a loss approximately once every eight years); the loss will most likely range from zero to some negative number (as shown above).

range of loss—How negative the expected loss will be on a calendar year basis; any given quarterly loss could be greater or less than what is shown.

recovery time—the projected number of months it will take for the loss to be made up and for you to be back at the "peak" point prior to the most recent loss.

A COUPLE OF POINTS TO KEEP IN MIND

As good as I believe this table to be, projecting or estimating future returns is part science and part art. Historical data, when viewed in proper context, can be a meaningful indicator of future expectations when your holding period is at least five years, but it is still an indication and not a guarantee or even strong assurance.

The longer your holding period, the more likely you will have similar returns to those shown above. An investor who stays the course for 10 years is much more likely to experience the kinds of gains shown above than another investor who only stays on board for four to six years.

The lower the risk level (i.e., a 10, 20 or 30), the more likely the outcome. Risk becomes much more predictable at these lower risk levels because the portfolio is comprised of investments that have very low or modest levels of volatility. As you might suspect, higher risk levels (i.e., a 70 or 80) are less predictable as to their overall returns and especially any market downturns. Still, the numbers shown at all levels are reasonable expectations.

Money Talks: One of the benefits of looking at risk and return (or simply risk-adjusted returns) is that you will now have an important shield to guard against brokers and advisors who try to steer you toward an investment that is not proper for your particular set of circumstances. This is of particular concern when you are investing during a very positive period of time for common stocks.

SUMMARY

This very brief, but important, chapter is something you can use as a yardstick for measuring return and risk for the next several years. It is also a chapter you will want to refer back to after you have read the chapter in the final section of this book on life cycle investing.

The next chapter describes investment portfolios for different age groups. No matter what the age range, the chapter includes a sample portfolio for a conservative, moderate, and aggressive investor.

The purpose of this chapter is twofold. First, the sample portfolios may open your eyes to some investment categories you had not previously thought of. Second, all of the portfolios are efficient—the risk-return trade-off is fair. There are certainly more investment possibilities than those listed in the following chapter. However, by sticking to these categories, you will greatly increase the chance of getting burned. Suffering a large loss in even part of your portfolio may cause you to do something truly terrible such as abandoning everything but "risk-free" investments or attempting to recover a loss by going into something that is just too risky for your temperament.

Dollars & $ense: You may feel that some of the rates of return, loss potential or recovery periods are a little high or a little low. There is nothing wrong with making up your own risk-reward table as long as you use data covering at least the last 15 years. Whether you use my table or come up with your own, this is the best way I have ever seen to quickly (and I believe accurately) determine someone's risk level.

LET'S REMEMBER THIS:

- ▶ There is a relationship between risk and return.
- ▶ There is a fair trade-off between risk and reward up to certain levels.
- ▶ Don't make the mistake of seeking returns beyond your comfort level.

INTRODUCTION TO LIFE CYCLE INVESTING

Each generation has different goals and objectives. For investors who are in their 20s and 30s, retirement is not a chief concern. Instead, younger investors focus on buying new cars, clothes and electronic equipment. These consumate consumers have just begun receiving meaningful paychecks and want to spend their newfound wealth. As these younger investors start to reach their mid-30s and early 40s, raising children and owning a home become their major goals. Job security is not much of a concern.

As we enter our late 40s, personal consumption becomes less important. The importance of owning a new car or owning the latest gadget diminishes; we have owned one or more homes and have gone through the process of buying drapes and remodeling the kitchen. Our attention shifts to providing for the children. Retirement planning starts to creep into our vocabulary as we see our parents enjoying (hopefully) their golden years. We can look ahead just a few more years when the kids go off to college or at least move out.

Somewhere in our early or mid-50s, the reality of retirement sets in. One or both of our parents appears to age more rapidly. Our career becomes less important as the daily routine becomes more predictable. Any future promotions or pay raises become more predictable and dreams of conquering the world are now reserved for our kids. A certain level of peacefulness sets in since there appears to be adequate time to prepare for leaving the work force.

Life in our 60s becomes very different because retirement is just a few years away. Our children are on their own and have lived away from home for a number of years (hopefully). We begin to think about moving into a smaller home. We contemplate what it would be like to live somewhere else, perhaps in a different state with a different climate. Finances take center stage. We realize that our options are limited since our past savings and investments will now greatly dictate our futures. We question the future and safety of our pensions and Social Security.

Dollars & $ense: As you read through the suggested case studies later in this chapter, keep in mind that there is no single "best" portfolio for a particular age or risk level, nor are there any "magic" categories or specific investments that must be included. A tremendous number of factors can influence how your portfolio should be structured, including things that only you are familiar with such as: (a) the health of you and/or your spouse; (b) the chances of you and/or your spouse getting a promotion; (c) the health of loved ones who might leave you an inheritance or who may need financial help from you; and (d) the likelihood of a divorce or separation.

Retirees in their 70s have now experienced a few years of not being part of the work force. Retirement checks have been coming in on a regular basis and the returns on our investments become more predictable as our risk level decreases. Our attention focuses on grandchildren, social friends, and recreational activities. Traveling to new lands is either a constant topic of discussion or something we have been experiencing.

As we reach our 80s and 90s, our attention once again shifts. We now concentrate on health and health care. Traveling takes much more effort and part or all of the appeal has worn off. The children and grandchildren come by less frequently because they have their own lives and friends. Death and estate planning become ideas that need to be discussed. We start to think about what it will be like if we survive our spouse or how we can best safeguard our spouse's quality of life if we die before him or her.

Our cycle of life involves financial decisions at every stage. For the first several stages, we must consciously decide the extent to which we are going to be consumers and savers. As we mature and current consumption becomes less important, deciding how conservatively or aggressively we want to invest our money is the central issue. As we age, safety and current income are paramount. Finally, as death approaches, setting up an organized estate is the business of the day.

The purpose of the next several sections of this chapter is to help guide you (or your clients if you are an advisor) in deciding how your investment portfolio should be structured. Each chapter includes model portfolios for the conservative moderate and aggressive investor. Each portfolio, for each cycle of life, includes the following:

▶ A structured portfolio for three different risk levels.

▶ A bar chart showing the historic year-by-year returns for each portfolio.

▶ A box that indicates the best and worst quarter and year over the past 15 years.

▶ A line chart that shows the growth of $10,000 for each portfolio.

▶ The growth of a $100, $500 and $1,000 monthly investment in each portfolio.

These sections and charts have multiple purposes. First, they will give you a good idea of what you can expect in the future. Second, the information should act as a form of motivation—showing you how much you could end up with if you play it smart. Third, some of the information provided will also show you what kind of losses are to be expected along the way. Finally, and most importantly, after you have reviewed those charts and graphs that apply to you (i.e., those that have a similar risk level, savings pattern and time horizon), you will discover that successful investing does not have to be overly risky or mysterious.

Recommended portfolio mixes will be derived from the following list of investments, ranked in order from the most conservative to the most aggressive. The percentage return figures you see in parentheses below represent average annualized returns using historical data from the last three years (ending 12/31/95):

▶ tax-free money market funds (4%)

▶ money market accounts (5%)

▶ residential real estate (5.5%)

▶ bank CDs (5.5%)

▶ tax-free municipal bonds (5.5%)

▶ fixed-rate annuities (6%)

▶ short-term government bonds (6%)

▶ intermediate-term government bonds (6.5%)

▶ long-term government bonds (7%)

▶ foreign government bonds (8%)

▶ high-yield corporate bonds (8.5%)

▶ all-cash leasing program (9.5%)

▶ real estate investment trust (10%)

▶ utility stocks (10.5%)

▶ balanced mutual funds (11%)

▶ equity-income mutual funds (11.5%)

▶ globally balanced mutual funds (11.5%)

▶ growth mutual funds (12%)

- ▶ blue chip stock portfolio (12.5%)
- ▶ global stock funds (13%)
- ▶ foreign stock funds (14%)
- ▶ small company stock funds (14.5%)
- ▶ aggressive growth funds (15%)
- ▶ emerging markets funds (16%)

Each of the next several sections is based on a certain age range. You should skip those sections that cover ages younger than yours. Such chapters may be useful to show your younger brothers and sisters or adult children, but other than that, they really have no relevance for you.

CASE STUDY NO. 1: INVESTING IN YOUR 20s AND 30s

General Profile:

Age: 25 to 35

Assumed Amount That Can Be Saved Each Year: $600 to $10,000

Chief Concerns: focus on career, get married and buy nice things

Secondary Concern: saving money for a down payment on a home

Not Very Concerned About: inflation, retirement plans, health insurance or life insurance

The younger you are, the greater the flexibility you have when it comes to investing. True, you probably do not have a lot of money to invest, but time is truly on your side. Ending up with a lot of money is not difficult, no matter how much you can save each year. A younger person or couple has the chance to see the true magic of compound interest.

Conceptually, investors in their 20s and 30s should be willing to take on moderate or high risk. They are young enough to recover from several declines in their lives. Their responsibilities are also less than older individuals and couples who have children and parents that may need to be helped financially. But, when I say "high risk," I mean investment categories that have done very well historically. I do not mean what are sometimes referred to as "flyers"—such as options, commodities, penny stocks or even securities from an industry group or country that might be up 40 to 300% one year and then down 40 to 90% the next year.

Conservative Portfolio

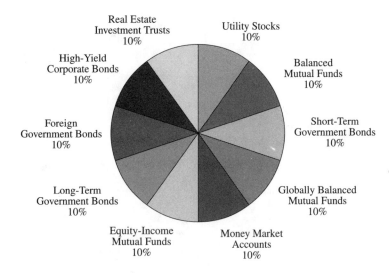

Real Estate Investment Trusts 10%

Utility Stocks 10%

High-Yield Corporate Bonds 10%

Balanced Mutual Funds 10%

Foreign Government Bonds 10%

Short-Term Government Bonds 10%

Long-Term Government Bonds 10%

Globally Balanced Mutual Funds 10%

Equity-Income Mutual Funds 10%

Money Market Accounts 10%

Moderate Portfolio

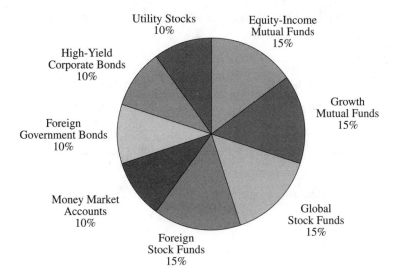

Utility Stocks 10%

Equity-Income Mutual Funds 15%

High-Yield Corporate Bonds 10%

Growth Mutual Funds 15%

Foreign Government Bonds 10%

Money Market Accounts 10%

Global Stock Funds 15%

Foreign Stock Funds 15%

Aggressive Portfolio

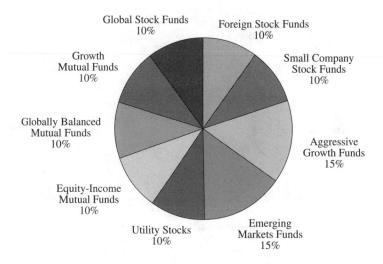

Global Stock Funds 10%

Foreign Stock Funds 10%

Growth Mutual Funds 10%

Small Company Stock Funds 10%

Globally Balanced Mutual Funds 10%

Aggressive Growth Funds 15%

Equity-Income Mutual Funds 10%

Utility Stocks 10%

Emerging Markets Funds 15%

Dollars & Sense: Once you become informed as to how an investment correlates to other investments, as well as the growth and loss potential, making a decision becomes much easier. Bottom line: If you don't feel you understand it, stay away from it.

CASE STUDY NO. 2: INVESTING IN YOUR 40s

General Profile:

Age: late 30s to late 40s

Assumed Amount That Can Be Saved Each Year: $2,000 to $20,000

Chief Concerns: life insurance, children's education, taking vacations, more free time

Secondary Concerns: fixing up the home, maintaining good relationship with your family

Not Very Concerned About: retirement or the financial well-being of your parents

Your 40s represent an odd period in life. You are no longer young (unless you figure life expectancy to be well over 100), but do not see yourself as middle-aged. If you have children, chances are that they are either in elementary or junior high school. The costs of raising these children have not been particularly great up to this point, unless there has been a large outlay for private education. Job stability is probably good. You have most likely owned a home for at least a few years. Expenses are fairly fixed and you have a pretty good idea as to how much can be saved for investments each year.

Despite the limitations investors in their late 30s to late 40s have (e.g., a large mortgage, raising children, working long hours, etc.), a risk level of moderate or aggressive is still recommended as a generality. I say "as a generality" because there are certainly a large number of people who want to remain conservative whether their time horizon is a few months or several decades. These are the kinds of investors that could easily lose sleep or become physically upset if their portfolio experienced even a modest loss.

Still, if you are not part of this group, strongly consider going at least "moderate." Keep in mind that if you are patient, any loss should be recovered within a few months or within a year or two (if we rely on history as a guide). A 45-year-old individual or couple who has a conservative portfolio that averages 8% a year will see that portfolio double in value every nine years. By the time the 45-year-old reaches age 63, the conservative portfolio would have doubled twice ($100,000 would grow to $200,000 and the $200,000 would compound to $400,000).

That same portfolio invested in moderate-risk assets that averaged 12% a year would double once every six years. This means that the 45-year-old would see his portfolio double three times over an 18-year period (from age 45 to age 63). Our hypothetical portfolio would go from $100,000 to $200,000, and from $200,000 to $400,000 (just like above), but it would double once more, from $400,000 to $800,000. Retiring with an $800,000 nest egg is very different than retiring with $400,000. By being too conservative you may miss out on one, two, or more doubling periods.

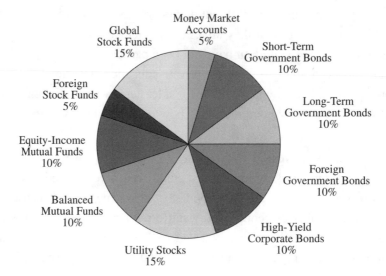

Conservative Portfolio

Money Market Accounts 5%

Short-Term Government Bonds 10%

Global Stock Funds 15%

Long-Term Government Bonds 10%

Foreign Stock Funds 5%

Equity-Income Mutual Funds 10%

Foreign Government Bonds 10%

Balanced Mutual Funds 10%

High-Yield Corporate Bonds 10%

Utility Stocks 15%

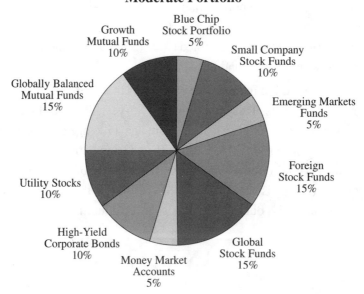

Moderate Portfolio

Blue Chip Stock Portfolio 5%

Growth Mutual Funds 10%

Small Company Stock Funds 10%

Globally Balanced Mutual Funds 15%

Emerging Markets Funds 5%

Foreign Stock Funds 15%

Utility Stocks 10%

High-Yield Corporate Bonds 10%

Global Stock Funds 15%

Money Market Accounts 5%

Aggressive Portfolio

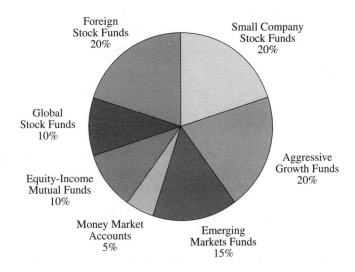

Foreign Stock Funds 20%

Small Company Stock Funds 20%

Global Stock Funds 10%

Aggressive Growth Funds 20%

Equity-Income Mutual Funds 10%

Money Market Accounts 5%

Emerging Markets Funds 15%

Dollars & Sense:

Stay away from anything if it sounds just too tempting. The worst investments I have ever seen, and I've seen most of them (and even invested in a couple myself), were the ones that appeal to one's sense of greed. The second worst investments I've encountered were those that I was told to recommend to my clients for just "5 to 15%" of their holdings in order to provide "valuable diversification." Most of these "diversifiers" turned out to diversify my clients' portfolio returns lower!

CASE STUDY NO. 3: INVESTING IN YOUR 50s

General Profile:

Age: 49 to 59

Assumed Amount That Can Be Saved Each Year: $4,000 to $25,000

Chief Concerns: finishing up on college bills, saving for retirement

Secondary Concern: how to deal with your parents if they need help

Not Very Concerned About: paying the mortgage or job security

By the time most people hit their 50s, they realize they are no longer young. The idea of being middle-aged and acting somewhat like your parents did when you were growing up begins to set in. You have generally come to grips with the way things are. You realize what the chances are that you will become president or senior vice president of the company you work for. Life, on the whole, seems to be good. Vacation and free time are now more frequent and predictable. It looks like the kids will finish four years of college in five years—six years at the worst. You hope they will not move back in after their school career ends but you are uncertain about the job market for new entrants.

If you were divorced (the divorce rate is 50% in some states), there is a good chance that you have remarried. The financial impact of a divorce was worse than you thought, but you have somehow survived and begun a "new" life with another mate.

Even at age 59, the "typical investor" should still have most of his or her assets in equity instruments. True, retirement may be just around the corner, but life does not end at retirement. You must look at your life expectancy. If a male makes it to age 65, his remaining life expectancy is about 15 years; for a female, it is about 19 years. These life expectancy figures are based on current medical technology and include smokers as well as non-smokers for determining life expectancy. It is for this reason that equities such as common stocks and certain forms of real estate be emphasized.

A 59-year-old does not have as many years to recover from a market loss as a 49-year-old, so even though I recommend a healthy, if not exclusive, weighting toward equities, portfolio volatility and risk can be greatly reduced by sticking to certain kinds of equities such as utility stocks, value growth funds (mutual funds that invest in depressed stocks that have already fallen in price), hybrids such as convertible securities and high-yield bonds and real estate investment trusts that have little or no leverage.

Conservative Portfolio

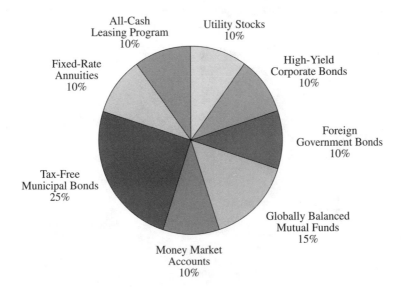

All-Cash Leasing Program 10%

Utility Stocks 10%

Fixed-Rate Annuities 10%

High-Yield Corporate Bonds 10%

Foreign Government Bonds 10%

Tax-Free Municipal Bonds 25%

Globally Balanced Mutual Funds 15%

Money Market Accounts 10%

Moderate Portfolio

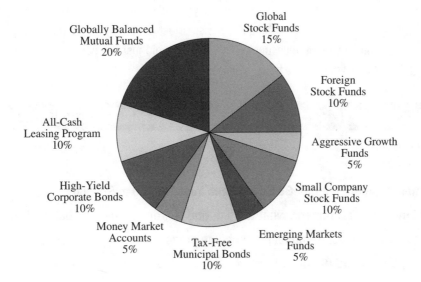

Globally Balanced Mutual Funds 20%

Global Stock Funds 15%

Foreign Stock Funds 10%

All-Cash Leasing Program 10%

Aggressive Growth Funds 5%

High-Yield Corporate Bonds 10%

Small Company Stock Funds 10%

Money Market Accounts 5%

Tax-Free Municipal Bonds 10%

Emerging Markets Funds 5%

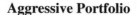

Aggressive Portfolio

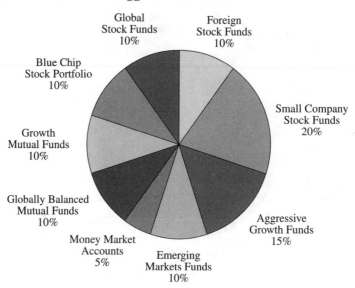

Dollars & $ense: If you just stay away from the bad stuff (generally anything not referred to in this book in a positive or neutral manner), you will be way ahead of your friends, neighbors, and co-workers. Some of the smartest people in the world have gone into some very dumb investments. If you can avoid just the bad ones, you are about 80% on your way to being a successful investor.

CASE STUDY NO. 4: INVESTING IN YOUR 60s

General Profile:

Age: 60 to 69

Assumed Amount That Can Be Saved Each Year: $5,000 to $25,000

Chief Concerns: retirement, what to do during retirement, helping out the kids

Secondary Concerns: remodeling the home or moving, health insurance

Not Very Concerned About: large ticket items (except possibly paying off part or all of any remaining mortgage)

Retirement is here or near at hand. You still have at least a few years worth of saving. These final three to ten years of investing can make a huge impact on the quality of retirement. A meeting with an investment advisor can help motivate you for the final stretch. One or both of your parents is deceased. You have learned to deal with visiting and taking care of an aged person. The idea of you or your spouse someday dying has also set in; the vague notion of some kind of immortality has given way to the way things really work. Your children are fully grown and have begun their own careers.

There comes a point in our lives when even a strongly equity-oriented investor and advisor such as myself realizes that some people die or become severely disabled in their 60s. There is also validity to the notion that life in your 60s is too short to continue worrying about the ups and downs of the stock market. It is for these and other reasons that I generally recommend this age group to be balanced in their portfolios. A blend of equities and debt instruments is warranted. The equity portion should provide the needed moderate- and long-term hedge against inflation that is critical to maintain one's purchasing power; the debt portion provides a steady stream of current income plus quite a bit of price stability with principal.

The overwhelming majority of financial writers and advisors would recommend that individuals and couples in their 60s should have most, if not all, of their assets in debt instruments. I do not agree with this point of view. I believe these other commentators and brokers either do not know the life expectancy of someone age 65, have not given any thought to what life expectancy might be with some kinds of medical breakthroughs or simply do not have a historical perspective of the markets.

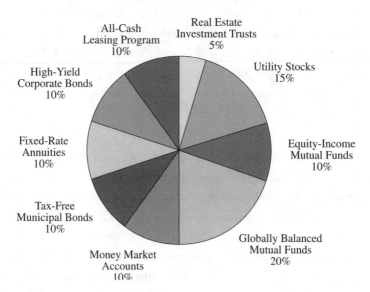

Conservative Portfolio

All-Cash Leasing Program 10%

Real Estate Investment Trusts 5%

High-Yield Corporate Bonds 10%

Utility Stocks 15%

Fixed-Rate Annuities 10%

Equity-Income Mutual Funds 10%

Tax-Free Municipal Bonds 10%

Money Market Accounts 10%

Globally Balanced Mutual Funds 20%

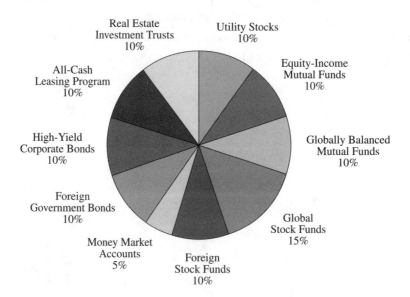

Moderate Portfolio

Real Estate Investment Trusts 10%

Utility Stocks 10%

All-Cash Leasing Program 10%

Equity-Income Mutual Funds 10%

High-Yield Corporate Bonds 10%

Globally Balanced Mutual Funds 10%

Foreign Government Bonds 10%

Global Stock Funds 15%

Money Market Accounts 5%

Foreign Stock Funds 10%

Aggressive Portfolio

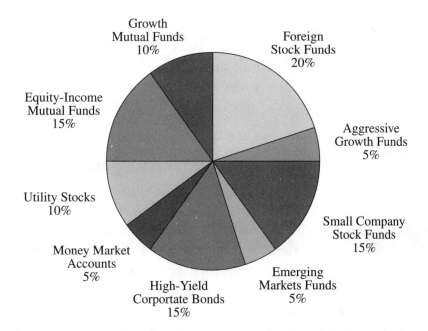

Growth Mutual Funds 10%

Foreign Stock Funds 20%

Equity-Income Mutual Funds 15%

Aggressive Growth Funds 5%

Utility Stocks 10%

Small Company Stock Funds 15%

Money Market Accounts 5%

Emerging Markets Funds 5%

High-Yield Corportate Bonds 15%

CASE STUDY NO. 5: INVESTING IN YOUR 70s

General Profile:

Age: 70 to 79

Assumed Amount That Can Be Saved Each Year: $0 to $15,000

Chief Concerns: health and estate planning

Secondary Concern: leisure time

Not Very Concerned About: making purchases

Retirement has now begun. Keeping investments conservative is of paramount importance. Equities still need to be included because you or your spouse may live another 10 to 15 years. A meeting with a healthcare specialist will help you ease into adjustments that may be necessary during the next several years. Relying on your children to later make decisions about care facilities or modifications to your home may be rushed and inadequate. Always remember that no one, not even your kids, will look out for you as much as you will (or should).

Although I cannot make a general recommendation for someone in their 70s to consider an aggressive portfolio like the one shown below, I can make a good case for such a portfolio for the right kind of investor. If your net worth is such that the quality of your remaining life would not be affected by a drop in your net worth of 15 to 20% (I am assuming that the roughly 30% exposure to equities in the aggressive portfolio below drops by 50 to 60% and never recovers), then you should at least consider being a little more aggressive than what is most likely being advised to you by other sources.

The reason why I can recommend the aggressive portfolio described below for a number of people is fourfold. First, someone who is 79 years old might live another 10 to 20 years and medical costs during some of those years are likely to be quite high. Second, if that "someone" is married, there is a very good likelihood that at least one spouse will live for several more years (enough time to recover from anything short of a market crash). Third, the equities recommended for this portfolio are not high risk; their volatility is modest—plus keep in mind that only about 30% of the portfolio will be in equities. Fourth, your estate does not end when you die. If you have loved ones, who are presumably younger than you are, you may feel it is important to pass on as large an estate as possible. True, a portfolio with even 30% exposure to equities could decline just before the 79-year-old dies, but the heirs have the time to see a recovery plus watch the portfolio go on to make new highs.

Conservative Portfolio

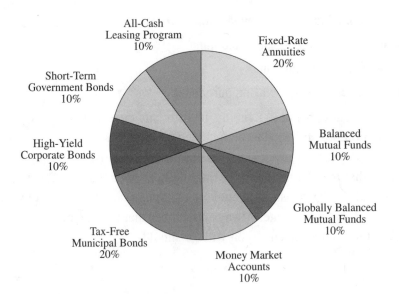

Moderate Portfolio

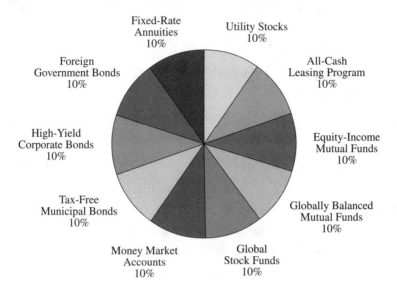

Fixed-Rate Annuities 10%
Utility Stocks 10%
Foreign Government Bonds 10%
All-Cash Leasing Program 10%
High-Yield Corporate Bonds 10%
Equity-Income Mutual Funds 10%
Tax-Free Municipal Bonds 10%
Globally Balanced Mutual Funds 10%
Money Market Accounts 10%
Global Stock Funds 10%

Aggressive Portfolio

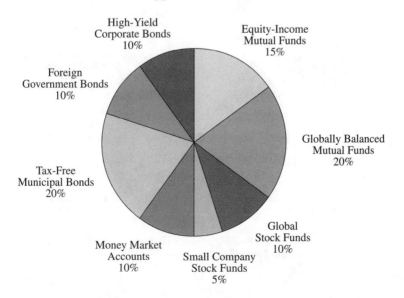

High-Yield Corporate Bonds 10%
Equity-Income Mutual Funds 15%
Foreign Government Bonds 10%
Globally Balanced Mutual Funds 20%
Tax-Free Municipal Bonds 20%
Global Stock Funds 10%
Money Market Accounts 10%
Small Company Stock Funds 5%

CASE STUDY NO. 7: INVESTING IN YOUR 80s AND 90s

General Profile:

Age: 80 to 99

Assumed Amount That Can Be Saved Each Year: $5,000 to $10,000

Chief Concerns: health

Secondary Concerns: spouse's health, the well-being of your children and grand-children

Not Very Concerned About: a mortgage, making a killing in the stock market

An "aggressive" portfolio is not even mentioned for this age group because it cannot be justified, even by someone who loves stocks and hates most categories of bonds. There have got to be more satisfying things at this point in life than trying to see your portfolio double in value just one more time.

The two recommended portfolios below provide a great deal of safety plus the opportunity for some modest growth by reinvesting part of the interest income. A debt portfolio is really a must at this point unless you have a tremendous net worth and can afford a loss (and probably never recover).

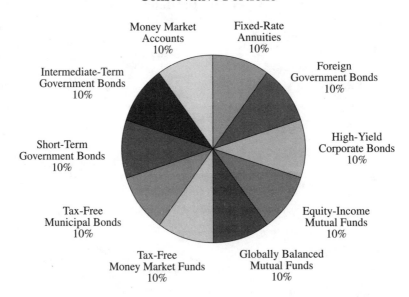

Conservative Portfolio

Moderate Portfolio

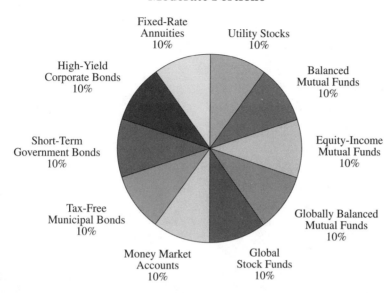

Fixed-Rate Annuities 10%
Utility Stocks 10%
High-Yield Corporate Bonds 10%
Balanced Mutual Funds 10%
Short-Term Government Bonds 10%
Equity-Income Mutual Funds 10%
Tax-Free Municipal Bonds 10%
Globally Balanced Mutual Funds 10%
Money Market Accounts 10%
Global Stock Funds 10%

Dollars & Sense: Wealthy individuals and couples have much more investment flexibility at any age than those who do not have millions. If losing 5% or 10% of your net worth over one, two or three years is going to result in your standard of living decreasing, don't do it, even if it's for the kids. Remember, people do not appreciate money given to them as much as they do when they earn it. Any sleepless nights or worrying you went through so that your kids or grandchildren might inherit an extra $1,000 or even $100,000 will not be appreciated as much as you think.

SUMMARY

As you can see from the recommended portfolios throughout this chapter, we have stayed true to some fundamental beliefs emphasized throughout this book: (1) stay diversified since no one can predict the future; (2) include tax-advantaged investments; (3) make sure you are "global" —despite what foreign stock and bond markets may have done the previous one to three years; and (4) try to match your lifestyle with your investment portfolio.

The next chapter looks at the issue of hidden fees, profits and commissions. As you will see, there is nothing wrong with such charges as long as you are receiving value.

▼

Paying Fees and Commissions

Investors are subject to a wide array of charges. Whenever something is bought or sold, a fee or commission is normally charged. Even if nothing changes in the portfolio, the investor could end up paying a quarterly or annual asset fee. The table below covers the most popular investments, showing what kind of charges or lost opportunities should be expected.

Investments and Fees	
Type of Investment	**What it Can "Cost" You**
Bank CDs	You could receive a non-competitive yield. The bank lends your money out, typically collecting 25 to 200% more than it is paying you.
Money Market Accounts	You could receive a non-competitive yield.
Corporate, Government & Municipal Bonds (includes GNMAs and FNMAs)	The commission is in the form of a "markup," which ranges from less than 1% up to 5%.
Individual Stocks	Traditional commissions vary greatly depending upon the brokerage firm, the number of shares and the price per share; figure approximately 1.5% to buy and 1.5% to sell.

continues

Investments and Fees [Continued]	
Type of Investment	*What it Can "Cost" You*
Individual Stocks Through a Super Discount Brokerage Firm or Using Your Computer	Virtually nothing, but look out for the "bid-ask" spread (they buy it at the bid price, say $10 a share, and sell it to you at the ask price, say $10.50 a share; or you sell at $10.00 and a traditional brokerage firm would have gotten you $10.25 or $10.50 a share)—this can be the most expensive trade of all (but hidden).
Mutual Funds	Anywhere from 0 to 8.5% depending upon whether you are buying a no-load fund or one that charges a commission; high ongoing operating costs can, over time, easily exceed any up-front commission—many funds have extremely low ongoing costs (less than .5% a year), others have annual costs that are more than 2% a year—the average is about 1% a year.
Mutual Funds (Large Purchases)	The majority of funds charge a commission, with 4 to 5% being the average; this can drop down to 1% or less, depending upon the dollar amount invested in the fund or the fund family.
Mutual Funds (Contingent Deferred Sales Charge)	No up-front charges, but normal annual costs are increased by about 1.25% a year (all of which are subtracted from your account) to cover the up-front commission paid to the broker (which is usually 4%)—this additional hidden fee usually disappears after six to seven years.
Mutual Funds ("C" Shares)	No up-front charges, broker receives 1% when you buy, plus 1% a year; your costs increase by at least 1% a year to cover this charge—the charge remains level, despite the value of your account, for as long as you own the fund.
Mutual Funds (Redemption)	No "back-end" charges or any other deferred costs unless you own shares that are associated with a contingent deferred sales charge and you've owned the shares for less than four to six years; a few funds charge a 1 to 2% redemption fee if shares are cashed in within a few years (in order to discourage trading).
Fixed-Rate Annuities	Investor pays nothing directly, broker gets paid 4%—the yield to the investor would be higher if the insurance company did not have to pay out any kind of commission.

Type of Investment	What it Can "Cost" You
Variable Annuities	Same as above but annual charges are 1.25% (or more) per year to pay for the guaranteed death benefit and as a profit to the insurance company; portfolio management fees are an added cost that averages about 1% per year (similar to mutual fund management).
Variable Life Insurance	Complex formula, but commissions are typically 5% of the amount of money going into the "investment side" of the insurance contract; the investor pays nothing up-front but faces severe penalties during the first several years of the contract plus pays "hidden" annual fees that are in the 3% range.
Limited Partnerships	Comes directly out of the investor's pocket; the broker gets 8 to 10%, plus the brokerage firm may get some of the partnership's back-end profits.
Gold or Silver Bullion	1 to 2% commission or fee when you buy plus 1 to 2% when you sell (plus assaying fees).
"Wrap Fee" (Also Known as "Managed") Accounts at Full Service and Discount Brokerage Firms	Client pays no brokerage fees to buy individual stocks or mutual funds but does pay a "management fee" whose typical charge is 1.5% a year but may be as high as 3% a year, fees are automatically debited from client's account balance and are based on the value of the account.

DON'T BE A SUCKER

Just as you have always heard, "There is no free lunch." The financial services industry is not a nonprofit group. They are in business to provide you a service and make a profit. Even your local bank can make a killing off of you. The typical checking account charges annual fees that approach $150 a year. Now this is not called a commission, but these service charges do come out of your pocket and quickly add up. Some banks now charge a fee if you simply want to talk to a teller (instead of using an ATM machine). One comedian has said that his bank is going to charge a fee if you just think about the bank.

The people that think they are getting the best deal are often getting taken advantage of the most. These are the do-it-yourselfers that use e-mail or a discount brokerage firm. There can be tremendous savings, but there can also be tremendous costs. First, when it comes to bonds, the mark up or mark down can be several percentage points when you buy or sell. Instead of buying a bond for $970, you might pay $1,000 per bond. When you go to sell the bond (prior to maturity) you may get $1,000, but the bond is really worth $1,040. These "spreads" do not show anywhere on your confirmation or monthly statement. They are a hidden cost to you since you paid more than you had to (when buying) or received less than you should have (when selling a bond prior to maturity).

When you buy a bank CD, there is no commission, but the bank lends out your money for several percentage points more than what they are paying you. This spread is also reoccurring; every time your money is lent out, a new spread is created. If you are getting 5% on your CD, be assured that the bank is lending out your money for 7 to 15% a year. For some reason, investors do not seem to mind a 2 to 10% annual spread but get very upset when a brokerage firm or mutual fund company charges a one-time 3 to 4% commission.

What Is Fair

The real question, however, is what are you getting for your money? Whether we are talking about spreads, up-front commissions, back-end commissions, termination fees or ongoing charges, the charges may or may not be fair, depending upon the level of service and the performance of the investment. As an example, I do not mind paying a 5% up-front commission plus 2% per year in operating costs if I end up netting 10 to 15% a year on my money. Similarly, if my bank is paying me 5 or 6% for investing $10,000 in one of their CDs, I should care if they lend my money out at 8% to someone who needs a new car loan.

When you are thinking about buying a $350 piece of software from Microsoft, I doubt part of your decision is based on whether or not Bill Gates is going to net $1 from the purchase or $320. After all, when was the last time you bought a no-load sofa or went to a no-fee dentist or bought some fast food at cost? You get paid for working, shouldn't other people?

Is it fair that you pay some broker, who may look younger than some of your kids (or grandchildren), a $230 commission for spending 30 to 60 minutes with you while you filled out an application for the XYZ Tax-Free Bond Fund? Is it even less fair that this kid appears to be earning a couple of hundred dollars an hour (at least while you're there) when you go back to work the next day earning $20 an hour? I don't know the answer to these questions, but I do know that the marketplace is efficient, even when it comes to salaries. A famous artist might be able to charge $20,000 for a painting he or she completes in a couple of hours. Such a fee may seem outrageous, but if people are willing to pay that kind of money for that kind of art, then the marketplace is efficient. How that artist got to $20,000 a painting is something we don't think about too much.

Picasso was once approached by someone who asked him to draw a quick sketch on a cocktail napkin. After completing the little drawing in less than a minute, Picasso told the stranger that the drawing would cost him several thousand dollars. The tourist asked Picasso if he was crazy or kidding—after all, it only took a few seconds to do! Picasso did not waver on his price but added, "You don't know how many years it took me to develop this style." The same thing is true with a good advisor, whether that advisor is acting as a lawyer, contractor, doctor, or stockbroker.

Fortunately for investors, there are a huge number of brokers, advisors, mutual fund companies and banks that would love to invest your money. Deciding which institution or which person gets to invest your money is the tough part. It becomes an even more difficult decision if you are also thinking about going it alone and not using any kind of advisor or broker.

GETTING HELP OR GOING IT ALONE

Once you have decided to make an investment, one of the next steps is determining how you are going to make the investment. Should you contact the company directly (if you are going to buy a mutual fund or variable annuity)? Should you see a stockbroker or go to a discount brokerage firm? Is an "advisor" better than a "registered representative" or "financial planner"? Should you pay a commission (also known as a sales charge or load) or go into a no-load (no commission) product? How the investment should be made is a two-decision process: (1) whether or not you should seek professional advice, and (2) whether or not you should pay a commission or sales charge to buy that product.

Seeking professional advice is a good idea if one or more of the following statements is true:

▶ The advisor is more knowledgeable about this kind of investment than you are.

► You believe the advisor you have interviewed can be more impartial and less emotional than you will be if the investment drops in value or does not increase in value as fast as you would expect.

► You do not have the financial background necessary to look at this and other investments to determine what is most appropriate for you.

► The amount of time (and the dollar value of your time) you will spend in fully understanding the investment and all of its ramifications (e.g., risk level, expected growth, loss potential, tax consequences, relationship or correlation to your other holdings, lost opportunity cost by not investing the money elsewhere) adds up to more than what you would spend on fees or commissions.

► You are confused because there are so many investment choices, pricing schedules, and advertisements where everyone claims to be number one.

► You need help establishing or reviewing your overall investment strategy.

Seeking out professional advice is a bad idea if the following points are true:

► The advisor appears to know less about the investment you are interested in than you do.

► The advisor does not seem to quite grasp your fears, hopes and concerns about investing.

► The advisor has a very limited product shelf (meaning there may be few, if any, competitively priced alternatives).

► The advisor seems to be pushing proprietary products (also known as "in-house" products).

► The advisor does not seem to have enough time and it appears that he or she will not be much, if any, help on an ongoing basis.

► The advisor seems to be evasive on points such as sales charges or any kind of fee structure.

► The advisor only tells you the good news and not what could happen to the investment or any of the investment's shortcomings (note: every investment has shortcomings).

One of the reasons you should seek out professional advice is to find out the positive and negative aspects of the investments you are considering (or those that are being recommended). As mentioned in the last bulleted point above, every investment has its shortcomings. The table below gives a quick overview of some of the shortcomings of a few different investments.

Investments and Their Shortcomings	
The Investment	*Some of its Shortcomings*
Bank CDs	Poor hedge against inflation plus all "growth" or income is currently taxable.
Money Market Accounts	You are at the mercy of interest rates; when rates are low, so are your returns.
Individual Stocks	Volatility can be enormous and the surprises can be great (e.g., who would have thought that IBM, a few years ago, could go from about $175 a share down to $45 a share in less than a year and then back up to the $100s a couple of years later?)
"Good" Mutual Funds	Impatient investors can end up with poor returns (while all the indexes are showing great returns) by changing from one fund to another too frequently.
Government Bonds	They sound very safe, but their daily, weekly, monthly, quarterly and annual price swings (changes in the value of your principal) can be greater than blue chip stocks.
Fixed-Rate Annuities	No up-front fees or commissions, but guaranteed rates of return are often lower than what you can get from a municipal (tax-free) bond that has no strings attached.

These are the kind of things you want your advisor to bring to your attention. There are lots of people who will try to get your account (your money) by telling you about "recent trends" in the market or by showing you a series of impressive, mountain charts. These "mountain" or performance charts often look very impressive, but the truth is that most investors rarely experience such returns because investors generally lack patience (or the broker becomes frustrated and wants someone else, the mutual fund perhaps, to take the blame for disappointing short-term results). Once the investor switches brokers, massive changes often take place and the process starts all over again.

Going it alone (doing your own investing) is kind of like giving yourself a haircut or reading a book about do-it-yourself brain surgery. These are things you shouldn't do on your own, evxen though it will certainly save you money—at least in the short run.

One of the problems with doing it on your own is that you do not know the shortcomings of the sources you are looking at for guidance. Every magazine, periodical or book has shortcomings as well as biases. Mainstream financial magazines appeal to the do-it-yourselfer; that is their audience. Naturally, they may be inclined to tell you bad things about brokers plus give you all sorts of ideas as to how you should invest your money. Their subscription rate (and therefore advertising revenue) would fall off steeply if they advocated a buy-and-hold strategy plus the use of a professional advisor. With these magazines, it is the "flavor of the month club"; each issue tells you what you should be doing (or at least considering) this month.

Financial Periodicals Revisited

Which periodicals offer better advice than others? Think about the number of possible conflicting sources. You can read *The Wall Street Journal* in the morning and get conflicting views almost every day. During the day you can hear market commentary on the radio or television (which may be different than what you read four hours earlier in the *Journal*). After the market closes there are more views expressed on "market wrap-up" shows. When you go home at night there are a couple of half-hour shows devoted to the stock and bond markets. A few hours later you can watch an interview show such as Charlie Rose (PBS) or Ted Koppel (ABC News) that might have a portfolio manager giving you his take on the market and what to expect in the future. If you are still awake at two or three in the morning, you can see how the overseas markets are doing plus get some commentary from the reporters or anchors. So far, I have just described what happens on Monday through Friday.

The weekend arrives and you go out and buy *Barron's*. This publication has several writers who have opinions about the market or have interviews with money managers across the country. There is also more weekly advice from magazines such as *Business Week, Time* and *Newsweek*. If you are not sure whether or not you should rely on hourly, daily or weekly advice, how about bi-weekly publications such as *Forbes?* If you are still uncertain, wait until the third week of the month for your monthly subscriptions of *Money Magazine, Kiplinger, Fortune*, etc. And for those do-it-yourselfers who are convinced that these magazines don't really have the inside track to what's really going on, there are a number of newsletters you can subscribe to, some of which have telephone "hot lines" to what is certain to amount to something close to insider information or, at the very least, some kind of holy financial message.

You say that you still can't decide between intra-day, daily, weekly, semi-weekly or monthly advice? Well, how about going to quarterly? Now you are looking at spending more, but if you spend more, then the advice must be only that much better! If *The Wall Street Journal* provides advice for about $100 a year, then a mutual fund subscription to Morningstar or Value Line for $300 to $400 a year must be three or four times as good. Still not quite sure? Well, how about looking at recently published books about investing. After all, if it's in print, particularly in an impressive-looking book, it must be "more true" than some flimsy periodical.

All Too Confusing

The fact that a lot of what you read will be contradictory should be of concern, but if you are like most investors, you can simply ignore this fact. Instead, most of these do-it-yourselfers will end up relying on one source or perhaps two sources (provided they are not in conflict). The sources selected are often based on what has just been read or some financial seminar that has just been attended.

If all of this sounds a little pessimistic and silly, it is. Yet, as amusing, ridiculous or sarcastic as it may sound, it is how most do-it-yourselfers make their investment decisions. The articles, books, seminar handouts, and performance tables suddenly become more legitimate once the do-it-yourselfer starts making his own charts or entering all the data into a software spreadsheet. It is thought that this stuff must be valid because hours and hours are spent drawing lines and making software computations.

These people believe that they have come up with some special way of looking at an investment — something that Wall Street hasn't figured out yet. This is the same kind of thinking as those who somehow think they know what the stock market is about to do. For some bizarre reason these feelings of the "gut" or "heart" are thought to be more accurate than what the traders on the floor of the New York Stock Exchange (or whatever exchange) are feeling or going through. The fact that these traders do this full-time and it is their source of livelihood and has probably been such for a number of years means little compared to what the do-it-yourselfer thinks right now. Do you now see how ridiculous and foolish it is to try this stuff on your own?

Even more prestigious publications that specialize in a particular area, such as Morningstar (which is the most publicized mutual fund advisory service), have their shortcomings. Despite Morningstar's disclaimers (which readers and subscribers apparently ignore), well over 90% of all mutual fund sales last year were funds ranked four or five stars by Morningstar. This is more than a coincidence. I have seen people at discount brokerage firms and libraries go through Morningstar. The pattern is the same every time. The reader skips all funds unless they have a four- or five-star rating. Yet, there is no relation between these ratings and future results. In fact, some studies indicate that the better performers are more likely to be those funds rated two or three stars.

Believe the Disclaimers

It seems that no one believes the statement that "past results are no guarantee of future returns." Even though this is required on mutual fund advertisements that mention performance figures, people don't seem to think the statement is true. Well, it is true. For the last half of the 1970s, the best performing fund was 44 Wall Street. This was also one of the "10 best" funds recommended by a well-known investment magazine. During the first half of the 1980s, this fund managed to lose well over half its value—a difficult feat when you consider how well the Dow did over this period.

A second reason why you do not want to go it alone is that you lack objectivity—we all do. Think about it. Most people think they have a good personality, are at least fairly smart and look average or better. The reality is that the majority of people are not that bright, are not that interesting and look average. How many people do you know think they could act as good as (pick some actor) because he or she makes it look so easy or that actor appears to have a limited acting range? The truth is that less than 5% of the Studio Actors Guild (SAG) works. These are people who have had training and have made some kind of commitment to the profession. If they only have a 1 in 20 shot at even a commercial or walk-on part, what makes some of your friends think they could do as well as someone starring in a movie or TV series?

When it comes to investment advisors, the same thing is true—a lot of people think they can do it. Giving investment advice and making investment decisions looks easy. In fact, a number of books and periodicals will tell you so. And, even if you believe this, input from a hopefully objective, or at least unemotional source, is invaluable.

When the stock market (or whatever market) falls and the do-it-yourselfers panic, they have no one to turn to. Do you think they are going to wait for the next monthly issue of *Money Magazine* or *Kiplinger?* Of course not. These people want action and they want it now. Their decision will largely be driven by short-term panic instead of relying on a long-term investment strategy. The short-term panic is always based on the same thought: Things are going to get worse, probably much worse, before it gets better. Downturns in the market should be viewed as a buying opportunity, not a time for panic selling.

At any point in time, I can give you a number of reasons why you should not invest in stocks, bonds or real estate. When things look bad I can show why things are probably going to get worse. When the market is flat, I can point to things that look like they can cause havoc for the market in the near future. And when the market is doing well, I can rattle off a host of reasons why investors are being "fooled" and that the end is near. Even though I and others can make convincing arguments as to why investing in the market at any time is a bad idea, this does not mean that what we say will come true. The reality is that the stock market has had an upward bias for well over a 100 years. You cannot say this about any other investment except "cash equivalents" that have clearly been a poor hedge against inflation.

STAY THE COURSE

Most of the time, when investors are frightened about their portfolio, the best thing to do is either make no changes or load up on the depressed security(s); this, of course, assumes that the losses are in something that is fundamentally good (e.g., an aggressive growth fund an S & P 500 index fund, a high-yield bond subaccount, an international fund or individual stocks that dominate their respective industry group) as opposed to something that was too chancy or begin with (e.g., penny stocks, individual growth stocks whose future was based on certain assumptions, almost all limited partnerships).

As simple or basic as it might sound, a good advisor who convinces you to stay in for the long haul is worth his or her weight in gold. Any kind of commissions or fees that he might have generated from you in the past or in the future can be small potatoes in comparison to the loss you would have suffered due to an emotional reaction. Think about all of the people who had no one to turn to on October 19th, 1987, when the stock market dropped well over 20% in one day, not to mention the beating it took during the couple of weeks leading up to October 19th. A number of these people exiting the market headed straight for bank CDs, money market funds, and short-term government securities, swearing that they would never go into stocks again—only to go back into stocks after the Dow had climbed another one or two thousand points. At least these people will do well over the long haul. Those that bailed into cash equivalents and stayed there may still be showing a loss today.

It is hard to measure the value or a dollar figure as to the worth of some simple advice given at a time when you and others around you are panicking. So far we have two good reasons to use an advisor: someone who can sort through all of the hype and someone who can be objective during chaotic times.

New Ideas

Another reason to consider an advisor is that you may be exposed to ideas you had never thought of before. The ideas or advice may be related to investments, income taxes, or estate planning. Just keeping an investor from buying things that are fundamentally bad is worth a lot of money (e.g., futures contracts, managed commodity accounts, many types of option trading, penny stocks, stocks selling at ridiculous price/earnings ratios in relation to their peers, leveraged real estate deals, oil and gas programs, research and development projects).

A Historical Perspective

Sometimes, just making a simple comparison or showing why certain things cannot appreciate as much as they did a decade ago is worth any fee or commission you might pay. Let us look at just two quick examples: our national debt and bond prices.

First, we are the largest debtor nation, but when compared to other nations, only Norway has a lower debt to gross domestic product (GDP). The ratio of our debt to our annual production is lower than any other member of the G-7 (the 7 major industrialized nations in the world), including Japan and Germany. The issue of debt is often cited by investors as to why they think the future looks bad for the economy as well as the stock and bond markets. Now, let us look at interest rates and bond prices compared to what happened in the 1980s.

The 1980s represented the best decade ever for U.S. bonds. No wonder: Interest rates went from 21.5% in 1981 to less than 7% by the end of the decade. When interest rates fall, bond prices rise. So, during the 1980s, interest rates fell about 14 points. It is now the 1990s and investors are wondering if bond returns will match, or at least be similar to, what they did in the 1980s. An advisor who understands what happened in the 1980s can point out to the prospective investor that it is literally impossible for bond prices to duplicate their 1980s returns. Why? Because interest rates are not going to fall below zero.

Whether the prime interest rate is at 7%, 8% or 9%, you cannot take it down another 13 or 14 points—it is just not possible. This does not mean that bonds should not be part of the portfolio; it does mean that the investor needs to be educated as to what the upside potential is compared to the downside potential. When prime is at 8%, it is not going to fall below zero (an eight point move). Yet, there is no guarantee that prime at 8% will not be 16% or 20% in a couple of years. After all, it was above 21% briefly in 1981 and there was nothing magical about 21%. In fact when it was at 21%, a lot of bright people thought it was going to 25%. What all of this means is that at 7 to 9%, bonds have some appreciation potential, but the possible gain is not nearly as great as the possible loss (prime heading upward several points). The risk-reward trade-off is not nearly as attractive as when the prime is at 10%, 11% or 12%.

WHAT'S A FAIR DEAL

Determining what's a fair fee or commission and what is excessive is not always clear cut. An investment that carries an 8% sales charge turns out to be fine if it ends up netting 10 to 20% for the year. An investment that includes a 3% commission is not looked at as favorably if its returns are low or minus for the year. Looking at performance and rationalizing or justifying a fee is not how you should determine if you got a "good deal." After all, the high commission asset may have lousy results the first year (perhaps because of the 8% drag) and then go up 45% the next year. An investment that has a 3% load may do well the first year and turn in below average results the same year something else is up 45%.

Determining what is a fair charge should be decided up-front. Assuming a fair fee is being charged, you should feel like you got your money's worth initially for one of the following reasons: (1) you were shown an investment that you had not thought of before and it fits in with your overall strategy; (2) you were given related investment advice that can help bring down the overall risk level of your portfolio without changing the return potential; (3) your are shown a way to reposition parts of your portfolio so that the overall risk level remains the same but the expected return is increased; (4) you were given tax or estate planning advice that could end up saving you or your heirs quite a bit of money; (5) the initial meetings with the advisor resulted in a comprehensive investment plan, one you would not have thought up on your own; or (6) the advisor agrees to provide you with ongoing monitoring of your portfolio plus advice along the way.

The paragraph above is prefaced on the investor being charged a fair fee. This means that if you are going into a limited partnership (which includes an 8 to 10% up-front commission plus means that you are in an investment that has little, most likely no, marketability) you should be paying less than the standard commission for any mutual fund purchases (3 to 4% being the standard) or individual security buys (1 to 2% being the standard for stocks and a 2 to 3% mark-up for long-term bonds). "Wrap fee" programs are a different story.

A wrap fee or managed account means that the investor is not charged a commission on any trades, including those mutual funds which normally have some sort of up-front charge. Instead, the investor is charged an annual management fee that is a percentage of the entire account. The fees are charged on a quarterly basis and are automatically deducted from the investor's money market account. If, for example, you are being charged 1% a year and your account at the end of the year has grown from $90,000 to $100,000 or shrunk from $110,000 to $100,000, your money market account will be debited $250 (one quarter of 1% in this example) at the very end of the year or the very beginning of the next year (to pay for the first quarter in the new year).

These management fees average .25 to .5% annually for accounts that are worth a couple of million dollars up to 2.5% for accounts that are worth less than $100,000. Although this is what they average, the actual fee you are charged can be a little higher or lower than what is described; it all depends upon the brokerage firm's policy and what latitude the broker has or is willing to give. However high or low the fee might be, you must still determine if you feel like it is fair. Obviously this is a highly subjective opinion, but one that must still be made if the relationship is to be long-term.

Who's Minding the Store

We have already talked about some of the ways in which a fee becomes a bargain or at least fair. Another way to help ensure that you are getting a fair shake is to make sure: (a) you get written reports or statements at least quarterly; (b) the broker or advisor returns your calls within a reasonable period of time; (c) you can meet with the broker on a regular basis if you feel it's necessary; and (d) if requested by you, there is some type of verbal or written review at least on an annual basis.

The review is one of the more important services you are looking for (and should demand) since you want to make sure that your investment goals will be later met. An underperforming portfolio can be altered to better the chances that financial objectives will be met. This does not mean that there needs to be changes made because of a bad quarter or even year, but it does mean that such underperformance needs to be noted and corrected if it continues for more than two to three years.

These periodic reviews will also help remind you of your risk level, what kinds of ups and downs your portfolio experienced over the past 3 or 12 months, how you are being impacted by taxes, and whether or not you need to save more or less money to reach your goals. These kinds of "reminders" may cause you to rightfully change your risk level, savings pattern, tax-advantaged investment mix or even lower or raise your projected expectations.

Summary

You now know more about investing than about 95% of the public. Armed with the information in this book, you can begin interviewing financial advisors and brokers. No institution is better than another, each has its own strengths and weaknesses. Instead, focus on the individual or team that will be overseeing your investment portfolio. Your portfolio will not be saved by the advisor's parent company.

There is a natural reluctance when it comes to investing. After all, this is not something we were taught about in school. A sense of terror, anxiety and uncertainty are natural whenever you are dealing with something you do not feel comfortable about. Nevertheless, investing is something you must get involved with in order to protect yourself as well as your loved ones. The human body can fix a number of mistakes caused by physicians or neglect; your portfolio may not make such a "natural" recovery.

Life cycle investing is exciting because it is ever-changing yet also stays the same in many respects. Historically good investments will continue to please the patient investor while fundamentally bad asset choices will always cause harm, despite some sporadic short-term surprises.

QUESTIONS & ANSWERS

▼

1. **What is the easiest way to categorize investments?**

   All investments fall into one of three categories: debt, equity or hybrid.

   When you invest in a debt instrument, you are lending your money to someone else. Buying a government bond means that you have lent the federal government some of your money; when you buy a municipal or corporate bond, you are lending the municipality or corporation your money. A certificate of deposit (CD) is evidence of a loan from you to a bank.

   When you invest in an equity instrument, you own part of something. Examples of equities include: common stocks, preferred stocks, real estate, metals, collectibles, mutual funds, variable annuity subaccounts and variable life insurance contracts that invest in common or preferred stocks.

   A hybrid is an investment that exhibits or possesses characteristics of both debt and equity instruments. The most common example of a hybrid is a balanced or income mutual fund that invests in both stocks and bonds. High-yield corporate bonds are sometimes categorized as hybrids, but such securities are really debt instruments.

2. **What is the difference between an investment's "yield," "return," "total return" and "real return"?**

   Stocks pay dividends quarterly and bonds pay interest semi-annually. By dividing the annual dividend or interest payments into the current value of the security, you can determine the investment's yield. As an example, if you own a stock that pays a 25¢ quarterly dividend ($1 per year) and its value is $20 a share, the stock has a yield of 5% ($1/$20).

   An investment's total return adds any dividend or interest paid during the calendar year to any change in underlying value (principal). As an example, if you bought a bond a year ago for $1,000 and that bond paid you interest over the past year that totaled $90 (a 9% yield) and that bond was now worth

$1,100 (the increase in value would most likely be due to falling interest rates), your total return would be 19% (9% in interest payments plus 10% appreciation of principal).

The term "return" is sometimes used synonymously with "yield" and "total return." More often than not, when you read that an investment had a "return of 13%," such a figure will include any interest or dividend payments plus any appreciation (or minus any loss of principal).

An investment's "real return" is not often quoted, but is perhaps the best measure of how you are really doing. Real return takes into account the following: (1) interest payments and/or dividends paid during the calendar year; (2) any positive or negative change in value (or price per share) of principal; (3) income taxes paid; and (4) the rate of inflation for the year. A dramatic example of this took place in 1981. At that time, money market funds had a yield that averaged about 14% for the year. Shares of money market funds remain at a constant $1 per share, so there is no appreciation or depreciation of principal. If you lived in California in 1981, the top marginal income tax bracket (state and federal combined) was 55.5%. Inflation for the year was 12%. The real return of this investment for 1981 was:

14%	(the interest payments for the year)
+ or - 00%	(no appreciation or loss of principal)
- 08%	(for income taxes)
- 12%	(for inflation)
- 6%	= the real return

It is difficult to imagine that a conservative investment such as a money market fund or bank CD could have a negative return. Nevertheless, this is what happened to a large number of investors in 1981. In fact, over the past 25 years, bank CDs have had more negative real returns than positive.

3. **How do you measure risk?**

There is no universal definition of risk since there are several types or kinds of risk (e.g., market risk, purchasing power risk, interest rate risk, currency risk, political risk, etc.). However, the most commonly used measurement of risk is standard deviation. Although it really measures the volatility or variance of returns, standard deviation is calculated by looking at an investment's average annual return over the past three years and the monthly variation of returns for the past 36 months. Unfortunately, the formula used in calculating standard deviation equally punishes an investment for extreme upward volatility (I have yet to meet someone who doesn't like such surprises) as well as downward price movements.

4. What does "risk-adjusted" return refer to?

Almost all sources that rank investments, particularly those publications that rate mutual funds, variable annuities, and variable life contracts, do so based on the particular investment's total return. Very little attention, if any, is given to the issue of risk. Few investors or advisors appear to be concerned about risk when things are going well. When there are losses, then risk becomes an issue.

You might be attracted to my track record if I told you that my portfolio has averaged a 200% return for each of the past three years. Such attraction would turn to hesitation (at the very least) if I then told you that my returns were based on betting a friend over the flip of a coin once each quarter.

Risk-adjusted returns look at how much risk was taken to obtain the results quoted. If an investment has a standard deviation of 9% and its average annual return over the past three years has been 12%, the investment has a good risk-adjusted return (meaning for every 1% of "risk," as measured by standard deviation, the investment has experienced 1.33% of return).

5. How should I invest my money?

Your portfolio, which includes all of your investments (i.e., your home, bank accounts, retirement plans, brokerage accounts, rare coin collection, etc.), should reflect your risk level, not someone else's notion of investing. Your risk level will most likely be influenced by the way you were raised, your own experiences in the different marketplaces, what you have read or heard, and the amount of time you have. All things being equal, the more time you have, the greater the percentage of your portfolio that should be in equities. A pure equity portfolio is certainly appropriate for an investor or couple who is age 60 or younger.

Although equities generally outperform debt instruments, short-term losses in equities such as common stocks can be substantially greater than similar period losses in debt instruments. Investors whose time horizon is only a few years should not have all of their money in equities unless their risk level can be described as "aggressive."

Stocks and bonds both experience a negative year about one out of every 12 years. For this reason, a balanced portfolio (roughly 50% in stocks and 50% in bonds) may be a proper mix for a somewhat conservative investor or an investor whose time horizon is only three to four years. If your time horizon is only two years or less, most, if not all, of your portfolio (excluding your personal residence) should be in short-term debt instruments such as bank CDs, money market accounts, and bonds that mature in two years or less. The reason why the portfolio should be so conservatively invested is that it may take more than a year or two to make up any losses from a correction or crash in stocks or real estate.

6. **What is the difference between short-, intermediate-, and long-term investing?**

Different people have different definitions as to what is short and what is long. In the bond market, traders and brokers refer to a bond with a remaining maturity of five years or less to be "short-term," bonds with a remaining maturity of six to ten years are "intermediate" and those debt instruments that have a remaining maturity of 11 years (over 16 years according to some financial writers) or more are said to be "long-term." Before making an investment, make sure you know how your advisor or broker defines short-term and long-term.

7. **A number of sources tell me that the stock market is too high; should I wait to invest?**

Probably not. I have been an investment advisor for over 15 years and not a month has gone by without a number of well-respected sources saying that a crash or correction will soon be coming. If you are worried about the daily, weekly, monthly, quarterly or annual ups and downs of the stock market, you should not invest in stocks—your peace of mind or lack of sleep is no substitute for any kind of stock market returns, no matter how good they may turn out to be.

8. **Are common stocks (or mutual funds, variable annuities or variable life accounts that invest in common stocks) a good investment?**

Historically, stocks have outperformed bonds, bank CDs, real estate, gold, diamonds, rare coins, and anything else you can think of. When you invest in common stocks, you own part of a business. The vast majority of businesses that have publicly traded stocks are quite profitable. And no matter how profitable they have become, they want to make an even greater profit next year. As a partial owner of such a company, you are able to participate in those profits. However, there are lots of examples each quarter and year where a company reports banner profits and yet its stock drops. It is for this and other reasons that stocks are best suited for the patient investor.

9. Should I own individual stocks and/or bonds or mutual funds?

Investors get a bigger kick out of owning an individual stock because they can identify more with a specific company than they can with a mutual fund that most likely owns stocks of 50 to 200 different companies. The return potential of individual stocks is only slightly better than a mutual fund that invests in similar securities. On a risk-adjusted basis, professionally managed equity portfolios such as mutual funds and variable annuities are a better way to go.

Bonds can be a very different story. Individual government bonds have greatly outperformed government bond funds for 15 years. The large difference is due to the overhead costs of running a mutual fund plus incorrect decisions by bond fund managers as to the direction of interest rates. Bond funds make sense if you are investing in high-yield securities or foreign bonds.

10. What are annuities?

There are two types of annuities: fixed-rate and variable. Fixed-rate annuities are similar to bank CDs. The investor locks in a guaranteed rate of return for a specific period. The specific period can range from one to ten years. Variable annuities are similar to mutual funds; the investor decides how his money is to be divided up among the different stock, bond, and money market portfolios.

All annuities share the following characteristics: (1) the investment grows and compounds tax deferred; (2) you only pay taxes on the growth or income portion and only when you make withdrawals; (3) you are not required to make withdrawals during your lifetime or the life of your spouse; (4) after the second spouse dies (assuming a married couple), distributions can be postponed for up to five more additional years; (5) the value of your annuity is not shown anywhere on your tax return; (6) the tax-deferred growth of your annuity is not used in calculating whether or not your social security benefits are taxable (unlike municipal bond interest); (7) the proceeds of your annuity pass free of probate; (8) you can take out part or all of your money at any time; and (9) the vast majority of annuities do not have a sales charge or commission (but most annuities have a back-end penalty that typically lasts from five to seven years).

11. Are annuities better than mutual funds?

Not necessarily; it depends upon your objective. If your goal is to have your portfolio grow for a number of years (ten year minimum) and then begin taking out income to live on, annuities can provide you with a larger income stream. If your goal is to pass on as large an estate as possible to your spouse, children or relatives, then mutual funds or individual stocks are a better way to go (annuities do not get a step-up in basis upon death).

Variable annuities include features that mutual funds do not (e.g., exchanges from one portfolio or one company to another are not taxable, most variable annuities have a guaranteed death benefit, etc.), but the operating expenses of the typical annuity are about 1% higher per year than a similar type of mutual fund. The performance of equity variable annuity portfolios is often greater than that of mutual funds, but debt portfolios (e.g., money market, government bonds, corporate bonds, high-yield bonds, and foreign bonds) of mutual funds are almost always better performers.

12. Why do I need to know how to use financial tables (such as the ones shown in the appendix)?

The four financial tables included in this book will show you if you are on target to reaching your goals. Whether you have a single lump-sum to invest, such as an inheritance, savings account or brokerage firm account, and/or you are able to save money on a regular basis (e.g., payroll deduction plans, retirement accounts, etc.), these tables will show what you will end up with at the end of any number of years. The tables will also show you how long your nest egg will last as well as the effects of inflation. It is important to have goals and a way to measure your progress in order to determine if changes need to be made. Such changes could include one or more of the following: (1) changing your risk level; (2) saving more or less each month or year; (3) retiring earlier or later than originally planned; or (4) accepting a higher or lower level of income in later years.

13. Why do I hear so many negative comments about the stock market?

The U.S. stock market has had an upward bias for well over a hundred years. An objective observer can make a better case for investing in stocks over the next 20 years than over the past 20 years. Financial writers and commentators will often talk negatively about the stock market because they think it is either too high or there has been a downturn, crash or correction and they think it is going to get worse. Despite the convincing nature of some of these "gurus," the reality is that no one knows what stocks will do over the next day, week, month, quarter or year.

People who watch television, listen to the radio, or read magazines or daily newspapers are not always conscious of the following points: (1) these sources of information are in the business of increasing their market share, not reporting the news; (2) good news does not sell—disasters, scandals and sex are the big sellers; (3) air time and periodicals must be filled and there would be little to write about (or little interest) concerning stocks if you kept telling people not to worry about short-term volatility and just keep patient; and (4) these commentators and writers know a lot less about the stock market than the people on the floor of the exchanges.

14. A large number of publications now regularly include their "favorite" mutual funds or investments. How do I choose from all of these lists?

These lists are a waste of time. These magazines and other periodicals must continually try to create excitement or some other reason to attract you. The track record of these lists and recommendations is ambiguous at best. In most cases, by the time a mutual fund appears as a recommendation, its days in the sun are either over or close to an end. For some bizarre reason, these publications think that an investment that has averaged some ridiculous figure like 20% a year or more will continue turning in such great results. The truth is that no one can turn in 20% or even 18% a year returns over a long period of time—not even Peter Lynch (who had one of the best intermediate-term records) or Sir John Templeton (who has the best long-term record in mutual funds).

15. What kind of returns should I expect from my portfolio?

Historically, high quality bonds end up averaging their coupon rate (the rate of interest the issuer pays twice a year). High-yield, or lower quality, bonds have done a little better than this. Over the past half-century, common stocks have averaged 12%. Over the past 15 years, common stocks have gone through extended periods when they have done significantly better than 12% annually. As a generality, you should avoid investments that have done a lot better than their peers over the past several years (such magic, luck and skill cannot last indefinitely).

16. Why are bank CDs and money market funds so popular, even when rates are low?

These investments, often referred to as "risk-free," are attractive for a number of reasons: (1) they are easy to understand; (2) it would be almost impossible to lose any principal; (3) they have a known rate of return; (4) few investors look at their after-tax returns; and (5) even fewer investors calculate their after-tax and after-inflation rate of return.

17. Should I look for an advisor or broker or invest on my own?

Seek out a qualified advisor. Few investors have the time, expertise or experience to make proper investment decisions. This kind of knowledge and breadth cannot be learned by simply reading books and attending seminars. Most importantly, a qualified advisor or broker can provide the objectivity that becomes criticial when the markets experience extreme volatility. Every business is a business.

18. What kinds of investments should I avoid?

Well over 90% of all limited partnerships are bad. The vast majority of people who buy options or deal in commodities lose money. Penny stocks are also a bad idea. People buy cheap stocks because they think about what kind of profit can be made when a stock goes from $1 a share to $5 a share. For some reason they do not seem to think about the kind of loss they would experience if the stock went from $1 a share down to 20¢ a share. Penny stocks (defined as stocks that sell for less than $5 a share) are considered so risky that most brokerage firms forbid their brokers from soliciting trades in such securities.

19. Are there any conservative investments I should avoid?

That depends on your time horizon. U.S. Treasury bills, bank CDs and money market accounts are a great place to park your money while you are deciding where to invest, but these debt instruments should not be considered investments if your time horizon is more than just a couple of years. The after-tax and after-inflation rate (the real return) of these investments is almost always less than 1% a year; the real return has actually been negative more often than not if you go back about five years or more when inflation was higher.

20. I want to stay very conservative. How can I get a yield better than CDs or money market accounts?

Although overlooked by most investors and a number of advisors and brokers, short-term bond funds may be just the ticket. These funds have yields that are about 1 to 2% higher than short-term CDs and money market accounts. A number of these funds also have free check-writing privileges. The volatility is minimal because the typical security in these portfolios is one to two years.

21. What do you think about high-yield (junk) bond funds?

They represent my favorite bond fund category. Their current yield is higher than government, municipal or high-quality corporate bond funds. High-yield bonds are less sensitive to interest rate changes. This reduced volatility is a real positive when interest rates are going up or are expected to go up. The lower volatility is a negative when interest rates are falling or are expected to fall. If rates remain level, high-yield bonds are again the winner. The only time you do not want to own high-yield bonds is when there is a severe recession and people temporarily lose confidence in the economy.

There is a big difference between "high-yield" and "junk" bonds. Junk bonds are much riskier than high-yield bonds, even though such terms are often used (incorrectly) interchangeably. Junk bonds can experience returns of well over 20% in a year right after a recession or market panic. High-yield bond funds are typically heavily weighted with bonds that are rated BB and B (just a notch or two below what is known as "investment grade" or "bank quality"). Some of the bonds in these portfolios may be what are known as fallen angels—bonds issued by corporations that were once investment grade but have at least temporarily fallen on hard times (e.g., Ford Motor Co. and Chrysler in the early 1980s, Occidental Petroleum in the mid-1990s). Junk bond funds normally are largely comprised of bonds that are either not rated (shown as "NR"), or rated CCC, CC, or C.

22. What period of time should I use to evaluate an investment's performance?

Ideally, a 15- or 20-year period should be used for a couple of reasons. First, the past several years have been particularly good for stocks and bad for real estate. Second, the 1980s represented the best decade ever for bonds—such returns cannot be repeated in the 1990s (it would be impossible for the prime interest rate to fall 14 points since the prime rate is well under 10%). Third, a longer time frame means that the investment(s) you are looking at have experienced some very good and bad periods.

23. My broker recommends market timing. What do you think?

Don't waste your time. Numerous neutral studies, domestic and international, clearly prove that trying to time the market is a waste of time. If someone could accurately determine when to buy and sell stocks, he or she would not need your money. If an institution such as Wells Fargo Bank, Merrill Lynch or Prudential Life Insurance could "predict" the market, they would not have any need or desire to have branch offices, employees or even retail customers. Assume for a moment that there was a timing service that was correct two-thirds of the time. If such a service existed, a large institution such as American Express or Dean Witter would pay tens of millions of dollars a year for such accuracy. None of these institutions believe in market timing and the best and even average mutual fund managers do not believe that you can predict when to buy and when to sell on any kind of consistent basis.

Your broker is recommending market timing to you for one of three reasons: (1) to get your account (or maintain your account) by providing you with a false sense of security; (2) the broker or advisor is simply ignorant; or (3) the advisor is trying to make more money off of your account. Market timing services typically charge about 2% a year; about half of that annual fee goes to the broker or advisor who signs up the sucker. If market timing worked, I would put my own clients in it and we would all get rich.

24. I've read some pretty amazing claims about investment newsletters. What do you think?

Pass. These writers offer an expensive means of finding out just some of the information you could get by reading *The Wall Street Journal* or *Barron's*. These newsletters are not regulated like stockbrokers or other financial advisors; consequently, they make false or misleading claims. People who subscribe to these newsletters may think that they are getting something that borders on inside information or that the writer has some kind of mystic powers, but the opposite is more likely to be true. If these writers had such good predictive abilities, I assure you they would be making millions of dollars a year working for a major financial institution.

25. Are foreign stocks and foreign bonds risky?

Not unless you are talking about the "emerging markets" (securities issued by third world countries). Most of the largest corporations are foreign. Foreign stock and bond markets outperform their U.S. counterparts more often than not. Currency fluctuations have benefited U.S. investors who own foreign securities more often than not. It is true that U.S. stocks have done better than most foreign country stocks, but there are still a number of countries that outperform the U.S. each year.

26. How can I reduce my portfolio's risk?

One of the easiest ways to reduce portfolio risk is to include foreign stocks and bonds. A global portfolio, which means a portfolio comprised of U.S. and foreign securities, is often less risky than one comprised only of domestic stocks and/or bonds. Another way to reduce risk is to add some new investment categories to your portfolio. These risk-reducing categories include: (1) real estate investment trusts (REITs); (2) short-term bonds; (3) high-yield bonds; (4) utility stocks; (5) natural resource funds; and (6) equity-income funds.

27. Do IRAs make much of a difference?

Yes. Recently passed legislation now allows non-working spouses to have up to $2,000 a year contributed to their own IRA. This means that a married couple can put away up to $4,000 in a tax-deferred vehicle. Most workers can deduct part or all of such contributions. What makes these accounts so great is the compounding effect and time.

As an example, assume a married couple, age 25, invests $4,000 a year for just five years. Further assume that there is no growth in the IRA accounts during those five years (something highly unlikely). If the accounts were invested in common stocks or equity mutual funds, a projected growth rate of 12% a year would be a fair assumption since that is what the S & P 500 has averaged over the past 50 years. If this couple were to retire at age 66, their IRA accounts alone would grow to $1.28 million (note: at a 12% growth rate, a portfolio doubles every six years and this couple has six doubling periods, from age 30 to 66, until retirement).

This is a pretty amazing figure, particularly in light of the following points: (1) investments into an IRA were only made for a total of five years—a cumulative investment of $20,000; (2) no additional contributions were made; (3) depending upon their level of income and participation in other retirement plans, part or all of the $20,000 was a tax deduction; and (4) the assumed or projected growth rate may actually end up being higher if the money was invested in foreign stocks, small company stocks or the couple was lucky and picked an equity mutual fund that ended up beating the S & P 500.

28. How do you feel about stock tips?

Throughout my career, I have been given a number of stock tips from brokers I respect as well as from friends and clients. Almost all of these tips have turned out to be bad; fortunately, I rarely acted on what were considered "sure things." In fact, the more exciting the story, the worse the stock ended up performing. A far better approach is to buy market leaders whose stocks have recently been in a slump.

29. Is it true that the stock market is riskier now than it was in the past?

No. Stock market volatility has decreased over the past 20 to 25 years and it is significantly lower than it was from 1926 to 1936. The market may appear more volatile because the daily point moves in the Dow are often greater now than they were a few years ago or a few decades ago. But keep in mind that the Dow is at a much higher level now than it was in the past. In the very early 1980s and late 1970s when the Dow was at about 1,000, a 50 point move represented a 5% change. Today, a 50 point move represents less than a 1% change.

30. Is beta a good way to measure risk?

Beta is a measurement of one type of risk. The S & P 500 maintains a constant beta of 1.00. No matter how high or low stocks climb or fall, the S & P 500's beta is 1.00; this is the benchmark. A stock or stock portfolio with a beta of less than 1.00 is considered by some to be less risky than the overall market. Conversely, a beta above 1.00 is thought to represent greater risk (e.g., a stock with a beta of 1.1 is considered to be 10% riskier than the stock market as a whole).

Beta is only applicable to U.S. stocks and only measures market-related risk. More importantly, a stock's beta can quickly change and therefore have little meaning to the analytical investor. Beta is a far better yardstick when comparing one domestic stock portfolio against another (e.g., the XYZ Growth Fund vs. the ABC Super Growth Fund).

You may occasionally see a beta figure for a bond fund or foreign equity fund; such a figure, no matter how high or low, is virtually worthless. As an example, gold mining stocks, most of which are foreign, often have low beta figures but this category of equities has well over twice the volatility (as measured by standard deviation) of aggressive growth or small cap growth funds.

31. Why do bonds and bond funds fall in value when interest rates go up?

Individual bonds and bond funds often drop in value when rates go up or if there is a belief that rates will be going up. Such beliefs may be short-term or may turn into reality. Between 1976 and 1981, when interest rates skyrocketed, the value of a 20- or 30-year U.S. government bond fell by 50%. From 1981 to the end of the 1980s, government bonds and government bond funds experienced some terrific appreciation because interest rates plummeted.

Bonds, and portfolios that invest in bonds, fall when rates increase because the income stream now becomes less competitive or desireable. As an example, suppose you bought a 20-year U.S. government bond a year ago and locked into a yield of 7%. At the time, 7% for each of 20 years, guaranteed by the U.S. government, was a fair deal. If, a year later, new 20-year government bonds are now being offered for sale with a yield of 8%, your 7% no longer looks attractive. No one in their right mind would pay you $1,000 (the original purchase price and eventual redemption price of the bond) in order to get $70 a year (7%) when they could pay $1,000 and get $80 a year (and eventually redeem the bond for $1,000). However, if you offered to sell your $1,000 bond for $920, the new owner would be tempted to buy your bond (instead of a new one that paid 8% a year) for two reasons: (1) their yield would be 7.5% ($70/$920 = 7.6%); and (2) the bond will mature for $70 more than the price paid by the new owner ($1,000 redemption value vs. a $920 purchase price).

32. Should I still worry about inflation?

Absolutely. The cumulative effects of inflation are still quite dangerous. Even the annual rates of inflation are probably much higher than what the U.S. government reports. Keep in mind it is in the government's best interest to downplay inflation numbers—a number of private and public sector salaries are affected by the rate of inflation. Inflation is often called the "cruelest tax of all" since it is not a tax you really see. From what I have observed, the true rate of inflation, at least for the middle, upper-middle, and upper classes is about twice the rate reported by the government.

33. Can I, or the mutual fund or variable annuity I invest in, beat the market?

There is a greater likelihood that you or a professionally managed portfolio will beat the market over a period of five years or less than there is that you or someone else will outperform the S & P 500 or the Dow over the next six to twenty years. Unfortunately, the chances of you, or anyone else, outperforming either market index over the next one to five years is about one in five or one in six. This does not mean that you should not try. Look at things in perspective: (1) the chances of you being born or becoming a U.S. citizen were certainly less than one in ten; (2) the odds of making an income of over $100,000 a year are less than one in twenty; and (3) you can think of a lot of other things that worked out well, despite the odds.

34. Why do you dislike most types of debt instruments?

I have an aversion for such investments in general because I believe that they are deceptive. These investments do not usually fare well once the effects of inflation and income taxes are factored in. Yet, things such as bank CDs, U.S. Treasury bills (T-bills), and money market accounts are considered to be "risk-free." The definition of risk-free needs to be expanded so that the typical investor starts to factor in other forms of risk when investing—risks such as purchasing power risk and interest rate risk.

Conceptually I dislike debt instruments because investors end up dealing with a "middle man" who can take advantage or at least highly profit from the transaction. As an example, when you buy a bank CD that yields say 6%, the bank turns around and lends your money out to someone buying a house for 8 or 9%, or to someone financing a car for perhaps 9 to 11%. Similarly, when you buy a General Motors corporate bond, you are lending your money to GM. General Motors then takes your money and increases its advertising, research, production, sales or whatever, and more often than not, makes a much higher profit on your money than what they are paying you in interest. If GM, IBM or whatever successful corporation you want to choose did not make at least a moderate profit off of your money, they would not be borrowing it.

35. What is a correlation coefficient?

First, no investment on its own has a correlation coefficient. A correlation coefficient is determined by looking at the performance of one investment against one or more other investments. Two or more investments that are highly (postively) correlated will generally move up or down in value to about the same degree at about the same time. Two or more investments whose prices tend to move in opposite directions are said to be negatively correlated. If there is no relationship between the price movement of two or more investments, then such investments are randomly correlated.

Having some appreciation and knowledge about correlation coefficients is good for any investor concerned with risk. It is fine and dandy when all of your investments appreciate at the same time, but your opinion of positive correlation will soon change if such investments were to all fall in price at or about the same time. Ideally, most investors should have a portfolio that, at a minimum, includes investments that are randomly correlated. Unfortunately, only a few investment categories are negatively correlated.

36. What is modern portfolio theory and should I use it?

The goal of modern portfolio theory is to get the investor the best risk-adjusted returns, regardless of the risk level. The first step is to determine your risk level. Next, historical data is gathered for different investment categories. The historical data needed is: (a) average annual return figures for at least the past ten years (15 or more years is preferable); (b) standard deviation (how volatile has the investment been over the past 36 months); and (c) how one investment category's returns, whether positive or negative or neutral, correlate to other investment categories.

You should not use modern portfolio theory, but you should utilize the services of an advisor or broker who is well-versed about this topic. Although modern portfolio theory (MPT) may well be the most scientific or accurate of predicting future returns and risk level, it is by no means foolproof and it does have its limitations and critics. An investment counselor who properly understands the pros and cons of MPT can recommend a portfolio mix to you that can provide better returns than MPT software programs. These software programs are obviously quite biased in favor of MPT and do not adequately protect or warn its users as to the shortcomings of the program or of MPT.

37. What is an efficient frontier?

The efficient frontier looks at historical data. A series of efficient portfolios are plotted on a computer or on graph paper. What makes a portfolio "efficient" is its risk-reward characteristics. If a portfolio has X amount of risk and X amount (or more) of return potential, it may well be considered efficient. Several portfolios are plotted because each level of risk represents a different portfolio mix that is more or less conservative or risky than the one above or below it. The line that connects all of these portfolios is called the efficient frontier. The number of points (or portfolios) used to construct the efficient frontier may be a handful or several dozen, it all depends upon what the user is trying to show.

38. Is it important for my portfolio to be on the efficient frontier?

Being on the efficient frontier implies maximum efficiency (the greatest return for that level of risk), but what actually happens may turn out to be different—a "non" efficient portfolio may end up outperforming the efficient one with the same amount of risk or even less. Just because portfolio X had a certain level of risk over the past three years does not mean that it will have the exact same level of risk over the next one, two, three or more years. The same point can be made about historical returns. When you read that "past results are no guarantee of future returns" you should believe it—it is a warning that is often very correct. Finally, correlation coefficients can change over time. As an example, historically, there has not been a strong relationship or correlation between interest rates and the stock market. Yet, over the past several years this relationship has been quite strong.

39. **If modern portfolio theory (MPT) has so many shortcomings, why should I (or some advisor) bother with it?**

For several reasons. First, there is no "system" or "theory" that can guarantee results or even make strong assurances. Second, MPT has been successfully used for several decades and has proved itself—when properly understood and implemented. Third, and most importantly, the chances of your portfolio obtaining its projected returns (at an acceptable risk level) are much more likely using MPT than other formulas or plans for the following reasons: (1) other approaches most likely do not look at correlation coefficients (which tend to be relatively consistent over time); (2) since MPT advocates using several investment categories, the investor will most likely learn, in hindsight, that some investments did better than expected, some worse, and some about average; and (3) the process makes intuitive sense.

DOLLARS & SENSE SUMMARY

▼

1. One of the quickest ways to explain asset allocation to my new clients is to tell them that their portfolio is like a garden, filled with different kinds of vegetables and fruits. My job is to make sure part of their garden is always in bloom. No investment should be expected to be in bloom the entire year. Asset allocation greatly increases the likelihood that parts of the portfolio will be in bloom throughout the year.

2. There has been an upward bias in the stock market for well over 100 years. If George Washington had $1 and had invested that $1 in U.S. stocks at the beginning of his presidency, today it would be worth over $15.4 billion, assuming stocks averaged the same 12% rate of return they have for the past half-century. If he had averaged 16.5%, which is what small company stocks have averaged over the past 50 years, his original $1 would have been worth $53 trillion by the end of 1996. A $53 trillion portfolio would pay off the national debt several times over.

3. To show you the absurdity of claiming to be able to time the market, let us go back 50 years to the beginning of 1946. Assume that 50 years ago you were able to correctly predict what the best performing asset category was going to be for every single month (12 months × 50 = 600 possible market moves). Finally, assume that your choices for investment were: small stocks, the S & P 500, long-term corporate bonds, long-term U.S. government bonds, intermediate-term government bonds and U.S. T-bills that had a remaining maturity of just one month.

   Starting with $1 (and never adding to this $1), by successfully switching into what would be that month's best peforming asset category (using one of the six categories described in the paragraph above), your $1 would have been worth $4,034 trillion or $4 quadrillion (70.05% annualized).

4. To get a better, hands-on feeling of why news stories and articles can be misleading as well as confusing, you need only to look at *The Wall Street Journal* or *Investor's Daily* for a week, any week. On any given day you will

find one or more positive articles or paragraphs and one or more negative viewpoints about the same company or stock.

5. Years ago I used to have a computer on my desk that was connected to a service that gave me stock quotes and market activity by the second. My performance and the performance of my clients suffered during this period because I made the critical mistake of being caught up in the moment. What I sometimes thought were positive or negative "trends" often turned out to be the exact oppositve an hour or day later.

6. I use these financial tables in my investment advisory practice on an almost daily basis. These tables are much easier, and often quicker, than relying on a software program. The beauty of these tables is that they never go out of date—interest rates and returns will change over time, but not these tables. The tables, shown in detail in the appendix, normally cost about $15 if you buy a complete book of them. The tables provided in the appendix, although only 20 pages in length, should satisfy 99% of all investors' and financial planners' needs.

7. All of the bar charts presented in this chapter (except two) are from neutral sources. The "Residential Real Estate" and "Art and Collectibles" are considered to be tainted because their respective sources represent entities that are considered self-serving.

8. If all this talk about risk tests and standard deviation just seem like too much, look at a one-page chart I use (see p.105). This chart presents risk and return in a real world context.

9. For more information about determining your risk level, consider contacting one or more of the following mutual fund companies. These companies provide a wide assortment of risk tests, brochures, worksheets and software (that is either free or sold for a nominal charge).

T. Rowe Price (800) 638-5660

Oppenheimer (800) 525-7048

Putnam (800) 345-2228

Franklin / Templeton (800) 342-5236

10. Despite its limitations, beta remains the best measurement of U.S. stock market-related risk. Still, this kind of risk can be small in comparison to other

things that can positively or negatively affect the entire market or select securities.

11. A rough guide to determining a bond's volatility is to simply remember that when interest rates move a full point, a long-term bond can be expected to drop or appreciate about 11%; an intermediate-term bond will rise or fall about half that amount (approximately 6%). This rule-of-thumb is not as accurate as the table in Chapter 9 (which is based on duration), but it is much easier to remember.

12. Whenever you buy an individual bond, unit trust (which is a fixed portfolio of securities), bond fund or any other kind of bond portfolio, always ask your broker what the yield-to-call and yield-to-maturity are. Investors often buy bonds based on an appealing yield, only to later find out (after it is too late), that the true yield (once the bond is called away) is much less than they bargained for.

13. If check-writing privileges are important to you, find out if the money market account or fund you are thinking about buying into charges on a per check basis (only a few funds have such a charge) or has a minimum amount for each check written (typically $100 to $250). These types of restrictions are quite common; the management company wants to keep expenses to a minimum in order to provide you, one of its shareholders, with the highest possible yield.

14. Money market yields are just like bank CD yields; they can vary all over the board. Phone several mutual funds, including Alger, Fidelity Spartan and Vanguard, and ask them what the highest yielding money market fund that they have is; find out if such a fund is "temporarily" waiving part or all of its current expenses. If it is, consider using another money market fund that is not using such a gimmick to attract new money.

15. For liquidity purposes, consider a short-term bond fund, one whose bonds have an average maturity of 1 to 2 years or less. These kinds of funds have very low volatility, often allow you to write checks against your account (for free), and may have a yield advantage of .5 to 1% over a traditional money market fund (and perhaps up to a 2 or 3% advantage over a bank's money market account).

16. Understanding the relationship between two or more investments is only important if you want to reduce your portfolio's risk level. Sometimes, maintaining your current risk exposure can result in increased returns by properly utilizing investments whose correlation is random or negative.

17. You may feel that some of the rates of return, loss potential or recovery periods are a little high or a little low. There is nothing wrong with making up your own risk-reward table as long as you use data covering at least the last 15 years. Whether you use my table or come up with your own, this is the best way I have ever seen to quickly (and I believe accurately) determine someone's risk level.

18. As you read through the suggested portfolios in the coming chapters, keep in mind that there is no single "best" portfolio for a particular age or risk level, nor are there any "magic" categories or specific investments that must be included. A tremendous number of factors can influence how your portfolio should be structured, including things that only you are familiar with such as: (a) the health of you and/or your spouse; (b) the chances of you and/or your spouse getting a promoion; (c) the health of loved ones who might leave you an inheritance or who may need financial help from you; and (d) the likelihood of a divorce or separation.

19. Once you become informed as to how an investment correlates with other investments, as well as with the growth and loss potential, making a decision becomes much easier. Bottom line: If you don't feel you understand it, stay away from it.

20. Stay away from anything if it sounds just too tempting. The worst investments I have ever seen, and I've seen most of them (and even invested in a couple myself), were the ones that appeal to one's sense of greed. The second worst investments I've encountered were those that I was told to recommend to my clients for just "5 to 15%" of their holdings in order to provide "valuable diversification." Most of these "diversifiers" turned out to diversify my clients' portfolio returns lower!

21. If you just stay away from the bad stuff (generally anything not referred to in this book in a positive or neutral manner), you will be way ahead of your friends, neighbors, and co-workers. Some of the smartest people in the world have gone into some very dumb investments. If you can avoid just the bad ones, you are about 80% on your way to being a successful investor.

MONEY TALKS SUMMARY

▼

1. The word "guarantee" is one that is used commonly. When it comes to investing, the word is often misused. There are only a handful of investments that the word "guarantee" can be used with: government securities (interest payments are guaranteed, but principal is only guaranteed if the security is held until its maturity date), fixed-rate annuities (principal is guaranteed at all times and so is the locked-in rate of return), bank CD interest rates (principal is not guaranteed because the potential penalty can eat into principal) and certain forms of life insurance (the death benefit and/or the growth rate of any cash value). The word "guarantee" cannot be used with municipal bonds, corporate bonds, common stocks, mutual funds, mortgages, real estate or collectibles.

2. When someone mentions "the stock market" to you, there is a strong likelihood that they are referring to the Dow Jones Industrial Average (also known as "the Dow"). The Dow is comprised of just 30 stocks; companies are not frequently added or taken off of this list. Most stock market performance charts use figures from the Standard & Poor's 500 (also known as the S & P 500). As you might suspect, this indice is much more representative of all U.S. stocks since it is comprised of 500 different issues and the list is revised on a more frequent basis. Most equity money managers are measured by their bosses against the S & P 500 and not the Dow.

3. There can be a huge difference between compound interest and simple interest. Compound interest means that interest is being earned on interest as well as principal. Simple interest means that only the principal is earning interest, not any previous interest payments or credits. As an example, if you had $100 earning 12% a year and such interest was compounding, the $100 would grow to $200 at the end of 6 years ($400 at the end of 12 years). If the same $100 were earning 12% simple interest, it would take a little over 8 years for $100 to grow to $200 (and a total of 25 years to get to $400).

4. One's "holding period" refers to how long you plan on keeping the investment before selling it. The financial advisor knows that you may have to sell part or all of your portfolio if an emergency arises, but since such occurences are rare, any anticipated holding period does not, and should not, take into account the possibility of a financial emergency (the issues of marketability and liquidity cover emergencies). Usually, expected holding periods coincide with a specfic event (i.e., retirement, a child entering college, a target date to pay off a loan or a mortgage) or round number (e.g., "If this investment acts like it's supposed to, I plan on keeping it for at least 10 years").

5. Although not frequently cited, the proper definition of "standard deviation" is variance or volatility of return from the investment's average annual rate of return. Most financial writers believe that standard deviation is synonymous with risk and although this may be true most of the time, it is not always the case. As an example, several years ago, a number of foreign equity mutual funds had some fantastic returns while experiencing few negative months. These funds were dubbed "high risk" because they had a large standard deviation — not from the negative months, which were modest in size and degree, but from some positive months' returns that were nothing short of fantastic.

6. A statistic you may find more useful than beta is alpha. The difference between beta and alpha is that alpha can be used for a wider range of investments, not just domestic stocks. Alpha does not rely on a single benchmark figure such as the S & P 500 (which always has a beta of 1.00), but instead looks at an investment's historical return and risk level.

7. The use of duration has become more widespread in recent years, but the term is still not widely used by the investing public. What turns people off to the concept of duration is that the formula for duration is based on the time value of money (i.e., a dollar today is worth more than a dollar tomorrow or next week). Duration discounts the future cash flows (the semi-annual interest payments of bonds) plus the eventual redemption price (face value) of a debt instrument and shows such cumulative discounts as a present value.

    Although you will probably never learn how to compute a bond's duration (and there is little reason why you should), simply understanding that whatever the figure might be, say someone tells you bond X has a duration of seven years, you know that "7" (or whatever the number is) represents the percentage of change the debt instrument will have if interest rates change by a full percentage point (or half that number if rates change by half a point).

8. A money market fund is virtually the same as a money market account you might have at a bank. Such accounts at banks may be insured by FDIC, but such insurance is of little importance or value. Since all money market funds and accounts, by definition and regulation, can only include short-term debt instruments whose ratings fall within the two highest categories, the odds of you losing any money (or any interest you were due) are several thousand to one.

9. Although the words "international" and "foreign" are interchangeable, the word "global" is not. A global portfolio includes U.S. securities, whereas a foreign (or international) fund does not. A global portfolio will usually have less risk than a foreign portfolio because the U.S. stock market is more stable than most, if not all, other markets around the world. Being the biggest and the most efficient has its advantages.

10. Correlation coefficients, the relationship between the price movement of two or more investments, are normally calculated based on an extensive period of time. Investors, or more likely advisors, are concerned with these relationships as a means of guiding the construction of a portfolio that will hopefully have either less risk or better risk-adjusted returns. Surprisingly, no one has yet isolated the negative periods of an investment (determining such months or quarters would be easy to do) and then calculated a correlation coefficient with another investment(s) over just such negative periods. This is surprising since there is little concern, or need for concern, about the risk level of a portfolio when things are going well.

11. The efficient frontier is determined by looking at historical information (past returns, standard deviation and correlation coefficients). The efficiency of such frontiers becomes highly questionable if the data used includes periods of time when performance figures of "risk-free" investments (e.g., money market funds, bank CDs, T-bills, etc.) have been particularly high (such as the early 1980s). Like other formulas or measurements, calculating an efficient frontier is a useful tool if it is properly understood and the user has an historical perspective and common sense.

12. One of the benefits of looking at risk and return (or simply risk-adjusted returns) is that you will now have an important shield to guard against brokers and advisors who try to steer you toward an investment that is not proper for your particular set of circumstances. This is of particular concern when you are investing during a very positive period of time for common stocks.

13. The words "liquidity" and "marketability" are often considered to be synonymous, but there is a big difference. An investment or asset is considered to be liquid if the investor can sell it for the same price he paid for it (or a price very close to the original purchase price). An investment is considered to be marketable if it can be easily bought and sold, regardless of price. Most common stocks you are familiar with are quite marketable—they can easily be sold by a brokerage firm on a major stock exchange. However, the price you receive for your shares of IBM or GM may be much less (or more) than what you paid for the shares last month or a decade ago. Money market funds are extremely liquid because their price per share remains at a constant one dollar. Money market funds have little marketability because the only one that will buy back your shares (plus the additional shares that represent interest) is the entity that issued the shares to begin with.

14. The term "financial tables" can end up referring to any set of numbers or figures. The four financial tables used in this book show you how to make some important but simple multiplication or division calculations. Your bookstore or local library should carry a number of books devoted solely to financial tables; a number of these books are designed to be used by people in specific areas (e.g., insurance, financial planning, banking, real estate, etc.).

RESOURCES

▼

Bank CDs

American Bankers Association
1120 Connecticut Ave., NW
Washington, DC 20036
(202) 663-5000

Bauer Financial Reports
P.O. Drawer 145510
Coral Gables, FL 33114-5510
(305) 441-2062

Money Market Funds

Alger Shareholder Services
30 Montgomery St., 13th Floor
Jersey City, NJ 07302
(800) 992-3863

Franklin Distributors
777 Mariners Island Blvd.
San Mateo, CA 94404
(800) 342-5236

U.S. Government Securities

Department of the Treasury
c/o Bureau of Public Debt
Information Center
13th and C sts., SW
Washington, DC 20228
(800) 287-4088

Federal Reserve Bank of Richmond
P.O. Box 27622
Richmond, VA 23261

Series EE and Series HH Bonds

U.S. Savings Bonds
Washington, DC 20226
(800) 872-6637

Federal Reserve Bank of Dallas
Public Affairs Department, Station K
Dallas, TX 75222
(214) 922-6000

Municipal Bonds

John Nuveen & Co., Inc.
333 W. Wacker Dr.
Chicago, IL 60606
(800) 351-4100

Van Kampen Merrit Investment
  Advisory
1 Parkview Rd.
Oakbrook Terrace, IL 60181
(800) 225-2222

GNMAs and FNMAs

GNMA
451 7th St. SW, Room 6100
Washington, DC 20410
(202) 708-0926

FNMA
Public Information Office
3900 Wisconsin Ave., NW
Washington, DC 20016
(202) 752-7000

Corporate Bonds

Neuberger & Berman Management
605 Third Ave., 2nd Floor
New York, NY 10158-0006
(800) 877-9700

Sanford C. Bernstein
767 Fifth Ave.
New York, NY 10153
(212) 756-4097

Annuities

All About Annuities and
The 100 Best Annuities You Can Buy
  both books by Gordon K. Williamson
  published by John Wiley Book
  Publishing
605 Third Ave., 10th Floor
New York, NY 10158
(212) 850-6000

Comparative Annuity Reports
P.O. Box 1268
Fair Oaks, CA 95628

A.M. Best Reports
Oldwick, NJ 08858
(908) 439-2200

Life Insurance

American Council of Life Insurance
1001 Pennsylvania Ave., NW
Washington, DC 20004-2599

National Insurance Consumer
  Organization
121 North Payne St.
Alexandria, VA 22314
(703) 549-8050

High-Yield Bonds

Kemper Financial Services
120 S. LaSalle St.
Chicago, IL 60603
(800) 621-1148

Lutheran Brotherhood Securities Corp.
625 4th Ave. South
Minneapolis, MN 55415
(800) 328-4552

Foreign Bonds

MFS Service Center
P.O. Box 2281
Boston, MA 02110
(800) 225-2606

Scudder, Stevens & Clark
175 Federal St.
Boston, MA 02110
(800) 225-2470

Residential Real Estate

Appraisal Institute
875 N. Michigan Ave., Suite 2400
Chicago, IL 60611-1980
(312) 335-4100

Commerce Clearing House
4025 West Peterson
Chicago, IL 60646
(312) 583-8500

Stocks

Merrill Lynch
c/o Marketing Communications
800 Scudder's Mill Rd.
Plainsboro, NJ 08540
(800) 637-7455

LPL Financial Services
5935 Cornerstone Court West
San Diego, CA 92121-3726
(619) 450-9240

Foreign Stocks

Capital Research & Management
333 S. Hope St.
Los Angeles, CA 90071
(800) 421-0180

Societe General Securities
50 Rockefeller Plaza, 3rd Floor
New York, NY 10020
(800) 334-2143

Convertible Securities

Value Line Convertible Survey
711 Third Ave., 4th Floor
New York, NY 10017
(800) 223-0818

Calamos Asset Management
2001 Spring Rd., Suite 750
Oak Brook, IL 60521
(800) 323-9943

REITs

NAREIT
1129 17th St., NW, Suite 705
Washington, DC 20036
(202) 785-8717

Variable Life Insurance

Morningstar
53 West Jackson Blvd., Suite 460
Chicago, IL 60604-3608
(312) 427-1985

Mutual Funds

Institute of Business & Finance
7911 Herschel Ave., Suite 201
La Jolla, CA 92037-4413
(800) 848-2029

▼

FINANCIAL TABLES

The next 20 pages are the financial tables referred to throughout Chapter 4. Each of these pages is identical in layout or format. What makes each page different is the rate of return (which ranges from "Rate 1%" to "Rate 20%").

Rate 1%

Year	Table 1 Compounding Factor for 1[1]	Table 2 Compounding Factor For 1 Per Annum[2]	Table 3 Sinking Fund Factor[3]	Table 4 Discount Factor[4]
1	1.01	1.00	1.00	.990
2	1.02	2.01	.498	.980
3	1.03	3.03	.330	.971
4	1.04	4.06	.246	.961
5	1.05	5.10	.196	.952
6	1.06	6.15	.163	.942
7	1.07	7.21	.139	.933
8	1.08	8.29	.121	.924
9	1.09	9.37	.107	.914
10	1.10	10.46	.096	.905
11	1.12	11.57	.087	.896
12	1.13	12.68	.079	.887
13	1.14	13.81	.072	.879
14	1.15	14.95	.067	.870

continues

Rate 1% (Continued)

Year	Table 1 Compounding Factor for 1[1]	Table 2 Compounding Factor For 1 Per Annum[2]	Table 3 Sinking Fund Factor[3]	Table 4 Discount Factor[4]
15	1.16	16.10	.062	.861
16	1.17	17.26	.058	.853
17	1.18	18.43	.054	.844
18	1.20	19.62	.051	.836
19	1.21	20.81	.048	.828
20	1.22	22.02	.045	.820
21	1.23	23.24	.043	.811
22	1.24	24.47	.041	.803
23	1.26	25.72	.039	.795
24	1.27	26.97	.037	.788
25	1.28	28.24	.035	.780

[1] What an initial amount becomes when growing at compound interest.

[2] Growth of equal year-end deposits all growing at compound interest.

[3] Level deposit required each year to reach 1 by a given year.

[4] How much 1 at a future date is worth today.

Rate 2%

Year	Table 1 Compounding Factor for 1[1]	Table 2 Compounding Factor For 1 Per Annum[2]	Table 3 Sinking Fund Factor[3]	Table 4 Discount Factor[4]
1	1.02	1.00	1.00	.980
2	1.04	2.02	.495	.961
3	1.06	3.06	.327	.942
4	1.08	4.12	.243	.924
5	1.10	5.20	.192	.906
6	1.13	6.31	.159	.888
7	1.15	7.43	.135	.871
8	1.17	8.58	.117	.854

Year	Table 1 Compounding Factor for 1[1]	Table 2 Compounding Factor For 1 Per Annum[2]	Table 3 Sinking Fund Factor[3]	Table 4 Discount Factor[4]
9	1.20	9.76	.103	.837
10	1.22	10.95	.091	.820
11	1.24	12.17	.082	.804
12	1.27	13.41	.075	.789
13	1.29	14.68	.068	.773
14	1.32	15.97	.063	.758
15	1.35	17.29	.058	.743
16	1.37	18.64	.054	.729
17	1.40	20.01	.050	.714
18	1.43	21.41	.047	.700
19	1.46	22.84	.044	.686
20	1.49	24.30	.041	.673
21	1.52	25.78	.039	.660
22	1.55	27.30	.037	.647
23	1.58	28.84	.035	.634
24	1.61	30.42	.033	.622
25	1.64	32.03	.031	.610

[1] What an initial amount becomes when growing at compound interest.

[2] Growth of equal year-end deposits all growing at compound interest.

[3] Level deposit required each year to reach 1 by a given year.

[4] How much 1 at a future date is worth today.

Rate 3%

Year	Table 1 Compounding Factor for 1[1]	Table 2 Compounding Factor For 1 Per Annum[2]	Table 3 Sinking Fund Factor[3]	Table 4 Discount Factor[4]
1	1.03	1.00	1.00	.971
2	1.06	2.03	.493	.943
3	1.09	3.09	.324	.915

continues

		Rate 3% (Continued)		
Year	Table 1 Compounding Factor for 1[1]	Table 2 Compounding Factor For 1 Per Annum[2]	Table 3 Sinking Fund Factor[3]	Table 4 Discount Factor[4]
4	1.13	4.18	.239	.889
5	1.16	5.31	.188	.863
6	1.19	6.47	.155	.838
7	1.23	7.66	.131	.813
8	1.27	8.89	.113	.789
9	1.31	10.16	.098	.766
10	1.34	11.46	.087	.744
11	1.38	12.81	.078	.722
12	1.43	14.19	.071	.701
13	1.47	15.62	.064	.681
14	1.51	17.09	.059	.661
15	1.56	18.60	.054	.642
16	1.61	20.16	.050	.623
17	1.65	21.76	.046	.605
18	1.70	23.41	.043	.587
19	1.75	25.12	.040	.570
20	1.81	26.87	.037	.554
21	1.86	28.68	.035	.538
22	1.92	30.54	.033	.522
23	1.97	32.45	.031	.507
24	2.03	34.43	.029	.492
25	2.09	36.46	.027	.478

[1] What an initial amount becomes when growing at compound interest.

[2] Growth of equal year-end deposits all growing at compound interest.

[3] Level deposit required each year to reach 1 by a given year.

[4] How much 1 at a future date is worth today.

Rate 4%

Year	Table 1 Compounding Factor for 1[1]	Table 2 Compounding Factor For 1 Per Annum[2]	Table 3 Sinking Fund Factor[3]	Table 4 Discount Factor[4]
1	1.04	1.00	1.00	.962
2	1.08	2.04	.490	.925
3	1.12	3.12	.320	.889
4	1.16	4.25	.236	.855
5	1.22	5.42	.185	.822
6	1.27	6.63	.151	.790
7	1.32	7.90	.127	.760
8	1.37	9.21	.109	.731
9	1.42	10.58	.095	.703
10	1.48	12.01	.083	.676
11	1.54	13.49	.074	.650
12	1.60	15.03	.067	.625
13	1.67	16.63	.060	.601
14	1.73	18.29	.055	.578
15	1.80	20.02	.050	.555
16	1.87	21.82	.046	.534
17	1.95	23.70	.042	.513
18	2.03	25.65	.039	.494
19	2.11	27.67	.036	.475
20	2.19	29.78	.034	.456
21	2.28	31.97	.031	.439
22	2.37	34.25	.029	.422
23	2.47	36.62	.027	.406
24	2.56	39.08	.026	.390
25	2.67	41.65	.024	.375

[1] What an initial amount becomes when growing at compound interest.

[2] Growth of equal year-end deposits all growing at compound interest.

[3] Level deposit required each year to reach 1 by a given year.

[4] How much 1 at a future date is worth today.

		Rate 5%		
Year	Table 1 *Compounding Factor for 1*[1]	Table 2 *Compounding Factor For 1 Per Annum*[2]	Table 3 *Sinking Fund Factor*[3]	Table 4 *Discount Factor*[4]
1	1.05	1.00	1.00	.952
2	1.10	2.05	.488	.907
3	1.16	3.15	.317	.864
4	1.22	4.31	.232	.823
5	1.28	5.53	.181	.784
6	1.34	6.80	.147	.746
7	1.41	8.14	.123	.711
8	1.48	9.55	.105	.677
9	1.55	11.03	.091	.645
10	1.63	12.58	.080	.614
11	1.71	14.21	.070	.585
12	1.80	15.92	.063	.557
13	1.89	17.71	.057	.530
14	1.98	19.60	.051	.505
15	2.08	21.58	.046	.481
16	2.18	23.68	.042	.458
17	2.29	25.84	.039	.436
18	2.41	28.13	.036	.416
19	2.53	30.54	.033	.396
20	2.65	33.07	.030	.377
21	2.79	35.72	.028	.359
22	2.93	38.51	.026	.342
23	3.07	41.43	.024	.326
24	3.23	44.50	.023	.310
25	3.39	47.73	.021	.295

[1] What an initial amount becomes when growing at compound interest.

[2] Growth of equal year-end deposits all growing at compound interest.

[3] Level deposit required each year to reach 1 by a given year.

[4] How much 1 at a future date is worth today.

Rate 6%

Year	Table 1 Compounding Factor for 1[1]	Table 2 Compounding Factor For 1 Per Annum[2]	Table 3 Sinking Fund Factor[3]	Table 4 Discount Factor[4]
1	1.06	1.00	1.00	.943
2	1.12	2.06	.485	.890
3	1.19	3.18	.314	.840
4	1.26	4.38	.229	.792
5	1.34	5.64	.177	.747
6	1.42	6.98	.143	.705
7	1.50	8.39	.119	.665
8	1.59	9.90	.101	.627
9	1.69	11.49	.087	.592
10	1.80	13.18	.076	.558
11	1.90	14.97	.067	.527
12	2.01	16.87	.059	.497
13	2.13	18.88	.053	.469
14	2.26	21.02	.048	.442
15	2.40	23.28	.043	.417
16	2.54	25.67	.039	.394
17	2.69	28.21	.036	.371
18	2.85	30.91	.032	.350
19	3.03	33.76	.030	.331
20	3.21	36.79	.027	.312
21	3.40	39.99	.025	.294
22	3.60	43.39	.023	.278
23	3.82	47.00	.021	.262
24	4.05	50.82	.020	.247
25	4.29	54.86	.018	.233

[1] What an initial amount becomes when growing at compound interest.

[2] Growth of equal year-end deposits all growing at compound interest.

[3] Level deposit required each year to reach 1 by a given year.

[4] How much 1 at a future date is worth today.

Rate 7%

Year	Table 1 Compounding Factor for 1[1]	Table 2 Compounding Factor For 1 Per Annum[2]	Table 3 Sinking Fund Factor[3]	Table 4 Discount Factor[4]
1	1.07	1.00	1.00	.935
2	1.15	2.07	.483	.873
3	1.23	3.22	.311	.816
4	1.31	4.44	.225	.763
5	1.40	5.75	.174	.713
6	1.50	7.15	.140	.666
7	1.61	8.65	.116	.623
8	1.72	10.26	.098	.582
9	1.84	11.98	.084	.544
10	1.97	13.82	.072	.508
11	2.11	15.78	.063	.475
12	2.25	17.89	.056	.444
13	2.41	20.14	.050	.415
14	2.58	22.55	.044	.388
15	2.76	25.13	.040	.363
16	2.95	27.89	.036	.339
17	3.16	30.84	.032	.317
18	3.38	34.00	.029	.296
19	3.62	37.38	.027	.277
20	3.87	41.00	.024	.258
21	4.14	44.87	.022	.242
22	4.43	49.01	.020	.226
23	4.74	53.44	.019	.211
24	5.07	58.18	.017	.197
25	5.43	63.25	.016	.184

[1] What an initial amount becomes when growing at compound interest.

[2] Growth of equal year-end deposits all growing at compound interest.

[3] Level deposit required each year to reach 1 by a given year.

[4] How much 1 at a future date is worth today.

Rate 8%

Year	Table 1 Compounding Factor for 1[1]	Table 2 Compounding Factor For 1 Per Annum[2]	Table 3 Sinking Fund Factor[3]	Table 4 Discount Factor[4]
1	1.08	1.00	1.00	.926
2	1.17	2.08	.481	.857
3	1.26	3.25	.308	.794
4	1.36	4.51	.222	.735
5	1.47	5.87	.171	.681
6	1.59	7.34	.136	.630
7	1.71	8.92	.112	.585
8	1.85	10.64	.094	.540
9	2.00	12.49	.080	.500
10	2.16	14.49	.069	.463
11	2.33	16.65	.060	.429
12	2.52	18.98	.053	.397
13	2.72	21.50	.047	.368
14	2.94	24.21	.041	.341
15	3.17	27.15	.037	.315
16	3.43	30.32	.033	.292
17	3.70	33.75	.030	.270
18	4.00	37.45	.027	.250
19	4.32	41.45	.024	.232
20	4.66	45.76	.022	.215
21	5.03	50.42	.020	.199
22	5.44	55.46	.018	.184
23	5.87	60.89	.016	.170
24	6.34	66.77	.015	.158
25	6.85	73.11	.014	.146

[1] What an initial amount becomes when growing at compound interest.

[2] Growth of equal year-end deposits all growing at compound interest.

[3] Level deposit required each year to reach 1 by a given year.

[4] How much 1 at a future date is worth today.

	Rate 9%			
Year	Table 1 Compounding Factor for 1[1]	Table 2 Compounding Factor For 1 Per Annum[2]	Table 3 Sinking Fund Factor[3]	Table 4 Discount Factor[4]
1	1.09	1.00	1.00	.917
2	1.19	2.09	.479	.842
3	1.30	3.28	.305	.772
4	1.41	4.57	.219	.708
5	1.54	5.99	.167	.650
6	1.68	7.52	.133	.596
7	1.83	9.20	.109	.547
8	2.00	11.03	.091	.502
9	2.17	13.02	.077	.460
10	2.37	15.19	.066	.422
11	2.58	17.56	.057	.388
12	2.81	20.14	.050	.356
13	3.07	22.95	.044	.326
14	3.34	26.02	.038	.299
15	3.64	29.36	.034	.275
16	3.97	33.00	.030	.252
17	4.33	36.97	.027	.231
18	4.72	41.30	.024	.212
19	5.14	46.02	.022	.195
20	5.60	51.16	.020	.178
21	6.11	56.77	.018	.164
22	6.66	62.87	.016	.150
23	7.26	69.53	.014	.138
24	7.91	76.79	.013	.126
25	8.62	84.70	.012	.116

[1] What an initial amount becomes when growing at compound interest.

[2] Growth of equal year-end deposits all growing at compound interest.

[3] Level deposit required each year to reach 1 by a given year.

[4] How much 1 at a future date is worth today.

Year	Table 1 Compounding Factor for 1[1]	Table 2 Compounding Factor For 1 Per Annum[2]	Table 3 Sinking Fund Factor[3]	Table 4 Discount Factor[4]
		Rate 10%		
1	1.10	1.00	1.00	.909
2	1.21	2.10	.476	.827
3	1.33	3.31	.302	.751
4	1.46	4.64	.216	.683
5	1.61	6.11	.164	.621
6	1.77	7.72	.130	.565
7	1.95	9.49	.105	.513
8	2.14	11.44	.087	.467
9	2.36	13.58	.074	.424
10	2.59	15.94	.063	.386
11	2.85	18.53	.054	.351
12	3.14	21.38	.047	.319
13	3.45	24.52	.041	.290
14	3.80	27.97	.036	.263
15	4.18	31.77	.032	.239
16	4.60	35.95	.028	.218
17	5.06	40.55	.025	.198
18	5.56	45.60	.022	.180
19	6.12	51.16	.020	.164
20	6.73	57.28	.018	.149
21	7.40	64.00	.016	.135
22	8.14	71.40	.014	.123
23	8.95	79.50	.013	.112
24	9.85	88.50	.011	.102
25	10.84	98.35	.010	.092

[1] What an initial amount becomes when growing at compound interest.

[2] Growth of equal year-end deposits all growing at compound interest.

[3] Level deposit required each year to reach 1 by a given year.

[4] How much 1 at a future date is worth today.

	Rate 11%			
Year	Table 1 Compounding Factor for 1[1]	Table 2 Compounding Factor For 1 Per Annum[2]	Table 3 Sinking Fund Factor[3]	Table 4 Discount Factor[4]
1	1.11	1.00	1.00	.901
2	1.23	2.11	.474	.812
3	1.37	3.34	.299	.731
4	1.52	4.71	.212	.659
5	1.69	6.23	.161	.594
6	1.87	7.91	.126	.535
7	2.08	9.78	.102	.482
8	2.31	11.86	.084	.434
9	2.56	14.16	.071	.391
10	2.84	16.72	.060	.352
11	3.15	19.56	.051	.317
12	3.50	22.71	.044	.286
13	3.88	26.21	.038	.258
14	4.31	30.10	.033	.232
15	4.79	34.41	.029	.209
16	5.31	39.19	.026	.188
17	5.90	44.50	.023	.170
18	6.54	50.40	.020	.153
19	7.26	56.94	.018	.138
20	8.06	64.20	.016	.124
21	8.95	72.27	.014	.112
22	9.93	81.21	.012	.101
23	11.03	91.15	.011	.091
24	12.24	102.17	.0098	.082
25	13.59	114.41	.0087	.074

[1] What an initial amount becomes when growing at compound interest.

[2] Growth of equal year-end deposits all growing at compound interest.

[3] Level deposit required each year to reach 1 by a given year.

[4] How much 1 at a future date is worth today.

Rate 12%

Year	Table 1 Compounding Factor for 1[1]	Table 2 Compounding Factor For 1 Per Annum[2]	Table 3 Sinking Fund Factor[3]	Table 4 Discount Factor[4]
1	1.12	1.00	1.00	.893
2	1.25	2.12	.472	.797
3	1.41	3.37	.296	.712
4	1.57	4.78	.209	.636
5	1.76	6.35	.157	.567
6	1.97	8.12	.123	.507
7	2.21	10.09	.099	.452
8	2.48	12.30	.081	.404
9	2.77	14.78	.068	.361
10	3.11	17.55	.057	.322
11	3.48	20.66	.048	.288
12	3.90	24.13	.041	.257
13	4.36	28.03	.036	.229
14	4.89	32.39	.031	.205
15	5.47	37.30	.027	.183
16	6.13	42.75	.023	.163
17	6.87	48.88	.021	.146
18	7.69	55.75	.018	.130
19	8.61	63.44	.016	.116
20	9.65	72.05	.014	.104
21	10.80	81.70	.012	.093
22	12.10	92.50	.011	.083
23	13.55	104.60	.0096	.074
24	15.18	118.16	.0085	.066
25	17.00	133.33	.0075	.059

[1] What an initial amount becomes when growing at compound interest.

[2] Growth of equal year-end deposits all growing at compound interest.

[3] Level deposit required each year to reach 1 by a given year.

[4] How much 1 at a future date is worth today.

Rate 13%

Year	Table 1 Compounding Factor for 1[1]	Table 2 Compounding Factor For 1 Per Annum[2]	Table 3 Sinking Fund Factor[3]	Table 4 Discount Factor[4]
1	1.13	1.00	1.00	.885
2	1.28	2.13	.470	.783
3	1.44	3.41	.294	.693
4	1.63	4.85	.206	.613
5	1.84	6.48	.154	.543
6	2.08	8.32	.120	.480
7	2.35	10.41	.096	.425
8	2.66	12.76	.078	.376
9	3.00	15.42	.065	.333
10	3.40	18.42	.054	.295
11	3.84	21.81	.046	.261
12	4.34	25.65	.039	.231
13	4.90	29.99	.033	.204
14	5.54	34.88	.029	.181
15	6.25	40.42	.025	.160
16	7.07	46.67	.021	.142
17	7.99	53.74	.019	.125
18	9.02	61.73	.016	.111
19	10.20	70.75	.014	.098
20	11.52	80.95	.012	.087
21	13.02	92.47	.011	.077
22	14.71	105.49	.0095	.068
23	16.63	120.20	.0083	.060
24	18.79	136.83	.0073	.053
25	21.23	155.62	.0064	.047

[1] What an initial amount becomes when growing at compound interest.

[2] Growth of equal year-end deposits all growing at compound interest.

[3] Level deposit required each year to reach 1 by a given year.

[4] How much 1 at a future date is worth today.

		Rate 14%		
Year	Table 1 Compounding Factor for 1[1]	Table 2 Compounding Factor For 1 Per Annum[2]	Table 3 Sinking Fund Factor[3]	Table 4 Discount Factor[4]
1	1.14	1.00	1.00	.877
2	1.30	2.14	.467	.770
3	1.48	3.44	.291	.675
4	1.69	4.92	.203	.592
5	1.93	6.61	.151	.519
6	2.20	8.54	.117	.456
7	2.50	10.73	.093	.400
8	2.85	13.23	.076	.351
9	3.25	16.09	.062	.308
10	3.71	19.34	.052	.270
11	4.23	23.05	.043	.237
12	4.82	27.27	.037	.208
13	5.49	32.09	.031	.182
14	6.26	37.58	.027	.160
15	7.14	43.84	.023	.141
16	8.14	50.98	.020	.123
17	9.28	59.12	.017	.108
18	10.58	68.39	.015	.095
19	12.06	78.97	.013	.083
20	13.74	91.03	.011	.073
21	15.67	104.77	.0096	.064
22	17.86	120.44	.0083	.056
23	20.36	138.30	.0072	.049
24	23.21	158.66	.0063	.043
25	26.46	181.87	.0055	.038

[1] What an initial amount becomes when growing at compound interest.

[2] Growth of equal year-end deposits all growing at compound interest.

[3] Level deposit required each year to reach 1 by a given year.

[4] How much 1 at a future date is worth today.

Rate 15%

Year	Table 1 Compounding Factor for 1[1]	Table 2 Compounding Factor For 1 Per Annum[2]	Table 3 Sinking Fund Factor[3]	Table 4 Discount Factor[4]
1	1.15	1.00	1.00	.870
2	1.32	2.15	.465	.756
3	1.52	3.47	.288	.658
4	1.75	4.99	.200	.572
5	2.01	6.74	.148	.497
6	2.31	8.75	.114	.432
7	2.66	11.07	.090	.376
8	3.06	13.73	.073	.327
9	3.52	16.79	.060	.284
10	4.05	20.30	.049	.247
11	4.65	24.35	.041	.215
12	5.35	29.00	.035	.187
13	6.15	34.51	.029	.163
14	7.08	40.51	.025	.141
15	8.14	47.58	.021	.123
16	9.36	55.72	.018	.107
17	10.76	65.08	.015	.093
18	12.38	75.84	.013	.081
19	14.23	88.21	.011	.070
20	16.37	102.44	.010	.061
21	18.82	118.81	.0084	.053
22	21.65	137.63	.0073	.046
23	24.89	159.28	.0063	.040
24	28.63	184.17	.0054	.035
25	32.92	212.79	.0047	.030

[1] What an initial amount becomes when growing at compound interest.

[2] Growth of equal year-end deposits all growing at compound interest.

[3] Level deposit required each year to reach 1 by a given year.

[4] How much 1 at a future date is worth today.

	Rate 16%			
Year	Table 1 Compounding Factor for 1[1]	Table 2 Compounding Factor For 1 Per Annum[2]	Table 3 Sinking Fund Factor[3]	Table 4 Discount Factor[4]
1	1.16	1.00	1.00	.862
2	1.35	2.16	.463	.743
3	1.56	3.51	.285	.641
4	1.81	5.07	.197	.552
5	2.10	6.88	.145	.476
6	2.44	8.98	.111	.410
7	2.83	11.41	.088	.354
8	3.28	14.24	.070	.305
9	3.80	17.52	.057	.263
10	4.41	21.32	.047	.227
11	5.12	25.73	.039	.195
12	5.94	30.85	.032	.169
13	6.89	36.79	.027	.145
14	7.99	43.67	.023	.125
15	9.27	51.66	.019	.108
16	10.75	60.93	.016	.093
17	12.47	71.67	.014	.080
18	14.46	84.10	.012	.069
19	16.78	98.60	.010	.060
20	19.46	115.38	.0087	.051
21	22.57	134.84	.0074	.044
22	26.19	157.42	.0064	.038
23	30.38	183.60	.0055	.033
24	35.24	213.98	.0047	.028
25	40.87	249.21	.0040	.025

[1] What an initial amount becomes when growing at compound interest.

[2] Growth of equal year-end deposits all growing at compound interest.

[3] Level deposit required each year to reach 1 by a given year.

[4] How much 1 at a future date is worth today.

Rate 17%

Year	Table 1 Compounding Factor for 1[1]	Table 2 Compounding Factor For 1 Per Annum[2]	Table 3 Sinking Fund Factor[3]	Table 4 Discount Factor[4]
1	1.17	1.00	1.00	.855
2	1.37	2.17	.461	.731
3	1.60	3.54	.283	.624
4	1.87	5.14	.195	.534
5	2.19	7.01	.143	.456
6	2.57	9.21	.109	.390
7	3.00	11.77	.085	.333
8	3.51	14.77	.068	.285
9	4.11	18.29	.055	.243
10	4.81	22.39	.045	.208
11	5.62	27.20	.037	.178
12	6.58	32.82	.031	.152
13	7.70	39.40	.025	.130
14	9.01	47.10	.021	.111
15	10.54	56.11	.018	.095
16	12.33	66.65	.015	.081
17	14.43	79.98	.013	.069
18	16.88	93.41	.011	.059
19	19.75	110.29	.0091	.051
20	23.11	130.03	.0077	.043
21	27.03	153.14	.0065	.037
22	31.63	180.17	.0056	.032
23	37.01	211.80	.0047	.027
24	43.30	248.81	.0040	.023
25	50.66	292.11	.0034	.020

[1] What an initial amount becomes when growing at compound interest.

[2] Growth of equal year-end deposits all growing at compound interest.

[3] Level deposit required each year to reach 1 by a given year.

[4] How much 1 at a future date is worth today.

		Rate 18%		
Year	Table 1 Compounding Factor for 1[1]	Table 2 Compounding Factor For 1 Per Annum[2]	Table 3 Sinking Fund Factor[3]	Table 4 Discount Factor[4]
1	1.18	1.00	1.00	.848
2	1.39	2.18	.459	.718
3	1.64	3.57	.280	.609
4	1.94	5.22	.192	.516
5	2.29	7.15	.140	.437
6	2.70	9.44	.106	.370
7	3.19	12.14	.082	.314
8	3.76	15.33	.065	.266
9	4.44	19.09	.052	.226
10	5.23	23.52	.043	.191
11	6.18	28.76	.035	.162
12	7.29	34.93	.029	.137
13	8.60	42.22	.024	.116
14	10.15	50.82	.020	.099
15	11.97	60.97	.016	.084
16	14.13	72.94	.014	.071
17	16.67	87.07	.012	.060
18	19.67	103.74	.010	.051
19	23.21	123.41	.0081	.043
20	27.39	146.63	.0068	.037
21	32.32	174.02	.0058	.031
22	38.14	206.34	.0049	.026
23	45.01	244.49	.0041	.022
24	53.11	289.50	.0035	.019
25	62.67	342.60	.0029	.016

[1] What an initial amount becomes when growing at compound interest.

[2] Growth of equal year-end deposits all growing at compound interest.

[3] Level deposit required each year to reach 1 by a given year.

[4] How much 1 at a future date is worth today.

Rate 19%

Year	Table 1 Compounding Factor for 1[1]	Table 2 Compounding Factor For 1 Per Annum[2]	Table 3 Sinking Fund Factor[3]	Table 4 Discount Factor[4]
1	1.19	1.00	1.00	.840
2	1.42	2.19	.457	.706
3	1.69	3.61	.277	.593
4	2.01	5.29	.189	.499
5	2.39	7.30	.137	.419
6	2.84	9.68	.103	.352
7	3.38	12.52	.080	.296
8	4.02	15.90	.063	.249
9	4.79	19.92	.050	.209
10	5.69	24.71	.041	.176
11	6.78	30.40	.033	.148
12	8.06	37.18	.027	.124
13	9.60	45.24	.022	.104
14	11.42	54.84	.018	.088
15	13.59	66.26	.015	.074
16	16.17	79.85	.013	.062
17	19.24	96.02	.010	.052
18	22.90	115.27	.0087	.044
19	27.25	138.17	.0072	.037
20	32.43	165.42	.0061	.031
21	38.59	197.85	.0051	.026
22	45.92	236.44	.0042	.022
23	54.65	282.36	.0035	.018
24	65.03	337.01	.0030	.014
25	77.39	402.04	.0025	.013

[1] What an initial amount becomes when growing at compound interest.

[2] Growth of equal year-end deposits all growing at compound interest.

[3] Level deposit required each year to reach 1 by a given year.

[4] How much 1 at a future date is worth today.

		Rate 20%		
Year	Table 1 Compounding Factor for 1[1]	Table 2 Compounding Factor For 1 Per Annum[2]	Table 3 Sinking Fund Factor[3]	Table 4 Discount Factor[4]
1	1.20	1.00	1.00	.833
2	1.44	2.20	.455	.694
3	1.73	3.64	.275	.579
4	2.07	5.37	.186	.482
5	2.49	7.44	.134	.402
6	2.99	9.93	.101	.335
7	3.58	12.92	.077	.279
8	4.30	16.50	.061	.233
9	5.16	20.80	.048	.194
10	6.19	25.96	.039	.162
11	7.43	32.15	.031	.135
12	8.92	39.58	.025	.112
13	10.70	48.50	.021	.094
14	12.84	59.20	.017	.078
15	15.41	72.04	.014	.065
16	18.49	87.44	.011	.054
17	22.19	105.93	.0094	.045
18	26.62	128.12	.0078	.038
19	31.95	154.74	.0065	.031
20	38.34	186.69	.0054	.026
21	46.01	225.03	.0044	.022
22	55.21	271.03	.0037	.018
23	66.25	326.24	.0031	.015
24	79.50	392.48	.0026	.013
25	95.40	471.98	.0021	.010

[1] What an initial amount becomes when growing at compound interest.

[2] Growth of equal year-end deposits all growing at compound interest.

[3] Level deposit required each year to reach 1 by a given year.

[4] How much 1 at a future date is worth today.

GLOSSARY

▼

Annual Return: Total return received from an investment over an annual period of time. This return includes all realized and unrealized capital gains/losses as well as dividend/interest income. The compound average annual return is an average return that is time-weighted; it measures the compounded rate of growth of an initial investment value over a certain period of time.

Annuitant: One of three parties named in the annuity contract. However, unlike the contract owner or beneficiary, the person (or persons) named as the annuitant (or co-annuitant) must be a living person (and not an entity such as a living trust, partnership, corporation, etc.). The person named as the "measuring life" does not have to be related to the beneficiary or owner. An annuity contract (investment) continues until terminated or liquidated by the contract owner(s) or when the annuitant dies, whichever happens first.

Annuitization: The orderly process of liquidating part or all of one's annuity contract. The contract owner decides whether distributions are to be made on a monthly, quarterly, semi-annual or annual basis. The duration of the distributions depends upon the value of the contract at the time of annuitization, the period selected and the amount of each distribution. The period selected, which is chosen by the contract owner, may be for three years or longer or based upon the lifetime of one or more persons (e.g., "Payments to continue as long as either me or my spouse are alive."). Some insurance companies allow the investor (contract owner) to have a specific dollar amount sent out each period (e.g., month, quarter, etc.) until the contract is completely depleted.

Annuity: A contract between an insurance company and an investor (individual, couple, trust, partnership, etc.). There are two ways to categorize annuities: type and method of payment. The two *types* of annuities are: (1) fixed-rate (which is similar to a bank CD, wherein the investor gets a set rate of return for a specific number of years) and (2) variable (which is similar to a mutual fund family, wherein the investor chooses one or more portfolios, ranging from conservative to aggressive). There are a couple of methods of payment: (a) deferred growth (wherein the annuity grows and compounds tax-deferred until the investor decides to make a partial or full redemption) and (b) immediate annuity (wherein the investor begins to receive a regular income stream, the amount of which depends upon the amount invested, the general level of interest rates and the competitiveness of the insurance company).

Arithmetic Mean: Average annual return of an investment over a series of time. This can be thought of as the investment's long-term expected rate of return.

Asset: For an investor, an asset is usually in the form of a security or portfolio of securities whose value is derived from the cash flow it can or potentially can produce over time.

Asset Allocation Mutual Fund: Funds that seek to produce a "total return" by deciding which asset classes to invest in and how much weight should be given to each one. Unlike balanced funds, which generally set proportions for their stock and bond allocations, asset allocation funds may change their mix within a predetermined range.

Barbell Portfolio: A strategy of investing in both short-term *and* long-term fixed-income securities for the purpose of locking in long-term rates while hedging against any potential rise in interest rates. Managers of a barbell portfolio can then adjust the average maturity of the portfolio based on their forecast of interest rate trends.

Basis: The total acquisition costs of an asset. It represents the actual cost when computing the gain or loss upon sale or redemption of the asset.

Bear Market: A prolonged period of market declines. Whereas a correction is a temporary adjustment in securities prices due to such things as overspeculation, a bear market represents a trend.

Beneficiary: One of three parties named in the annuity contract. The beneficiary can be an individual, couple, series of people (e.g., children, relatives, friends, etc.) or entity such as a living trust. The beneficiary has no rights or voice in any annuity matter. The beneficiary does receive the value of the annuity (or death benefit) upon the annuitant's death.

Beta: Measures the stock market–related risk of a security or portfolio. The S & P 500 always has a beta of 1.00, even when the market is going up, down or moving sideways. The security or portfolio being measured against the market (the S & P 500) may also end up having a beta of 1.00 or a beta that is below or above 1.00. If the portfolio has a beta that is greater than 1.00, this means that its market-related risk is higher than the S & P 500; a beta of less than 1.00 means that the market-related risk is lower than that of the S & P 500. A higher than average (1.00) beta means that the portfolio or security is likely to outperform the market during good periods and underperform it (drop more than the S & P 500) during bad times. A lower than average beta means that the portfolio or security will have a tendency to underperform the market during good periods (e.g., not go up as much), but perform better (not drop as much) during stock market declines.

Blue Chip: Well-established companies that have a long history of earnings growth and consistent growth of dividends. Such companies usually have a large market capitalization and possess a greater share of the market than their industry counterparts. Investing in blue chip stocks is considered to be a conservative approach to equity investing.

Bond: A security issued by a borrower that promises to pay the holder a fixed level of interest payments over a certain period. Many bonds are issued in the coupon-variety, where coupon payments are made over the life of the bond along with the repayment of principal upon maturity. Bonds are considered to be a safer form of investment than stocks mainly because of the higher certainty associated with their future cash flows (as opposed to the uncertainty of a company's earnings or stream of dividend payouts).

Bond Rating: Rating assigned to a company's debt and designed to provide information on the borrower's ability to meet the timely payment of interest and principal. Rating agencies such as Standard & Poor's and Moody's are retained by borrowers to evaluate their credit risk by analyzing the borrower's financial condition and growing concern as a business. Bonds with lower ratings command a higher yield in order to entice lenders (investors) to take on the extra risk.

Bull Market: Prolonged rise in the prices of stocks, bonds or commodities that reflect a fundamental trend of upward valuation. Bull markets for different asset classes might not coincide with one another. A bull market for stocks might represent a period of rising earnings, economic growth or lower interest rates while a bull market for bonds might represent a period of declining economic growth.

Buying on Margin: A form of financial leverage for investors who wish to purchase a security through credit. Buying on margin requires that an investor put up an initial amount for purchase and may borrow an additional amount from his/her broker to purchase additional shares. This action is heavily regulated by the Federal Reserve Board as it sets the margin requirements needed to establish such a position. As with any form of leverage, such activity can magnify gains as well as losses.

Capital Gains Distribution: When mutual funds sell assets for a gain over the course of the year, these gains must be distributed to the shareholders. These realized gains are capital gains distributions and are classified as either short-term or long-term capital gains for tax purposes. The share price, or net asset value, of the fund is then adjusted to reflect this distribution. Unless the fund is held in a tax-sheltered account, investors should not invest in funds right before a distribution is made because they will ultimately owe taxes on gains they did not truly realize over the course of the year.

CFS: Also known as Certified Fund Specialist, this is the only designation awarded to brokers, financial planners, CPAs, insurance agents, and other investment advisors who either recommend or sell variable annuities or mutual funds. There are fewer than 2,500 people across the country who have passed this certification program. For additional information about the CFS program or to get the name of a CFS in your area, call (800) 848-2029.

Common Stock: A security that represents ownership interest in a public corporation. Common stocks are actively traded in various secondary markets such as the New York Stock Exchange and NASDAQ. Stocks are commonly valued at the present value of their future cash flows such as dividends and earnings.

Compound Annual Return: Average return that is time-weighted; it measures the cumulative rate of growth of an initial investment value over a certain period of time.

Compound Interest: Commonly known as "interest on interest," it is the interest earned on both the principal and interest of an investment assuming a reinvestment of both. This means that the growth of an investment, even with a constant rate of return, can increase exponentially over time. This is a key concept for retirement planning as it understates the importance of saving early.

Constant-Dollar Plan: Known as "dollar-cost averaging," a constant-dollar plan is based on investing a fixed amount of money in a mutual fund at specific intervals. The premise is that if several purchases of a fund are made over an extended period of time, the unpredictable highs and lows will "average out." The investor ends up buying more shares when the market price is low and less shares when it is up. When this program is followed, losses during market declines are limited, while the ability to participate in good markets is maintained.

Contract Owner: One of four parties named in an annuity contract (note: the other parties named are the annuitant, the beneficiary and the insurance company). The contract owner can be an individual or entity. Some contracts allow co-ownership, meaning that spouses could equally own or control the investment. It is the contract owner who decides how the money is to be invested, when changes are to be made, and, until the annuitant's death, how long the contract (investment) should last.

Contrarian: An investor who resists the "herd-mentality" and seeks to invest in securities or sectors that are "out-of-favor" but are due for a rebound. They feel the best investment opportunities are those that not too many people notice or pay attention to. Contrarians try to avoid sectors that might be popular but overvalued and instead focus on assets selling close to their intrinsic value in the hopes that the market will bid up their prices to reflect their full potential value.

Convertibles: A hybrid security that pays the investor a below-average yield but gives him/her the right to exchange the convertible for a set number of common shares. Usually this exercise price is set much higher than what the shares are currently trading for. Such securities can help diversify a fixed-income portfolio because of their link to performance of the equity market.

Corporate Bond: Debt instruments issued by corporations. The yields offered on corporate bonds differ based on their credit risk. Such credit risk is established by the rating a company is issued by such firms as Standard & Poor's and Moody's. Companies that have high credit risk are assigned lower ratings—ratings that are BB or Baa and lower are considered speculative-grade as opposed to investment-grade. Investors usually demand a higher yield from such companies so as to compensate them for the higher credit risk.

Correlation Coefficient: This is a statistical measure of the co-movement of asset returns. The range for this measure is -1 to +1 where a -1 means the two assets' returns are negatively correlated while a +1 means their returns are perfectly correlated. Ideally, a portfolio seeks to acquire assets that have a negative or no correlation with one another because this can reduce the overall risk of the portfolio without compromising its return.

Countercyclical Stocks: Stocks that trade counter to the performance of the economy. Such companies include so-called defensive stocks such as tobacco and agriculture because they attract investors looking for safety from a downturn in the business cycle (people still eat and drink in a recession).

Coupon: The stated interest rate of a bond payable to the debt holder. The coupon rate is the stated rate of the bond sold at par and differs from the current yield which is the yield adjusted for the bond price's premium or discount. A bond would command a premium if interest rates had fallen or were expected to fall; a discount is warranted if rates went up or were expected to possibly increase.

CPI: The Consumer Price Index (CPI) is the mostly commonly used yardstick to measure the rate of inflation in the U.S.

Cumulative Preferred: Preferred stock shareholders are paid dividends before common stock owners and are considered a more senior obligation of the corporation. For preferred shares that are cumulative, any dividend payments that the company cannot meet accumulate until the company can pay them out from earnings. Most preferred shares issued today are cumulative.

Current Yield: The current yield is the annual rate of interest received divided by the bond price. A bond bought at a discount will have a higher current yield than the coupon rate and vice versa for a bond bought at a premium.

Cyclical Stocks: Stocks that trade in sync with the overall economy. These companies usually operate in cyclical sectors such as heavy industry, transportation and consumer durables. They benefit tremendously from an expanding economy but are often hurt during a recession.

Derivative: Instrument whose value is derived from the price of an underlying security that it follows. Common derivatives include: options, swaps and futures contracts; such instruments are not a claim on a specific asset but rather the right to buy or sell that asset at a given price. Because of their highly volatile nature, speculators use derivatives to leverage themselves for higher returns. However, derivatives are also commonly used as hedging instruments to reduce exposure to price fluctuations. Such users include farmers who wish to lock in a price for the sale of their crop or portfolio managers who want to hedge against a possible drop in the market.

Disposable Income: The after-tax personal income that people choose to consume or save. The percentage of personal income used for savings has been historically low in the United States, especially when compared to other industrial countries such as Japan.

Dividend: Distribution of a company's earnings to shareholders. The board of directors decide what portion of after-tax net income will be paid to shareholders with the remaining portion kept as retained earnings. Retained earnings are essentially reinvested dividends that the corporation uses to expand its growth output—that's why many fast growing companies have little or no dividend payouts. Dividends are taxed at the individual's income tax bracket. Mutual funds that receive dividends must distribute them to shareholders on a per share basis. These dividends are also taxed at the individual bracket.

Dollar-Cost Averaging: The practice of investing equal amounts of money at regular intervals regardless of whether securities markets are moving up or down. This procedure reduces average unit (share) costs to the investor who acquires more units in the periods of lower securities prices and fewer units in periods of higher prices (see appendix for a more detailed explanation and example).

Dressing Up a Portfolio: Also known as "window-dressing," this is a practice where money managers dump the past year's losers and replace them with the winners so as to make their portfolio look better than it actually is. This practice has commonly led to an arbitrage strategy known as the "January effect" where as a result of this dressing up, the price of many of these "losers" gets depressed at the end of the year but then picks up at the beginning after the dressing (buying) ends.

Duration: Weighted-average of the time periods over which a bond pays out interest and principal. It is a time measure of interest rate sensitivity and will usually be shorter than the maturity. The concept of duration can be associated with beta because it measures the price sensitivity of a bond to interest rate changes (bond market) while beta measures the sensitivity of stock prices to changes in the overall market. Fixed-income managers adjust the duration of their portfolios in relation to a bond index based on their projection of where they think interest rates will move.

Efficient Market: A theory that states all securities fully reflect available information. Strategies such as buying undervalued stocks or timing the market will not produce an excess return in an efficient market. There are various forms of this theory ranging from a weak form that states securities reflect all past information to the strong form that states securities reflect all information both public and private. Those who follow this theory believe that picking a random set of stocks has as much of a chance of beating the market as picking a portfolio of stocks based on some market strategy.

Efficient Portfolio: A portfolio that maximizes return given a certain risk level usually represented by the standard deviation. A set of these portfolios with different risk levels makes up what is commonly known as the efficient frontier. Based on this risk-reward relationship, one can go along this curve and find efficient portfolios (meaning the maximum return potential for a given level of risk).

Equity REIT: The most common type of REIT, the equity REIT emphasizes actual ownership of income-producing properties such as commercial real estate rather than investing in mortgages backed by real estate. Investors can earn dividends from the rental income derived from the properties as well as any realized gains from the sale of appreciated property. Since real estate is not as highly correlated with inflation as most other types of fixed-income instruments, investors might look to equity REITs to diversify their fixed-income portfolio.

Eurobond: A bond denominated in the domestic currency issued by companies or commercial interests to be sold outside of the domestic market. Some common Eurobonds include Samurai bonds which are Eurobonds issued by Japanese corporations to be sold to U.S. investors.

Face Value: The par value of the bond when issued. This is the value that will be redeemed to bondholders at maturity. Bonds that trade in the secondary market usually trade at prices above or below the face value, due to changes in interest rates.

Fallen Angels: Bonds whose ratings have fallen due to declining financial conditions along with the borrower's ability to meet timely payments of interest and principal. Many contrarians look for turnaround opportunities in the fallen angel category by purchasing corporate debt at a deep discount, hoping for an eventual return to better conditions.

Fixed-Rate Annuity: A fixed-rate annuity is different from a variable annuity in that the fixed-rate contract offers the investor a locked-in rate of return (similar to a bank CD rate); the investor's only investment choice is whether to lock in a rate for 1 to 10 years (or whatever the periods of time offered by the annuity contract). A variable annuity allows the investor to choose among one or more stock, bond or money market portfolios—similar to a mutual fund family. Money in all annuities grows and compounds tax-deferred (not tax-free).

Flight to Quality: Investor reaction to adverse financial or economic conditions by shifting funds from more speculative investments to safer ones. This can result in higher financing costs for less-than-quality businesses who must offer investors a higher risk premium to maintain their financing. Such a flight tends to increase the yield margin between investment-grade debt and speculative-grade debt.

Fundamental Analysis: Research into the company's financial statements used to forecast the stock's future price. Several factors taken into account include: earnings, efficiency of operations and management, market share, accounting techniques, cash flow, etc. Those who practice fundamental analysis argue that their research uncovers the intrinsic risk and value of the firm.

Index Fund: A mutual fund that invests in the securities of a stock or bond market index. Some index funds, such as the Vanguard Index 500, own shares of every security that comprises the index; other index funds own enough securities of the index so that any price movements are either similar or very similar to the index. Index funds provide a low-cost investment opportunity for followers of the efficient market hypothesis who believe that excess returns over the market cannot be achieved in the long run given that security prices already reflect all available information.

Inflation: Rate at which the general level of prices for goods and services is rising and is calculated by an index comprised of a basket of goods. Inflation is the purchasing power risk that reduces the value of financial assets. It is a key component of interest and currency rate fluctuations and cost-of-living-adjustments (COLA) for federal programs. The 1954 calendar year was the last time the rate of inflation was negative (meaning the costs of goods and services actually declined).

Initial Public Offering (IPO): A company's first public offering of equity to the general public. These companies go through an underwriting process where several underwriters market the company's shares to investors looking to participate at an aggressive, venture-capital level.

Insurer: The insurance company that offers or packages the annuity. The term is also applicable when describing different forms of life insurance.

Interest-Rate Risk: The major risk faced by fixed-income investors (and to some extent equity investors). Higher interest rates cause existing debt instruments to drop in value while raising the financing costs of business activity. Fixed-income portfolios can reduce their exposure to interest-rate risk by decreasing the maturity of their bond holdings or purchasing interest-rate futures and options.

Investment Company: A corporation, trust, or partnership that invests the owners' money in securities appropriate to a stated objective. Among the benefits of investment companies, compared to direct investments, are professional management and diversification. Mutual funds (also known as "open-end" investment companies) are the most popular type of investment company.

Investment Objective: The goal—e.g., long-term capital growth, current income, etc.—that the investor and management company (mutual fund or variable annuity) pursue together.

Investment Philosophy: Style of investment that many investors and money managers follow when establishing a stock-picking strategy. Such styles range from market capitalization (small cap vs. large cap), asset valuation (value vs. growth) and timing (buy-and-hold vs. market-timing). Each style has its advocates and has at various times outperformed each other over the course of the history of the markets. Investors should ultimately pay attention to investment philosophy and invest in a style that they feel most comfortable with.

January Effect: A historical trend of stock pricing that usually results in the increase of stock prices whose shares have been depressed from year-end trading. Many portfolio managers dump stocks at the end of the year for various reasons, including: to create tax losses, realize capital gains, window-dress, or raise cash for year-end fund share redemptions. In other words, the decline in stock prices has nothing to do with fundamental factors relating to the company or the market. This effect is cited as proof that markets are not as efficient as some would believe.

Junk Bonds: Corporate bonds that have been assigned a speculative rating (BB or Ba and lower) or whose ratings have been adjusted downward due to deteriorating financial conditions. Such shares offer a higher yield due to the additional default risk associated with investing in such instruments. During the 1980s, junk bonds were a popular means of financing.

Large Cap Stocks: These are equities issued by companies that have a net worth of at least several billion dollars.

Limit Order: An order to buy or sell a security or commodity at a specified price. Although not commonly used by the general investing public, limit orders can help to lock in a gain or minimize a loss.

Management Fee: The amount paid by a mutual fund investor (shareholder) to the investment advisor for his/her services. The average annual fee industrywide is about 1% of the fund's assets.

Monetary Policy: Policy established by the central bank (the Federal Reserve) that controls the money supply of the country. Control of the money supply has far-reaching consequences on the economy as it influences the demand for credit as well as short-term interest rates. Excessive money supply over that of the economic growth rate can lead to high inflation ("Too many dollars chasing too few goods") while a low money supply can hinder economic growth by making it too hard for people to borrow.

Money Supply: The total stock of money circulating in the economy. There are several tiers of money supply in the United States. M1 includes just basic checking and savings account balances while M2 and M3 include other cash equivalents such as CDs and money market accounts. The Federal Reserve controls the money supply through monetary policy.

Mortgage REIT: These REITs (real estate investment trusts) invest in mortgage loans collateralized by real estate. They are actually considered to be less conservative than equity REITs because they are highly affected by interest movements. They also don't offer actual ownership in real estate assets, so there is little potential for capital appreciation of the REIT—unless interest rates fall.

Mutual Fund: Mutual funds come in several forms. The closed-end fund has a fixed initial capitalization and number of shares issued to the public. Because closed-end shares are not continuously redeemed, shareholders cannot obtain the net asset value of their shares from the company. Many closed-end shares trade in the secondary market where the fund's assets can be bought at a premium or discount depending on the share price in relation to net asset value. Open-end funds maintain a policy of continuously issuing redeeming shares at net asset value (NAV), which is determined at the closing session of market trading. Open-end funds are much more popular than closed-end funds. No matter what type of mutual fund you own, all shareholders share equally in the gains and losses generated by the fund.

National Debt: The total debt owed by the federal government. As of the end of 1996, the national debt stood at approximately $5 trillion dollars.

Nonrated: Bonds that have not been assigned a rating by a major rating agency such as Standard & Poor's and Moody's. Such debt might be considered too small to justify the expenses of having to get a rating assignment.

Par: The face value of a bond. When a bond is selling at par, which is usually $1,000, it is selling at neither a discount (any price below $1,000) nor a premium (any price above $1,000). Par value also represents the redemption value.

Portfolio: A collection of securities owned by an individual or an institution. A portfolio may include a combination of stocks, bonds and money market securities.

Small Cap Stocks: These are equities (stocks) issued by corporations that you and I might consider large, but the marketplace considers "small." Some financial writers consider a company that has a capitalization of $500 million or less to be "small cap"; other writers have a cut-off point of $1 billion or less.

Standard Deviation: A means of measuring how volatile an investment is from its norm. A high standard deviation indicates a large swing in price or movement; a low standard deviation means that the investment's return is more predictable.

Subaccount: A portfolio offered by a variable annuity, similar to a fund within a mutual fund family. How the money is invested depends upon the number of subaccounts offered by the insurance company (e.g., world bonds, utilities, growth, etc.) and how the investor determines to divide up his money (e.g., 25% in growth and income, 30% in international stocks, 40% in government bonds, and 5% in a balanced portfolio).

1035 Exchange: Refers to the Internal Revenue Code (IRC) section that allows contract owners to switch their existing annuity or insurance policy for a contract (or policy) offered by another company without triggering a taxable event. The key to a 1035 exchange (also known as a "tax-free exchange") is to make sure that the money or account is not touched by the investor (contract owner) during the exchange process.

Withdrawal Plan: A program in which shareholders receive payments from their mutual fund(s) or variable annuity(s) at regular intervals (usually monthly). The frequency of payments is determined by the investor and may be either monthly, quarterly, semi-annually or annually. There are two methods to choose from: a systematic withdrawal plan or annuitization.

INDEX

▼

A

Acampora, Ralph, 40
Adjustable-rate securities, 142
Advisors, financial, 42–44, 213–15, 219–20, 223, 232
Age. *See* Life cycle investing
Aggressive investing, 6, 9, 30, 100–102, 156, 157, 163, 167–70, 175, 179, 204, 227
Alger Shareholder Services, 251
Alpha, 115, 248
A.M. Best Reports, 252
American Bankers Association, 251
American Council of Life Insurance, 252
American Stock Exchange (AMEX), 82
Annual returns, 26, 103–04
  risk table and, 186
Annuities, 229–30, 247
  fees, 210–11
  mutual funds versus, 230
  resources for, 252
  tax-deferred growth, 76
Appraisal Institute, 252
Art and collectibles, 94
Asset allocation, 1–19, 78, 179
  components to, 155
  definitions of, 1, 12, 19, 243
  dynamic, 18–19
  process of, 6–10, 78–79, 162
  reallocation and, 178–79
  as series of trade-offs, 12
  types of, 16–19

B

Bank CDs. *See* Certificates of deposit (CDs)
Barron's, 40, 216, 235
Bauer Financial Reports, 251
Bear market, 36, 39, 112
Beta, 109–15, 237, 244–45
  how to use, 113–14
  sampling of mutual fund, 114
  shortcomings of, 113
Biases, 9, 78
Blue chip stocks, 11, 61, 185, 215
Bond funds, 229
  dropping in value, 237–38
Bonds, 142. *See also* Interest rates; *specific types of bonds*
  call feature of, 125–27
  coupon rates, 118, 123, 124, 127, 144, 184, 232
  dropping in value, 237–39
  duration, 127–29, 248–49
  fees, 209, 212
  five best and five worst years for, 2–4
  high yield, 127
  intermediate-term, 143, 228, 245
  issuer of, 87, 123, 125, 126
  long-term bonds, 5, 8, 24, 143, 228, 245
  low yield, 127
  maturity date of, 24–27, 123–27, 142–43
  performance, 183–84, 220–21, 234

  portfolios, total returns in, 129–30
  ratings, 87, 142, 144
  returns expected, 232
  risk-reward characteristics, 5
  selling at discount, 118–21
  short-term bonds, 143–43, 146, 228, 235
  volatility of, 122–24, 128, 142–43, 245
Brokerage firms, discount, 210–13
Brokers, financial, 42–44, 213–15, 219–20, 223
Buffett, Warren, 42
Bull market, 39, 40
Business Week, 42

C

Calamos Asset Management, 253
Call feature. *See* Bonds
Capital appreciation, 91
Capital gains, 10, 174
Capital Research & Management, 253
Cash equivalents, 11, 169–70. *See also* Certificates of deposit (CDs); Money market accounts/funds; Treasury bills, U.S. (T-bills)
  performance, 184–85
CDA/Weisenberger, 31, 113
Certificates of deposit (CDs), 86, 225